Flies
The Best One Thousand

By Randle Scott Stetzer

Frank Amato Publications
Portland, Oregon

Dedication

This book is dedicated to my wife, Patricia, and my sons, Joshua and Benjamin. For their support and endurance with my absence from family activities and evenings together. Also to my parents, Mel and Laurene Wirth.

Special Acknowledgements

I would like to thank Bill McMillan for writing the foreword. Bill has been my mentor and guiding influence, not only in fly fishing but in life also.

Marty Sherman and John Hazel have been very important influences. Both are special fishing partners who's friendships I hold very dear. And my father Stephen Stetzer for providing the computer, which without, this project would have almost been impossible. Jim Schollmeyer, who's expertise with shutter, light and lens have made these fly patterns come alive.

Special thanks also to Dave Hall at Umpqua Feather Merchants, Randall Kaufmann at Kaufmann's Streamborn Flies, Bill Black at Spirit River Inc., Kathy Johnson at Amato Publications, Joyce Sherman for her computer help, and my publisher Frank Amato, for the original concept and his patience.

I would also like to thank all the innovator's of the fly patterns listed here. Their expertise and tying skills have made fly tying what it is today.

The people listed below are all tiers who's special skills appear in this book. I would like to thank them for their time, effort and expertise in tying many of the flies pictured here: Bob Aid, Larry Atchison, Christine Cutz Baxter, Bill Beardsley, Bill Black, Joe Branham, Richard Bunse, Brad Burden, Joe Butoric, Doug Canfield, Greg Carrier, Bill Chinn, Lee Clark, George Cook, Jim Cope, Scott Dawkins, Jim Dionne, Kevin Erickson, John Farrar, Tony Fox, Ken Fujii, René Harrop and family, John Hazel, Jeff Johnston, Doug Jorgensen, John Kistler, Harry Lemire, Tim Martin, Bill McMillan, Dave McNeese, Skip Morris, Gordon Nash, Jim Schollmeyer, Marty Sherman, John Shewey, Umpqua Feather Merchants, Bob Wagoner, Dick Williamson.

❖

All Flies Tied By Randle Scott Stetzer Unless Credited Otherwise

❖

See Photo Credits On Page 127

❖

Cover Photo and Fly Plates: Jim Schollmeyer
Book and Cover Design: Kathy Johnson
Printed in Hong Kong
10 9 8 7 6 5 4 3 2

ISBN NUMBER: Softbound 1-878175-20-3   Hardbound 1-878175-21-1

Table of Contents

❖

Foreword

My 1962 edition of Ray Bergman's *Trout* has 17 colored fly plates painted by Dr. Edgar Burke. This book with its 687 listed patterns and painted color plates was the most complete reference book for the era. The plates are still impressive for the sheer number of patterns depicted and the dedicated process involved in the painting of each. But, despite the efforts of Dr. Burke, the simplistic paintings captured nothing of the subtleties of coloring or construction of the patterns depicted. In spite of this failing *Trout* was essential to North American anglers and fly tiers because of the quantity of flies listed.

Since the publication of *Trout* the scope of fly fishing and fly tying has greatly increased and many anglers now seek salt water fish that can weigh over 100 pounds. In Ray Bergman's era, roughly the 1920's to 1960's, most anglers were little-travelled and salt water fly fishing was rarely done. Bergman was an East Coast angler of modest means, yet he did manage several fishing adventures out West. It was the breadth of his North American fly fishing experience (at least at the time) that made *Trout* such an important book, and the breadth of that experience resulted in the long list of fly patterns he compiled. While the fly plates left much to be desired, the extensive listing of patterns and dressings was remarkable and has remained a challenge to equal, let alone surpass.

I first met Randy Stetzer while fishing the Washougal River in the mid-1970's. Randy was 17 or 18 years old at the time and as I worked a favorite piece of steelhead water, he quietly watched. When I waded to shore he moderated an eagerness to ask questions with a self consciousness that did not want to intrude. We've been friends ever since, with as many hours spent astream together collecting wild steelhead spawning data as in the actual activity of fishing.

Challenges have been nothing new to Randy. While in his early twenties Randy became president of the Clark-Skamania Flyfishers (CSF) of Vancouver, Washington. With an unusual sense of voluntary duty and obligation for a person of any age, he may well have been the youngest person to preside over a major fly fishing organization. More importantly, he adeptly did so during the most tumultuous (and significant) year in that organiza-

tion's history. It is to CSF's credit, under Randy's presidency, that Wind River was made the first stream to be managed entirely for wild steelhead in the state of Washington in the pivotal year of 1981. It was a landmark decision at the time, and though hatchery steelhead were planted again several years later, that initial Wind River decision permanently changed the steelhead management process in Washington—and with ramifications throughout the Northwest.

When a mere tyke, Randy began tying flies of lashed grass and dog hair in imitation of what he saw in tackle shops. By the time we met he was hard hit by the steelhead mystique, and shortly after he began to tie steelhead flies commercially. In the late 1970's he was tying Spey-type flies and full-dressed Atlantic salmon patterns, and we often provided each other with suggestions and criticisms in the design, materials, and on-the-water fishability of surface steelhead flies that had captured our fascination.

In late 1982, Randy again volunteered to be president of the CSF. This was also about the time that he went to work for the Kaufmann brothers at Streamborn Flies in Tigard, Oregon where he has become a welcome figure to customers seeking advice on flies and fly tying. Whether beginners choosing their first tools, experts focused on some specific need such as the correct setting of a married wing, or anglers wondering how to pick or design flies to fish a certain way, his good council is well known and sought by many.

For ten years Randy has worked summers and falls at the Kaufmann house on the Deschutes River where he has guided and taught fly fishing schools with customers that come from throughout North America as well as other continents. Combined with occasional guiding stints for saltwater fish in Belize and the hardy exploration of remote steelhead streams along the coast of southeastern Alaska, Randy has either experienced, or become verbally familiar with, much of the breadth of fly fishing both within and outside North America.

His early interest in fly tying, combined with the breadth of his experience and fly fishing contacts, provides the necessary background for the scope of a fly tying book that provides the North American fly tier with 1000 fly patterns that are

skillfully tied on the hooks and in the manner they are intended to be fished. Selected to represent contemporary importance within nineteen categories of fly pattern groupings, it is the most complete single-volume reference available.

The majority of the 1000 patterns were tied by Randy; the others were tied either by their originators or tiers known for their special skills. The research required for making pattern choices, and then tying, took five years. The quality of the tying speaks for itself.

The flies are shown to best advantage through the photography of Jim Schollmeyer who has created unusual lighting that seems to make the patterns glow from within. This is in great contrast to the frustrations of Bergman's **Trout** in which the fly tier is perpetually at a loss to determine the coloration of materials.

Thanks to the even quality of both the photography and the tying of the patterns, the tier who uses this book has the best models to work from I've yet seen for such a comprehensive range of North American flies.

Although the book contains 1000 fly patterns, there is no excess fluff. These are proven working flies, not some quick whim of a talented tier designed to please the camera. That is an important difference from some recent books that have great value from the standpoint of fly tying art and visual esthetics, but have less value as functional fishing flies—with a significant angler following or proven history of angling success.

While it is true that just about any fly one can conceive will take some type of fish when in the right hands, most fly tiers are looking for patterns that have proven fish-appeal quality in appearance and/or materials, thus helping angling success. Whether the pattern is then duplicated or deviated from, the tier generally likes to have a known point of angling success from which to begin. Randy Stetzer has taken great care to provide the tier with proven patterns. Some are very old, some are contemporary favorites, and some are cutting edge...but all have a known reputation in one corner or another of North America for catching fish.

Bill McMillan
Washougal River, Washington

Chapter 1

Miscellaneous Dries
❖

Mayfly Dries
❖

Caddisfly Dries
❖

Stonefly Dries
❖

BLACK GNAT

Tier: Skip Morris
Hook: TMC 100, Mustad 94845, sizes 12-20
Thread: Black 6/0 prewaxed
Tail: Black hackle fibers
Body: Black rabbit or poly dubbing
Wings: Natural gray duck quill
Hackle: Natural or dyed black hackle

ADAM'S

Originator: Leonard Halladay
Hook: TMC 100, Mustad 94845, sizes 10-20
Thread: Black 6/0 prewaxed
Tail: Brown and grizzly hackle fibers mixed
Body: Gray muskrat underfur
Wings: Grizzly hen hackle tips
Hackle: Brown and grizzly hackle, mixed

MOSQUITO

Tier: Skip Morris
Hook: TMC 100, Mustad 94845, sizes 12-18
Thread: Black 6/0 prewaxed
Tail: Grizzly hackle fibers
Body: Dark and light moose mane, wrapped
Wings: Grizzly hen hackle tips
Hackle: Grizzly hackle

RED TAIL MOSQUITO

Tier: Skip Morris
Hook: TMC 100, Mustad 94845, sizes 12-18
Thread: Black 6/0 prewaxed
Tail: Red hackle fibers
Rib: Black floss, 1 strand
Body: White floss, thin
Wings: Grizzly hen hackle tips, tied over back
Hackle: Grizzly hackle

CALIFORNIA MOSQUITO

Hook: TMC 100, Mustad 94845, sizes 10-18
Thread: Black 6/0 prewaxed
Tail: Grizzly hackle fibers
Rib: Black floss, one strand
Body: White floss.
Wings: Grizzly hen hackle tips, over the back
Hackle: Grizzly hackle

MISCELLANEOUS DRY FLIES

BLACK GNAT

WHITE MILLER

ADAM'S

RIO GRANDE KING

MOSQUITO

ROYAL COACHMAN

RED TAIL MOSQUITO

BENTZ COACHMAN

CALIFORNIA MOSQUITO

FEMALE ADAM'S

WHITE MILLER

Tier: Umpqua Feather Merchants
Hook: TMC 100, Mustad 94845, sizes10-16
Thread: White 6/0 prewaxed
Tail: White hackle fibers
Rib: Fine copper wire
Body: White Floss
Wings: White duck quills
Hackle: White hackle

RIO GRANDE KING

Tier: Skip Morris
Hook: TMC 100, Mustad 94845, sizes 10-18
Thread: Brown 6/0 prewaxed
Tail: Golden pheasant tippet fibers
Body: Fine black chenille
Wings: White duck quill
Hackle: Brown hackle

ROYAL COACHMAN

Originator: John Haily
Hook: TMC 100, Mustad 94845, sizes 6-14
Thread: Black 6/0 prewaxed
Tail: Golden pheasant tippet fibers
Butt: Peacock herl
Body: Red floss
Shoulder: Peacock herl
Wings: White duck quill
Hackle: Coachman brown hackle

BENTZ COACHMAN

Originator Ted Bentz
Hook: TMC 100, Mustad 94845, sizes 10-12
Thread: Black 6/0 prewaxed
Tail: Golden pheasant tippet fibers
Butt: Peacock herl
Body: Gray floss
Shoulder: Peacock herl
Wings: Natural gray duck quill
Hackle: Grizzly hackle

FEMALE ADAM'S

Tier: Umpqua Feather Merchants
Hook: TMC 100, Mustad 94845, sizes10-18
Thread: Gray 6/0 prewaxed
Tail: Grizzly hackle fibers
Butt: Yellow poly dubbing
Body: Gray poly dubbing
Wings: Grizzly hen hackle tips
Hackle: Brown and grizzly hackle, mixed

SUPER SKATER

Originator: Al Troth
Hook: TMC 100, Mustad 94845, sizes 8-12
Thread: Yellow 6/0 prewaxed
Body: Yellow thread
Hackle: Spun elk hair, front and back

TOM THUMB

Hook: TMC 100, Mustad 94845, sizes 6-8
Thread: Black 6/0 prewaxed
Tail: Deer body hair
Body: Deer body hair
Wing: Deer body hair, tips from body

HUMPY

Tier: Skip Morris
Hook: TMC 100, Mustad 94845, sizes 8-14
Thread: Black 6/0 prewaxed
Tail: Dark moose body hair
Shellback: Dark moose body hair
Body: Black thread
Wings: Moose hair, tips from overbody
Hackle: Natural or dyed black hackle

ADAM'S HUMPY

Tier: Skip Morris
Hook: TMC 100, Mustad 94845, sizes 8-14
Thread: Gray 6/0 prewaxed
Tail: Dark Moose hair
Shellback: Deer hair
Body: Gray thread
Wings: Deer hair tips from overbody
Hackle: Brown and grizzly hackle, mixed

TRUDE HUMPY

Tier: Skip Morris
Hook: TMC 100, Mustad 94845, sizes 12-20
Thread: Yellow 6/0 prewaxed
Tail: Dark moose hair
Shellback: Dark moose body hair
Body: Yellow thread
Wing: White calf body hair
Hackle: Badger hackle

MISCELLANEOUS DRY FLIES

SUPER SKATER

WATER WALKER

TOM THUMB

RAT-FACED McDOUGAL

HUMPY

IRRESISTIBLE WULFF

ADAM'S HUMPY

ROYAL HUMPY

TRUDE HUMPY

GREEN HUMPY

WATER WALKER

Originator: Frank Johnson
Tier: Skip Morris
Hook: TMC 100, Mustad 94845, sizes 6-14
Thread: Tan 6/0 prewaxed
Tail: Natural tan elk hair
Body: Tan rabbit dubbing
Wings: Natural tan elk hair, divided
Hackle: Dark ginger, tied parachute, one around each wing

RAT-FACED McDOUGAL

Originator: Harry Darbee
Tier: Skip Morris
Hook: TMC 100, Mustad 94845, sizes 6-14
Thread: Tan 6/0 prewaxed
Tail: Light tan elk hair
Body: Natural light gray deer hair, spun and clipped
Wings: Light grizzly hen hackle tips
Hackle: Light ginger hackle

IRRESISTIBLE WULFF

Tier: Umpqua Feather Merchants
Hook: TMC 100, Mustad 94845, sizes 8-14
Thread: Black 6/0 prewaxed
Tail: Moose body hair
Body: Spun deer hair
Wings: White calf body hair
Hackle: Brown hackle

ROYAL HUMPY

Tier: Umpqua Feather Merchants
Hook: TMC 100, Mustad 94845, sizes 8-14
Thread: Red 6/0 prewaxed
Tail: Dark moose body hair
Shellback: Dark moose body hair
Body: Red floss
Wings: White calf body hair
Hackle: Brown hackle

GREEN HUMPY

Tier: Umpqua Feather Merchants
Hook: TMC 100, Mustad 94845, sizes 8-14
Thread: Black 6/0 prewaxed
Tail: Moose body hair.
Shellback: Moose body hair
Body: Fluorescent green floss
Wings: White calf body hair
Hackle: Brown hackle

BURR'S BRIGHT

Originator: Walter Burr
Hook: TMC 100, Mustad 94845, sizes 12-16
Thread: Black 6/0 prewaxed
Tail: White hackle fibers
Body: Fluorescent green wool yarn
Hackle: Grizzly hackle

DUN BIVISIBLE

Hook: TMC 100, Mustad 94845, sizes 10-14
Thread: Black 6/0 prewaxed
Tail: Blue dun hackle fibers
Body: Blue dun hackle, tightly palmered
Hackle: Cream hackle

BROWN BIVISIBLE

Hook: TMC 100, Mustad 94845, sizes 10-14
Thread: Black 6/0 prewaxed
Tail: Brown hackle fibers
Body: Brown hackle, tightly palmered
Hackle: Cream hackle

BADGER HACKLE PEACOCK

Hook: TMC 100, Mustad 94845, sizes 10-18
Thread: Black 6/0 prewaxed
Tail: Lady Amherst tippet fibers
Rib: Fine gold wire, reversed
Body: Peacock herl
Hackle: Badger hackle

BADGER VARIANT

Hook: TMC 100, Mustad 94845, sizes 10-16
Thread: Black 6/0 prewaxed
Tail: Badger hackle fibers
Rib: Gray 3/0 thread
Body: Black floss
Wings: Natural gray duck quill, short
Hackle: Badger hackle, oversized

MISCELLANEOUS DRY FLIES

BURR'S BRIGHT

DUN BIVISIBLE

FORE AND AFT

RENEGADE

BROWN BIVISIBLE

SIERRA BRIGHT DOT

BADGER HACKLE PEACOCK

DESCHUTES CRANE

BADGER VARIANT

CDC CRANE FLY

FORE AND AFT

Tier: Skip Morris
Hook: TMC 100, Mustad 94845, sizes 16-18
Thread: Gray 6/0 prewaxed
Aft-hackle: Dark dun hackle, shiny side facing forward
Body: Gray muskrat underfur
Fore-hackle: Dark dun hackle, shiny side facing towards rear

RENEGADE

Originator: Taylor Williams
Tier: Umpqua Feather Merchants
Hook: TMC 100, Mustad 94845, sizes 6-18
Thread: Black 6/0 prewaxed
Tip: Fine flat gold tinsel
Rear Hackle: Brown hackle
Body: Peacock herl
Front Hackle: White hackle

SIERRA BRIGHT DOT

Hook: TMC 100, Mustad 94845, sizes 10-16
Thread: Black 6/0 prewaxed
Tail: Golden pheasant tippets
Aft-hackle: Grizzly hackle, 2 sizes undersize
Body: Red floss, thin
Hackle: Grizzly hackle

DESCHUTES CRANE

Originator: Scott Dawkins
Tier: Scott Dawkins
Hook: TMC 100, Mustad 94845, sizes 10-16
Thread: Tan 6/0 prewaxed
Abdomen: Bleached moose hair
Legs: Bleached moose hair
Thorax: Rust poly dubbing
Wings: Pale watery dun hen hackle tips

CDC CRANE FLY

Originator: Ken Shimazaki
Tier: Umpqua Feather Merchants
Hook: TMC 900BL, sizes 10-16
Thread: Brown 6/0 prewaxed
Butt: Brown thread
Rib: Black thread
Body: Cream rabbit dubbing
Wings: White Z-lon
Hackle: Light blue dun CDC feather, wrapped

STIMULATOR, olive

Originator: Randall Kaufmann
Tier: Umpqua Feather Merchants
Hook: TMC 200R, sizes 6-16
Thread: Fluorescent fire orange 6/0 prewaxed
Tail: Gray elk hair
Rib: Brown hackle, palmered and counter-wound with fine gold wire
Body: Olive Haretron dubbing
Wing: Gray elk hair
Head: Amber goat dubbing
Hackle: Grizzly hackle, wrapped over head

STIMULATOR, orange

Originator: Randall Kaufmann
Tier: Umpqua Feather Merchants
Hook: TMC 200R, sizes 4-16
Thread: Fluorescent fire orange 6/0 pre-waxed
Tail: Dark elk hair
Rib: Furnace hackle, palmered and counterwound with fine gold wire
Body: Rusty orange Haretron or fluorescent fire orange antron
Wing: Dark elk hair
Head: Amber goat dubbing
Hackle: Grizzly hackle, wrapped over head

STIMULATOR, royal

Originator: Randall Kaufmann
Tier: Umpqua Feather Merchants
Hook: TMC 200R, sizes 10-16
Thread: Fluorescent fire orange 6/0 prewaxed
Tail: Medium or dark elk hair
Rib: Furnace hackle, palmered and counterwound with fine gold wire
Body: Peacock herl, fluorescent fire orange floss, peacock herl
Wing: Medium or dark elk hair
Hackle: Grizzly hackle, three to four turns over thorax
Thorax: Fluorescent fire orange antron dubbing

FALK

Originator: Dale LaFollette
Hook: TMC 5212, Mustad 94831, sizes 8-14
Thread: Black 6/0 prewaxed
Tail: Golden pheasant tippet fibers
Rib: Grizzly hackle, palmered
Body: Burnt orange floss
Wing: Natural deer hair, blunt ends left as a head

MONTANA BUCKTAIL

Hook: TMC 5212, Mustad 94831, sizes 6-10
Thread: Fire orange 6/0 prewaxed
Tail: Golden pheasant tippet fibers
Rib: Fine gold wire
Body: Orange floss
Hackle: Grizzly hackle, palmered over the body
Wing: Natural deer hair

MISCELLANEOUS DRY FLIES

STIMULATOR, olive

PARACHUTE ADAMS

STIMULATOR, orange

FLOAT-N-FOOL

STIMULATOR, royal

HARE'S EAR PARACHUTE

FALK

ADAMS IRRESISTIBLE

MONTANA BUCKTAIL

RIO GRANDE TRUDE

PARACHUTE ADAMS

Tier: Umpqua Feather Merchants
Hook: TMC 100, Mustad 94845, sizes 10-18
Thread: Gray 6/0 prewaxed
Tail: Grizzly hackle fibers
Body: Gray muskrat dubbing
Wing: White calf body hair
Hackle: Brown and grizzly hackle, parachute style

FLOAT-N-FOOL

Originator: Wayne Buszek
Tier: Skip Morris
Hook: TMC 100, Mustad 94845, sizes 10-16
Thread: Black 6/0 prewaxed
Tail: White calf body hair, butt ends form wing post
Rib: Fine gold wire, reverse wrapped
Body: Peacock herl
Wing: Butt ends of tail
Hackle: Brown and grizzly hackle, mixed, tied parachute style

HARE'S EAR PARACHUTE

Originator: Ed Schroeder
Tier: Umpqua Feather Merchants
Hook: TMC 900BL sizes 10-18
Thread: Gray 6/0 prewaxed
Tail: Natural dark deer hair
Rib: Fine silver wire
Body: Natural Hare's ear dubbing
Wing: White calf body hair
Hackle: Grizzly hackle, parachute style

ADAMS IRRESISTIBLE

Tier: Umpqua Feather Merchants
Hook: TMC 100, Mustad 94845, sizes 8-14
Thread: Black 6/0 prewaxed
Tail: Moose body hair
Body: Spun deer hair
Wings: Grizzly hackle tips
Hackle: Brown and grizzly hackles, mixed

RIO GRANDE TRUDE

Tier: Umpqua Feather Merchants
Hook: TMC 100, Mustad 94845, sizes 10-16
Thread: Black 6/0 prewaxed
Tail: Golden Pheasant tippets
Body: Black rabbit dubbing
Wing: White calftail
Hackle: Coachman brown hackle

BLONDE WULFF

Tier: Skip Morris
Hook: TMC 100, Mustad 94845, sizes 4-14
Thread: Black 6/0 prewaxed
Tail: Natural tan elk hair
Body: Light tan rabbit fur
Wings: Natural tan elk hair
Hackle: Light ginger hackle

GRIZZLY WULFF

Originator: Dan Bailey
Tier: Skip Morris
Hook: TMC 100, Mustad 94845, sizes 8-14
Thread: Black 6/0 prewaxed
Tail: Natural brown bucktail
Body: Yellow floss
Wings: Natural brown bucktail
Hackle: Brown and grizzly hackle, mixed

BROWN WULFF

Originator: Lee Wulff
Hook: TMC 100, Mustad 94845, sizes 8-12
Thread: Black 6/0 prewaxed
Tail: Brown bucktail
Body: Brown or cream rabbit fur
Wings: Natural brown bucktail
Hackle: Brown hackle

GRAY WULFF

Originator: Lee Wulff
Hook: TMC 100, Mustad 94845, sizes 8-14
Thread: Black 6/0 prewaxed
Tail: Natural brown bucktail
Body: Gray muskrat underfur
Wings: Natural brown bucktail
Hackle: Medium blue dun hackle

COLORADO CAPTAIN

Tier: Skip Morris
Hook: TMC 100, Mustad 94845, sizes 8-18
Thread: Black 6/0 prewaxed
Tag: Fine flat gold tinsel
Tail: Golden pheasant tippet fibers
Body: Black ostrich herl, 3 strands
Wings: White calf body hair
Hackle: Coachman brown hackle

MISCELLANEOUS DRY FLIES

BLONDE WULFF

WHITE WULFF

GRIZZLY WULFF

HOUSE AND LOT VARIANT

BROWN WULFF

REVEREND LANG

GRAY WULFF

ROYAL WULFF

COLORADO CAPTAIN

AUSABLE WULFF

WHITE WULFF

Originator: Lee Wulff
Tier: Umpqua Feather Merchants
Hook: TMC 100, Mustad 94845, sizes 6-16
Thread: White 6/0 prewaxed
Tail: White calf body hair
Body: White rabbit dubbing
Wings: White calf body hair
Hackle: Cream badger hackle

HOUSE AND LOT VARIANT

Hook: TMC 100, Mustad 94845, sizes 10-16
Thread: Black 6/0 prewaxed
Rib: Fine gold wire, reverse wrapped
Tail: White calf body hair
Body: Rear 1/2; stripped peacock herl, front 1/2; peacock herl
Wings: White calf body hair
Hackle: Badger hackle

REVEREND LANG

Tier: Skip Morris
Hook: TMC 100, Mustad 94845, sizes 8-14
Thread: Black 6/0 prewaxed
Tail: White calf body hair
Body: Black rabbit or poly dubbing
Wings: White calf body hair
Hackle: Furnace hackle

ROYAL WULFF

Originator: Lee Wulff
Tier: Umpqua Feather Merchants
Hook: TMC 100, Mustad 94845, sizes 8-14
Thread: Black 6/0 prewaxed
Tail: Natural brown bucktail
Butt: Peacock herl
Body: Red floss
Shoulder: Peacock herl
Wings: White calf body hair
Hackle: Coachman brown hackle

AUSABLE WULFF

Originator: Francis Betters
Hook: TMC 100, Mustad 94845, sizes 8-14
Thread: Red 6/0 prewaxed
Tail: Moose body hair
Body: Bleached Australian opossum
Wings: White calf body hair
Hackle: Brown and grizzly hackles, mixed

BLUE QUILL

Tier: Umpqua Feather Merchants
Hook: TMC 100, Mustad 94845, sizes 12-18
Thread: Black 6/0 prewaxed
Tail: Medium blue dun hackle fibers
Body: Stripped peacock quill
Wings: Natural gray duck quill
Hackle: Medium blue dun hackle

GINGER QUILL

Tier: Skip Morris
Hook: TMC 100, Mustad 94845, sizes 12-18
Thread: Yellow 6/0 prewaxed
Tail: Golden ginger hackle fibers
Body: Stripped peacock quill
Wings: Natural gray duck quill
Hackle: Golden ginger hackle

MARCH BROWN

Hook: TMC 100, Mustad 94845, sizes 10-14
Thread: Brown 6/0 prewaxed
Tail: Dark ginger hackle fibers
Rib: Yellow thread
Body: Brown rabbit dubbing
Wings: Turkey wing quill
Hackle: Dark ginger hackle

MALE BEAVERKILL

Hook: TMC 100, Mustad 94845, sizes 12-14
Thread: Black 6/0 prewaxed
Tail: Dark ginger hackle fibers
Rib: Brown hackle, palmered
  and undersized
Body: White floss
Wings: Natural gray duck quill
Hackle: Dark brown hackle

PINK LADY

Hook: TMC 100, Mustad 94845, sizes 12-16
Thread: Cream 6/0 prewaxed
Tail: Golden pheasant tippets
Rib: Fine flat gold tinsel
Body: Pink floss
Wings: Natural gray duck quill
Hackle: Golden badger hackle

MAYFLY DRIES

BLUE QUILL

LADY BEAVERKILL

GINGER QUILL

LITTLE MARRYATT

MARCH BROWN

BLUE DUN

MALE BEAVERKILL

DUSTY MILLER

PINK LADY

PALE WATERY DUN

LADY BEAVERKILL

Hook: TMC 100, Mustad 94845, sizes 12-16
Thread: Black 6/0 prewaxed
Tail: Ginger hackle fibers
Butt: Yellow wool
Body: Gray muskrat fur
Wings: Natural gray duck quill
Hackle: Ginger hackle

LITTLE MARRYATT

Hook: TMC 100, Mustad 94845, sizes 10-18
Thread: Cream 6/0 prewaxed
Tail: Brown hackle fibers
Body: Light gray rabbit dubbing
Wings: Natural gray duck quill
Hackle: Brown hackle

BLUE DUN

Tier: Umpqua Feather Merchants
Hook: TMC 100, Mustad 94845, sizes 12-18
Thread: Gray 6/0 prewaxed
Tail: Medium blue dun hackle fibers
Body: Gray muskrat fur
Wings: Natural gray duck quill
Hackle: Medium blue dun hackle

DUSTY MILLER

Hook: TMC 100, Mustad 94845, sizes 10-14
Thread: Gray 6/0 prewaxed
Tail: Light blue dun hackle fibers
Body: Muskrat fur and hare's ear fur, mixed
Wings: Natural gray duck quill
Hackle: Light blue dun and dark ginger
  hackle, mixed

PALE WATERY DUN

Hook: TMC 100, Mustad 94845, sizes 16-18
Thread: Gray 6/0 prewaxed
Tail: Sandy dun hackle fibers
Body: Light gray muskrat fur
Wings: Natural gray duck quills
Hackle: Sandy dun hackle

GRAY QUILL

Tier: Skip Morris
Hook: TMC 100, Mustad 94845, sizes 12-18
Thread: Black 6/0 prewaxed
Tail: Dark grizzly hackle fibers
Body: Badger hackle stem, stripped
Wings: Barred teal flank
Hackle: Dark grizzly hackle

QUILL GORDON

Originator: Theodore Gordon
Tier: Umpqua Feather Merchants
Hook: TMC 100, Mustad 94845, sizes 12-14
Thread: Black 6/0 prewaxed
Tail: Dark blue dun hackle fibers
Body: Stripped peacock quill, lacquered
Wings: Lemon woodduck flank fibers
Hackle: Dark blue dun hackle

RED QUILL

Originator: Art Flick
Tier: Skip Morris
Hook: TMC 100, Mustad 94845, sizes 12-16
Thread: Gray 6/0 prewaxed
Tail: Medium bronze dun hackle fibers
Body: Coachman brown hackle stem, stripped
Wings: Lemon woodduck flank fibers
Hackle: Medium bronze dun hackle

AMERICAN MARCH BROWN

Originator: Preston Jennings
Tier: Skip Morris
Hook: TMC 100, Mustad 94845, sizes 10-14
Thread: Orange 6/0 prewaxed
Tail: Dark brown hackle fibers
Rib: Brown thread
Body: Tannish-red rabbit dubbing
Wings: Woodduck flank feathers
Hackle: Brown and grizzly hackle, mixed

DARK CAHILL

Hook: TMC 100, Mustad 94845, sizes 12-18
Thread: Tan 6/0 prewaxed
Tail: Dark ginger hackle fibers
Body: Gray muskrat fur
Wings: Lemon woodduck flank
Hackle: Dark ginger hackle

MAYFLY DRIES

GRAY QUILL

QUILL GORDON

DARK HENDRICKSON

GRAY FOX

RED QUILL

LIGHT HENDRICKSON

AMERICAN MARCH BROWN

FLICK'S MARCH BROWN

DARK CAHILL

PINK CAHILL

DARK HENDRICKSON

Originator: Roy Steenrod
Tier: Skip Morris
Hook: TMC 100, Mustad 94845, sizes 12-18
Thread: Gray 6/0 prewaxed
Tail: Dark blue dun hackle fibers
Body: Dark gray muskrat fur
Wings: Lemon woodduck flank fibers
Hackle: Dark blue dun hackle

GRAY FOX

Originator: Preston Jennings
Tier: Umpqua Feather Merchants
Hook: TMC 100, Mustad 94845, sizes 12-14
Thread: Primrose 6/0 prewaxed
Tail: Golden ginger hackle fibers
Body: Light red fox fur
Wings: Mallard flank fibers
Hackle: Golden ginger and light grizzly hackle, mixed

LIGHT HENDRICKSON

Originator: Roy Steenrod
Tier: Umpqua Feather Merchants
Hook: TMC 100, Mustad 94845, sizes 12-18
Thread: Tan 6/0 prewaxed
Tail: Medium blue dun hackle fibers
Body: Urine stained fox belly fur
Wings: Lemon woodduck flank fibers
Hackle: Medium blue dun hackle

FLICK'S MARCH BROWN

Originator: Art Flick
Tier: Umpqua Feather Merchants
Hook: TMC 100, Mustad 94845, sizes 10-14
Thread: Tan 6/0 prewaxed
Tail: Dark ginger hackle fibers
Body: Tan rabbit or poly dubbing.
Wings: Woodduck flank fibers
Hackle: Brown and grizzly hackle

PINK CAHILL

Tier: Umpqua Feather Merchants
Hook: TMC 100, Mustad 94845, sizes 12-18
Thread: Tan 6/0 prewaxed
Tail: Pale ginger hackle fibers
Body: Tannish pink poly dubbing
Wings: Woodduck flank fibers
Hackle: Pale ginger hackle

BLACK QUILL

Originator: Ernest Schwiebert
Hook: TMC 100, Mustad 94845, sizes 10-14
Thread: Black 6/0 prewaxed
Tail: Dark blue dun hackle fibers
Body: Stripped badger hackle stem
Wings: Black hen hackle tips
Hackle: Dark blue dun hackle

FFF MAY

Originator: Fenton Roskelley
Hook: TMC 100, Mustad 94845, sizes 12-18
Thread: Black 6/0 prewaxed
Tail: Coachman brown and black hackle
   fibers, mixed
Rib: Tan thread
Body: Dark brown rabbit dubbing
Wings: Grizzly hen hackle tips
Hackle: Coachman brown and black hackle,
   mixed

BORCHER SPECIAL

Originator: Ernie Borcher
Tier: Skip Morris
Hook: TMC 100, Mustad 94845, sizes 10-18
Thread: Black 6/0 prewaxed
Tail: Mahogany ringneck pheasant tail
   fibers
Body: Mottled turkey wing quill fibers
Wings: Blue dun hen hackle tips
Hackle: Brown and grizzly hackle, mixed

LITTLE OLIVE

Hook: TMC 100, Mustad 94845, sizes 18-22
Thread: Olive 6/0 prewaxed
Tail: Blue dun hackle fibers
Body: Tannish-olive rabbit dubbing
Wing: Blue dun hen hackle tips
Hackle: Blue dun hackle

LITTLE SULPHUR DUN

Hook: TMC 100, Mustad 94845, sizes 16-18
Thread: Yellow 6/0 prewaxed
Tail: Dark cream hackle fibers
Body: Creamish-yellow rabbit dubbing
   plus a touch of orange rabbit, mixed
Wings: Light blue dun hen hackle tips
Hackle: Dark cream hackle

MAYFLY DRIES

BLACK QUILL

SULPHUR DUN

FFF MAY

PALE MORNING DUN

BORCHER SPECIAL

PALE EVENING DUN

LITTLE OLIVE

LIGHT CAHILL

LITTLE SULPHUR DUN

FALL RIVER SPECIAL

SULPHUR DUN

Originator: Charles Fox
Hook: TMC 100, Mustad 94845, sizes 16-18
Thread: Cream 6/0 prewaxed
Tail: Pale blue dun hackle fibers
Body: Cream fox fur
Wings: Cream hen hackle tips
Hackle: Pale blue dun hackle

PALE MORNING DUN

Tier: Umpqua Feather Merchants
Hook: TMC 100, Mustad 94845, sizes 12-18
Thread: Cream 6/0 prewaxed
Tail: Very light dun hackle fibers
Body: Cream rabbit dubbing
Wings: Light dun hen hackle tips
Hackle: Very light dun hackle

PALE EVENING DUN

Originator: Charles Fox and Ray
   Bergman
Tier: Umpqua Feather Merchants
Hook: TMC 100, Mustad 94845, sizes 14-20
Thread: Cream 6/0 prewaxed
Tail: Light blue dun hackle fibers
Body: Pale yellow rabbit dubbing
Wings: Light blue dun hackle tips
Hackle: Medium blue dun hackle

LIGHT CAHILL

Originator: Dan Cahill
Tier: Umpqua Feather Merchants
Hook: TMC 100, Mustad 94845, sizes 10-20
Thread: Cream 6/0 prewaxed
Tail: Light ginger hackle fibers
Body: Cream badger underfur
Wings: Lemon woodduck flank
Hackle: Light ginger hackle

FALL RIVER SPECIAL

Tier: Skip Morris
Hook: TMC 100, Mustad 94845, sizes 12-22
Thread: Cream 6/0 prewaxed
Tail: Bleached elk, 5 hairs
Body: Cream thread, tapered
Wings: Lemon woodduck flank
Hackle: Light ginger hackle

CALLIBAETIS ZINGER

Originator: Scott Dawkins
Tier: Scott Dawkins
Hook: TMC 100, Mustad 94845, sizes 10-16
Thread: Tan 6/0 prewaxed
Tail: Light dun hackle fibers or micro-fibetts
Body: Tan poly dubbing
Wings: Clear zing (Taiwanese packing twine) streaked with waterproof marker
Hackle: Light dun hackle, parachute style

BAETIS ZINGER

Originator: Scott Dawkins
Tier: Scott Dawkins
Hook: TMC 100, Mustad 94845, sizes 16-20
Thread: Black 6/0 prewaxed
Tail: Sandy dun hackle fibers or micro-fibetts
Abdomen: Stripped peacock eye, from near the eye
Wings: Zing (Taiwanese packing twine), colored gray
Hackle: Sandy dun hackle, wrapped over the thorax
Thorax: Olive dun poly dubbing

HENDRICKSON THORAX

Hook: TMC 100, Mustad 94845, sizes 12-16
Thread: Olive 6/0 prewaxed
Tail: Bronze dun hackle fibers, forked
Body: Grayish-tan fox fur
Wing: Medium dun turkey flats
Hackle: Bronze dun hackle, clipped on bottom

MAHOGANY DUN THORAX

Hook: TMC 100, Mustad 94845, sizes 12-16
Thread: Brown 6/0 prewaxed
Tail: Medium blue dun hackle fibers, forked
Body: Mahogany rabbit dubbing
Wing: Dark blue dun turkey flats
Hackle: Medium blue dun hackle, clipped on bottom

SLATE OLIVE THORAX

Tier: Umpqua Feather Merchants
Hook: TMC 100, Mustad 94845, sizes 14-20
Thread: Olive 6/0 prewaxed
Tail: Medium blue dun hackle fibers, forked
Body: Medium olive rabbit dubbing
Wing: Dark dun turkey flats
Hackle: Medium blue dun hackle, clipped on bottom

MAYFLY DRIES

CALLIBAETIS ZINGER

PMD ZINGER

BAETIS ZINGER

PALE MORNING DUN THORAX

HENDRICKSON THORAX

SCOTT'S PMD

MAHOGANY DUN THORAX

CUTWING BLUE WING OLIVE

SLATE OLIVE THORAX

CUTWING PALE MORNING DUN

PMD ZINGER

Originator: Scott Dawkins
Tier: Scott Dawkins
Hook: TMC 100, Mustad 94845, sizes 14-18
Thread: Cream 6/0 prewaxed
Tail: Pale watery dun hackle fibers or micro-fibetts
Abdomen: Stripped dyed yellow hackle stem
Thorax: Pale yellow poly dubbing
Wings: Clear zing (Taiwanese packing twine) colored yellow
Hackle: Pale watery dun hackle, tied parachute

PALE MORNING DUN THORAX

Tier: Umpqua Feather Merchants
Hook: TMC 100, Mustad 94845, sizes 14-20
Thread: Pale yellow 6/0 prewaxed
Tail: Light blue dun hackle fibers, forked
Body: Pale yellow rabbit dubbing
Wing: Light dun turkey flats
Hackle: Light blue dun hackle clipped on bottom

SCOTT'S PMD

Originator: Scott Dawkins
Tier: Scott Dawkins
Hook: TMC 100, Mustad 94845, sizes 14-18
Thread: Pale yellow 6/0 prewaxed
Tail: Pale watery dun hackle fibers or micro-fibetts
Abdomen: Stripped dyed yellow hackle stem
Thorax: Pale yellow poly dubbing
Hackle: Pale watery dun hackle, wrapped over the thorax
Wings: Pale watery dun hen hackle, clipped to shape

CUTWING BLUE WING OLIVE

Tier: Umpqua Feather Merchants
Hook: TMC 100, Mustad 94845, sizes 14
Thread: Dark olive 6/0 prewaxed
Tail: Dark dun hackle fibers
Body: Medium olive poly dubbing
Wings: Mottled brown hen hackle tips, cut to shape
Legs: Dark dun hackle fibers

CUTWING PALE MORNING DUN

Originator: Ken Iwamasa
Tier: Umpqua Feather Merchants
Hook: TMC 100, Mustad 94845, sizes 14
Thread: White 6/0 prewaxed
Tail: Light ginger hackle fibers
Body: Cream poly dubbing
Wings: White hen hackle tips, cut to shape
Legs: Light ginger hackle fibers

BROWN DRAKE

Originator: Mike Lawson
Tier: Umpqua Feather Merchants
Hook: TMC 100, Mustad 94845, sizes 6-16
Thread: Brown 6/0 prewaxed
Tail: Dark moose body hair
Rib: Yellow floss, thin
Body: Olive rabbit or poly dubbing
Wings: Light brown elk hair
Hackle: Dyed yellow-tan grizzly hackle

WESTERN GREEN DRAKE

Originator: Mike Lawson
Tier: Umpqua Feather Merchants
Hook: TMC 100, Mustad 94845, sizes 10-12
Thread: Olive 6/0 prewaxed
Tail: Dark moose body hair
Rib: Bright olive floss, thin
Body: Olive rabbit dubbing
Wings: Dark moose body hair
Hackle: Grizzly hackle dyed olive

CRIPPLE OLIVE

Originator: Bob Quigley
Tier: Umpqua Feather Merchants
Hook: TMC 100, Mustad 94845, sizes 10-18
Thread: Tan 6/0 prewaxed
Tail: Light olive ostrich herl
Body: Light olive ostrich herl
Thorax: Dark olive rabbit dubbing
Wing: Tan deer hair, butt ends showing
Hackle: Dyed olive grizzly hackle

GULPHER SPECIAL

Originator: Al Troth
Tier: Umpqua Feather Merchants
Hook: TMC 100, Mustad 94845, sizes 14-18
Thread: Brown 6/0 prewaxed
Tail: Grizzly hackle fibers
Body: Dark beaver fur
Wing: White poly pro yarn
Hackle: Grizzly hackle, parachute style

SPECKLED-WING PARACHUTE

Originator: Pret Frazier
Hook: TMC 100, Mustad 94845, sizes 10-18
Thread: 6/0 prewaxed, to match body
Tail: Micro-fibetts, to match natural
Body: Rabbit dubbing, to match natural
Wing: Mallard flank, trimmed to shape
Hackle: Neck hackle, to match natural,
parachute style

MAYFLY DRIES

BROWN DRAKE

MORRIS MAY LIGHT

WESTERN GREEN DRAKE

MORRIS MAY DARK

CRIPPLE OLIVE

RUSTY SPINNER

GULPHER SPECIAL

CDC CALLIBAETIS BIOT SPINNER

SPECKLED-WING PARACHUTE

SPARKLE SPINNER

MORRIS MAY LIGHT

Originator: Skip Morris
Tier: Skip Morris
Hook: TMC 100, Mustad 94845, sizes 8-24
Thread: Pale yellow 6/0 prewaxed
Tail: 2 to 6 ginger hackle fibers, split
Abdomen: Tan poly dubbing
Wing: Gray poly yarn
Thorax: Tan poly dubbing
Hackle: Ginger hackle, wrapped over
the thorax

MORRIS MAY DARK

Originator: Skip Morris
Tier: Skip Morris
Hook: TMC 100, Mustad 94845, sizes 8-24
Thread: Dark brown 6/0 prewaxed
Tail: 2 to 6 hackle fibers, split
Abdomen: Brown poly dubbing
Wing: Gray poly yarn
Thorax: Brown poly dubbing
Hackle: Brown hackle, wrapped over
the thorax

RUSTY SPINNER

Hook: TMC 5230, Mustad 94833,
sizes 12-24
Thread: Tan 6/0 prewaxed
Tail: Medium dun hackle fibers
Body: Rusty brown rabbit dubbing
Wings: Light gray poly pro yarn

CDC *CALLIBAETIS* BIOT SPINNER

Originator: René Harrop & Family
Tier: René Harrop
Hook: TMC 5230, Mustad 94833,
sizes 12-16
Thread: Tan 6/0 prewaxed
Tail: Ginger cock hackle fibers
Wings: White CDC feathers with brown
Z-lon over the top
Abdomen: Brown goose biot, wrapped
Thorax: Tan rabbit dubbing.

SPARKLE SPINNER

Hook: TMC 5230, Mustad 94833,
sizes 12-18
Thread: 6/0 prewaxed, to match body
Tail: Micro-fibetts, to match natural, forked
Body: Rabbit dubbing, to match natural
Wings: Pearl Krystal Flash

CDC PMD CRIPPLE DUN

Originator: René Harrop & Family
Tier: René Harrop
Hook: TMC 100, Mustad 94845, sizes 16-22
Thread: Yellow 6/0 prewaxed
Tail: Woodduck flank, yellow and brown Z-lon, sparse
Abdomen: Medium brown rabbit dubbing
Wing: White CDC feather with yellow Z-lon on the sides
Thorax: Pale yellow rabbit dubbing

HEN SPINNER

Originators: Doug Swisher and Carl Richards
Tier: Umpqua Feather Merchants
Hook: TMC 5230, Mustad 94833, sizes 10-20
Thread: 6/0 prewaxed, to match body
Tail: Hackle fibers, to match natural, forked
Body: Rabbit dubbing, to match natural
Wings: Hen hackle tips, to match natural

BAETIS CUT-WING

Originator: Scott Dawkins
Tier: Scott Dawkins
Hook: TMC 100, Mustad 94845, sizes 16-20
Thread: Olive 6/0 prewaxed
Tail: Sandy dun hackle fibers or micro-fibetts
Abdomen: Stripped peacock quill, from near the eye
Hackle: Grizzly hackle, wrapped over thorax
Thorax: Olive dun poly dubbing
Wing: Center section from dun turkey flat, cut to shape

CUTWING TRICO

Originator: Ken Iwamasa
Tier: Umpqua Feather Merchants
Hook: TMC 100, Mustad 94845, sizes 18
Thread: Black 6/0 prewaxed
Tail: Black hackle fibers
Body: Black poly dubbing
Wings: White hen hackle tips, cut to shape
Legs: Black hackle fibers

TRICO PARACHUTE

Hook: TMC 101, Mustad 94859, sizes 20-24
Thread: White 6/0 prewaxed
Tail: Grizzly hackle fibers
Body: White thread
Thorax: Black rabbit dubbing
Wing: White turkey flats
Hackle: Grizzly dun hackle, parachute style

MAYFLY DRIES

CDC PMD CRIPPLE DUN

EXTENDED PALE MORNING DUN

HEN SPINNER

CDC RUSTY SPINNER

BAETIS CUT-WING

TRUSTY RUSTY

CUTWING TRICO

TRICO SPINNER

TRICO PARACHUTE

TRICO POLY SPINNER

EXTENDED PALE MORNING DUN

Originator: Bing Lempke
Tier: Umpqua Feather Merchants
Hook: TMC 100, Mustad 94845, sizes 14-18
Thread: Pale yellow 6/0 prewaxed
Tail: Clear micro-fibetts, 3 strands
Body: Pale yellow poly dubbing, extended
Wings: Natural gray duck quill
Hackle: Light ginger hackle, clipped on the bottom.

CDC RUSTY SPINNER

Originator: René Harrop & Family
Tier: René Harrop
Hook: TMC 5230, Mustad 94833, sizes 12-24
Thread: Orange 6/0 prewaxed
Tail: Pale gray cock hackle fibers
Wings: White CDC feathers with light dun Z-lon over the top
Abdomen: Rusty brown goose biot, wrapped
Thorax: Rusty brown rabbit dubbing

TRUSTY RUSTY

Originator: Scott Dawkins
Tier: Scott Dawkins
Hook: TMC 100, Mustad 94845, sizes 14-22
Thread: Brown 6/0 prewaxed
Tail: Pale watery dun hackle fibers
Abdomen: Stripped brown hackle stem
Thorax: Rust poly dubbing
Wings: Pale watery dun hen hackle

TRICO SPINNER

Tier: Umpqua Feather Merchants
Hook: TMC 5230, Mustad 94833, sizes 20-26
Thread: White 6/0 prewaxed
Tail: Light micro fibetts
Body: White thread
Thorax: Black rabbit dubbing
Wings: Light dun hen hackle tips

TRICO POLY SPINNER

Hook: TMC 5230, Mustad 94833, sizes 20-26
Thread: Black 6/0 prewaxed
Tail: Dark dun micro-fibetts, forked
Abdomen: White rabbit dubbing
Thorax: Black rabbit dubbing
Wings: White poly pro yarn

NO HACKLE

Originators: Doug Swisher and
 Carl Richards
Tier: Umpqua Feather Merchants
Hook: TMC 5230, Mustad 94833,
 sizes 14-20
Thread: 6/0 prewaxed, to match body
Tail: Hackle fibers, forked, to
 match natural
Body: Rabbit dubbing, to match natural
Wings: Natural gray duck quill

CDC *CALLIBAETIS* CRIPPLE DUN

Originator: René Harrop & Family
Tier: René Harrop
Hook: TMC 100, Mustad 94845, sizes 12-16
Thread: Brown 6/0 prewaxed
Tail: Three lemon woodduck flank fibers,
 with olive Z-lon
Abdomen: Light olive gray rabbit dubbing
Wing: White CDC feathers with brown
 Z-lon on the sides
Thorax: Tan rabbit dubbing

DARK HAYSTACK

Hook: TMC 100, Mustad 94845, sizes 10-18
Thread: Tan 6/0 prewaxed
Tail: Dark deer hair
Body: Brown Australian opossum fur
Wing: Dark deer hair, flared 180 degrees

MARCH BROWN COMPARA DUN

Hook: TMC 5230, Mustad 94833,
 sizes 12-14
Thread: Tan 6/0 prewaxed
Tail: Beaver fur guard hairs
Body: Tan hare's ear dubbing
Wing: Tan deer hair, flared 180 degrees

HAIRWING NO HACKLE

Originator: René Harrop & Family
Tier: Umpqua Feather Merchants
Hook: TMC 100, Mustad 94845, sizes 14-18
Thread: Gray 6/0 prewaxed
Tails: Dark dun hackle fibers
Body: Slate gray poly dubbing
Wing: Natural light deer hair

MAYFLY DRIES

NO HACKLE

PMD HAIRWING DUN

CDC *CALLIBAETIS* CRIPPLE DUN

HAIRWING DUN

DARK HAYSTACK

DOWNWING GREEN DRAKE

MARCH BROWN COMPARA DUN

LOOP-WING BLUE DUN

HAIRWING NO HACKLE

LOOP-WING MARCH BROWN

PMD HAIRWING DUN

Originator: René Harrop & Family
Tier: Umpqua Feather Merchants
Hook: TMC 100, Mustad 94845, sizes 14-18
Thread: Pale yellow hackle fibers
Tail: Light ginger hackle fibers
Body: Pale yellow poly dubbing
Hackle: Ginger hackle, clipped on
 the bottom
Wing: Natural light elk hair
Head: Natural light elk hair, butts to
 form head

HAIRWING DUN

Originator: René Harrop & Family
Tier: Umpqua Feather Merchants
Hook: TMC 100, Mustad 94845, sizes 14-18
Thread: Olive 6/0 prewaxed
Tail: Dark blue dun hackle fibers, forked
Body: Olive rabbit dubbing
Hackle: Dark blue dun hackle, clipped on
 the bottom
Wing: Dyed dark gray deer hair, butts to
 form head

DOWNWING GREEN DRAKE

Originator: René Harrop & Family
Tier: Umpqua Feather Merchants
Hook: TMC 100, Mustad 94845, sizes 8-12
Thread: Olive 6/0 prewaxed
Tail: Dyed olive grizzly hackle fibers, forked
Rib: Bright olive floss, thin
Body: Olive rabbit dubbing
Hackle: Dyed olive grizzly hackle, clipped
 on the bottom
Wing: Black moose body hair, clipped
 butts form head

LOOP-WING BLUE DUN

Hook: TMC 100, Mustad 94845, sizes 12-18
Thread: Gray 6/0 prewaxed
Tail: Medium blue dun hackle fibers
Body: Gray muskrat fur
Wings: Clipped, gray mallard flank
 stem, looped
Hackle: Medium blue dun hackle

LOOP-WING MARCH BROWN

Hook: TMC 100, Mustad 94845, sizes 10-14
Thread: Tan 6/0 prewaxed
Tail: Dark ginger hackle fibers
Body: Tan rabbit dubbing
Wings: Clipped, woodduck flank
 stem, looped
Hackle: Dark ginger hackle

CLARKS GREEN DRAKE PARACHUTE

Originator: Lee Clark
Tier: Lee Clark
Hook: TMC 100, Mustad 94845, sizes 10-12
Thread: Green 6/0 prewaxed
Body: Flat gold tinsel, with green and brown macramé' yarn, combed and twisted
Wing: Dyed green deer hair
Hackle: Dyed olive grizzly hackle, parachute style

NATURAL DUN

Originator: Richard Bunse
Tier: Richard Bunse
Hook: Mustad 94838, size 12
Thread: Black 6/0 prewaxed
Tail: Beaver fur guard hair fibers
Body: Packing foam, colored with a waterproof marking pen, extended
Wing: Natural gray dun deer hair

COLORADO GREEN DRAKE

Tier: Umpqua Feather Merchants
Hook: TMC 100, Mustad 94845, sizes 10-12
Thread: Dark olive 6/0 prewaxed
Tail: Dark moose body hair
Rib: Dark olive floss
Body: Olive-brown rabbit dubbing
Wings: Medium blue dun hen hackles
Hackle: Dyed olive grizzly and brown hackle

GRAY DRAKE DUN

Originator: Doug Swisher and Carl Richards
Hook: TMC 5230, Mustad 94833, size 12
Thread: Gray 6/0 prewaxed
Tail: Dark gray hackle fibers
Body: Natural gray deer hair, extended
Wings: Gray partridge feathers, cut to shape
Hackle: Dark blue dun hackle, clipped on the bottom

HATCHMASTER

Hook: TMC 100, Mustad 94845, sizes 12-18
Thread: 6/0 prewaxed, to match body
Tail, Body, Wing: Same mallard flank feather, dyed to match natural
Hackle: To match natural

MAYFLY DRIES

CLARKS GREEN DRAKE PARACHUTE

BIG YELLOW MAY SPINNER

NATURAL DUN

BIG YELLOW MAY DUN

COLORADO GREEN DRAKE

CLARKS BIG YELLOW MAYFLY PARACHUTE

GRAY DRAKE DUN

BROWN PARA-DRAKE

HATCHMASTER

GREEN PARA-DRAKE

BIG YELLOW MAY SPINNER

Originator: Polly Rosborough
Hook: TMC 5212, Mustad 94831, size 8
Thread: Tan 6/0 prewaxed
Tail: Yellow and ginger hackle fibers
Body: Yellow rabbit dubbing
Wings: Yellow deer hair, semi spent
Hackle: Yellow and ginger hackle, mixed

BIG YELLOW MAY DUN

Originator: Polly Rosborough
Hook: TMC 5212, Mustad 94831, size 8
Thread: Yellow 6/0 prewaxed
Tail: Woodduck flank fibers
Rib: Yellow thread
Shellback: Woodduck flank fibers
Body: Yellow rabbit dubbing
Wings: Pale yellow hen hackle tips
Hackle: Yellow and light ginger hackle, mixed

CLARKS BIG YELLOW MAYFLY PARACHUTE

Originator: Lee Clark
Tier: Lee Clark
Hook: TMC 5262, Mustad 9671, sizes 8-10
Thread: Yellow 6/0 prewaxed
Body: Flat gold tinsel, with brown and yellow macramé yarn, combed and twisted
Wing: Dyed yellow deer hair
Hackle: Dyed yellow grizzly hackle, parachute style

BROWN PARA-DRAKE

Originator: Mike Lawson
Tier: Umpqua Feather Merchants
Hook: TMC 100, Mustad 94845, sizes 10-12
Thread: Pale yellow 6/0 prewaxed
Tail: Dark moose body hair, 3 fibers
Body: Dyed brown elk hair, extended
Wing: Natural dark elk hair
Hackle: Dyed light brown grizzly hack

GREEN PARA-DRAKE

Originator: Mike Lawson
Tier: Umpqua Feather Merchants
Hook: TMC 100, Mustad 94845, sizes 10-12
Thread: Olive 6/0 prewaxed
Tail: Dark moose body hair, 3 fibers
Rib: Olive thread, cross ribbed
Body: Dyed olive elk hair, extended
Wing: Moose body hair
Hackle: Dyed light olive grizzly hackle

SPENT PARTRIDGE CADDIS

Originator: Sheralee Lawson
Hook: TMC 100, Mustad 94845, sizes 14-20
Thread: Olive 6/0 prewaxed
Body: Dark olive rabbit dubbing
Wing: Two mottled partridge feathers, one on top of the other
Thorax: Peacock herl
Hackle: Brown and grizzly hackle, mixed, wrapped over the thorax

WOODCHUCK CADDIS

Hook: TMC 100, Mustad 94845, sizes 12-18
Thread: Orange 6/0 prewaxed
Body: Dirty orange rabbit dubbing
Wing: Woodchuck guard hairs
Hackle: Brown and grizzly hackle, mixed

PM CADDIS

Hook: TMC 100, Mustad 94845, sizes 10-18
Thread: Olive 6/0 prewaxed
Body: Olive rabbit dubbing
Wing: Natural fine brown deer hair
Hackle: Brown and grizzly hackle, mixed

HAIRWING CADDIS

Tier: Umpqua Feather Merchants
Hook: TMC 100, Mustad 94845, sizes 12-20
Thread: Black 6/0 prewaxed
Body: Muskrat fur
Wing: Natural dark deer hair
Hackle: Brown hackle

PEACOCK CADDIS

Originator: Jim Bonnett
Tier: Umpqua Feather Merchants
Hook: TMC 100, Mustad 94845, sizes 8-14
Thread: Black 6/0 prewaxed
Body: Peacock herl
Wing: Tan elk hair
Hackle: Brown and grizzly hackle, mixed

CADDIS FLY DRIES

SPENT PARTRIDGE CADDIS

GRAY CADDIS

WOODCHUCK CADDIS

POLY CADDIS

PM CADDIS

DELTA WING CADDIS

HAIRWING CADDIS

CANADIAN SEDGE

PEACOCK CADDIS

GRAY ELK CADDIS

GRAY CADDIS

Hook: TMC 100, Mustad 94845, sizes 10-16
Thread: Gray 6/0 prewaxed
Tail: Blue dun hackle fibers
Body: Brown olive poly dubbing
Shellback: Natural gray deer hair
Wing: Blue dun hackle fibers
Hackle: Blue dun hackle

POLY CADDIS

Originator: Gary Borger
Hook: TMC 100, Mustad 94845, sizes 10-18
Thread: Brown 6/0 prewaxed
Body: Medium brown rabbit dubbing
Hackle: Brown hackle, wrapped over thorax area
Wing: Golden tan poly yarn, butt end forms head

DELTA WING CADDIS

Originator: Larry Solomon
Hook: TMC 100, Mustad 94845, sizes 10-22
Thread: Gray 6/0 prewaxed
Body: Gray rabbit dubbing
Wings: Blue dun hen hackle tips, delta style
Hackle: Bronze dun hackle

CANADIAN SEDGE

Hook: TMC 100, Mustad 94845, sizes 6-10
Thread: Black 6/0 prewaxed
Body: Mallard breast feather or yarn to match natural
Rib: Gray, black or green floss
Wing: Mallard flank fibers
Hackle: Grizzly hackle

GRAY ELK CADDIS

Hook: TMC 100, Mustad 94845, sizes 12-20
Thread: Olive 6/0 prewaxed
Body: Insect green rabbit dubbing
Rib: Brown hackle, palmered over body and clipped short
Wing: Dyed gray elk hair
Hackle: Brown hackle

ELK HAIR CADDIS, tan

Originator: Al Troth
Tier: Umpqua Feather Merchants
Hook: TMC 100, Mustad 94845, sizes 10-20
Thread: Tan 6/0 prewaxed
Rib: Fine gold wire
Body: Tan rabbit dubbing
Hackle: Ginger hackle, palmered over body
Wing: Light elk hair, leave butts to form head

ELK HAIR CADDIS, black

Originator: Al Troth
Tier: Umpqua Feather Merchants
Hook: TMC 100, Mustad 94845, sizes 10-20
Thread: Black 6/0 prewaxed
Rib: Fine gold wire
Body: Black rabbit dubbing
Hackle: Black hackle, palmered over body
Wing: Light elk hair, leave butts to form head

DEER HAIR CADDIS

Originator: Jim Schollmeyer
Hook: TMC 100, Mustad 94845, sizes 10-20
Thread: Gray 6/0 prewaxed
Body: Olive rabbit dubbing
Hackle: Blue dun hackle, palmered over body
Wing: Natural dun deer hair

ELK HAIR CADDIS, olive

Originator: Al Troth
Tier: Umpqua Feather Merchants
Hook: TMC 100, Mustad 94845, sizes 10-20
Thread: Olive 6/0 prewaxed
Rib: Fine gold wire
Body: Olive rabbit dubbing
Hackle: Dyed olive grizzly hackle, palmered over body
Wing: Light elk hair, leave butts to form head

SUMMER CADDIS

Originator: Randle Scott Stetzer, color variation on Al Troth's Elk Hair Caddis.
Hook: TMC 100, Mustad 94845, sizes 12-22
Thread: Tan 6/0 prewaxed
Body: Peacock herl
Rib: Fine gold wire
Hackle: Grizzly hackle, palmered over body
Wing: Elk hair dyed dark cinnamon, butts to form head

CADDIS FLY DRIES

ELK HAIR CADDIS, tan

PARACHUTE CADDIS BUCK

ELK HAIR CADDIS, black

PARACHUTE CADDIS

DEER HAIR CADDIS

BUCKTAIL CADDIS, orange

ELK HAIR CADDIS, olive

BUCKTAIL CADDIS, yellow

SUMMER CADDIS

COLORADO KING

PARACHUTE CADDIS BUCK

Hook: TMC 100, Mustad 94845, sizes 12-18
Thread: Tan 6/0 prewaxed
Body: Gray rabbit dubbing
Wing: Natural brown elk hair, butt ends form post
Hackle: Ginger hackle, parachute style

PARACHUTE CADDIS

Originator: Ed Schroeder
Tier: Umpqua Feather Merchants
Hook: TMC 100, Mustad 94845, sizes 10-16
Thread: Gray 6/0 prewaxed
Body: Hare's mask dubbing
Wing: Mottled turkey wing quill, tented over the body
Post: White calf body hair
Hackle: Grizzly hackle, parachute style

BUCKTAIL CADDIS, orange

Tier: Umpqua Feather Merchants
Hook: TMC 100, Mustad 94845, sizes 6-12
Thread: Orange 6/0 prewaxed
Tail: Moose body hair
Body: Orange wool yarn
Hackle: Brown hackle, palmered over body
Wing: Deer hair

BUCKTAIL CADDIS, yellow

Tier: Umpqua Feather Merchants
Hook: TMC 100, Mustad 94845, sizes 6-12
Thread: Yellow 6/0 prewaxed
Tail: Moose body hair
Body: Yellow wool yarn
Hackle: Brown hackle, palmered over body
Wing: Deer hair

COLORADO KING

Originator: George Bodmer
Hook: TMC 100, Mustad 94845, sizes 10-18
Thread: Black 6/0 prewaxed
Tail: Two peccary fibers, long and forked
Body: Yellow rabbit dubbing
Hackle: Grizzly hackle, palmered over body
Wing: Elk hair, slightly longer than shank

STILLBORN ELK CADDIS

Hook: TMC 100, Mustad 94845, sizes 12-20
Thread: Brown 6/0 prewaxed
Body: Tan haretron dubbing
Wing: Elk hair
Head: Dark brown haretron dubbing

MICRO SUSPENDER CADDIS

Originator: Randle Scott Stetzer
Hook: TMC 5230, Mustad 94833,
    sizes 16-22
Thread: Black 6/0 prewaxed
Body: Fine black dubbing
Wing: Natural dark deer hair, up at 90
    degree angle, butts form head

ELK HAIR CADDIS

Hook: TMC 100, Mustad 94845,
    sizes 10-20
Thread: Black 6/0 prewaxed
Body: Black rabbit dubbing
Rib: Black hackle, undersized, clipped
    on top
Wing: Black elk hair
Hackle: Black hackle, clipped on top

DANCING CADDIS

Originator: Gary LaFontaine
Hook: Partridge K3A, sizes 12-18
Thread: Black 6/0 prewaxed
Body: Rabbit dubbing to match natural
Wing: Dark gray deer hair
Hackle: To match natural

STILLBORN CADDIS

Hook: TMC 5230, Mustad 94833,
    sizes 12-18
Thread: Olive 6/0 prewaxed
Tail: Dark brown hen hackle tip
Body: Tan rabbit dubbing
Shellback: Natural gray duck quill
Hackle: Dark ginger hackle

CADDIS FLY DRIES

STILLBORN ELK CADDIS

PARKANY DEER HAIR CADDIS

MICRO SUSPENDER CADDIS

CADDIS CRIPPLE, gray

ELK HAIR CADDIS

CADDIS CRIPPLE, olive

DANCING CADDIS

SKITTERING CADDIS

STILLBORN CADDIS

CADDIS TAIL FLY

PARKANY DEER HAIR CADDIS

Originator: Ken Parkany
Hook: TMC 100, Mustad 94845, sizes 8-16
Thread: Brown 6/0 prewaxed
Body: Light brown deer hair, spun and
    clipped
Wing: Mottled deer hair tips
Head: Mottled deer hair, butts from wing

CADDIS CRIPPLE, gray

Originator: Bob Quigley
Tier: Umpqua Feather Merchants
Hook: TMC 100, Mustad 94845, sizes 12-18
Thread: Gray 6/0 prewaxed
Tail: Gray marabou
Rib: Fine copper wire
Abdomen: Gray marabou, wrapped
Thorax: Dark gray rabbit dubbing
Wings: Cree hackle tips, to the sides
Head: Natural deer hair, spun and clipped
    box shape, tips on top to form overwing

CADDIS CRIPPLE, olive

Originator: Bob Quigley
Tier: Umpqua Feather Merchants
Hook: TMC 100, Mustad 94845, sizes 12-18
Thread: Olive 6/0 prewaxed
Tail: Dark olive marabou
Rib: Fine Copper wire
Abdomen: Dark olive marabou, wrapped
Thorax: Dark olive rabbit dubbing
Wings: Cree hackle tips, to the sides
Head: Natural deer hair, spun and clipped
    box shape, tips on top to form overwing

SKITTERING CADDIS

Originator: William R. Priest
Hook: TMC 100, Mustad 94845, sizes 14-18
Thread: Black 6/0 prewaxed
Body: Gray rabbit dubbing
Wing: White poly pro yarn, tied spent
Hackle: Brown and grizzly hackle, mixed

CADDIS TAIL FLY

Originator: Warren Johns
Hook: TMC 100, Mustad 94845, sizes 12-18
Thread: Brown 6/0 prewaxed
Tail: Mottled brown turkey quill, cut in a
    "V" and lacquered
Body: Gray-brown hare's ear fur
Rib: Grizzly hackle, palmered over body
Hackle: Brown hackle

CDC ADULT CADDIS, tan

Originator: René Harrop & Family
Tier: René Harrop
Hook: TMC 100, Mustad 94845, sizes 14-18
Thread: Tan 6/0 prewaxed
Body: Tan poly dubbing
Underwing: White Z-lon
Wing: Ginger CDC feather
Legs: Ginger CDC feather
Thorax: Tan poly dubbing

CDC ADULT CADDIS, olive

Originator: René Harrop & Family
Tier: René Harrop
Hook: TMC 100, Mustad 94345, sizes 14-18
Thread: Olive 6/0 prewaxed
Body: Olive poly dubbing
Underwing: Light dun Z-lon
Wing: Medium dun CDC feather
Legs: Medium dun CDC feather
Thorax: Olive poly dubbing

CDC ADULT CADDIS, black

Originator: René Harrop & Family
Tier: René Harrop
Hook: TMC 100, Mustad 94845, sizes 16-22
Thread: Black 6/0 prewaxed
Body: Black poly dubbing
Underwing: Black Z-lon
Wing: Black CDC feather
Legs: Black CDC feather
Thorax: Black poly dubbing

FLUTTERING CADDIS, ginger

Originator: Leonard Wright
Hook: TMC 100, Mustad 94845, sizes 12-16
Thread: Tan 6/0 prewaxed
Body: Ginger rabbit dubbing
Wing: Ginger mink tail guard hairs
Hackle: Ginger hackle

FLUTTERING CADDIS, black

Originator: Leonard Wright
Hook: TMC 100, Mustad 94845, sizes 12-16
Thread: Black 6/0 prewaxed
Body: Black rabbit dubbing
Wing: Black mink tail guard hairs
Hackle: Dark rusty dun hackle

CADDIS FLY DRIES

CDC ADULT CADDIS, tan

SPARKLE CADDIS, tan

CDC ADULT CADDIS, olive

SPARKLE CADDIS, olive

CDC ADULT CADDIS, black

DELTA CADDIS

FLUTTERING CADDIS, ginger

SLOW WATER CADDIS, brown

FLUTTERING CADDIS, black

SLOW WATER CADDIS, olive

SPARKLE CADDIS, tan

Originator: Craig Matthews
Tier: Umpqua Feather Merchants
Hook: TMC 100, Mustad 94845, sizes 14-18
Thread: Tan 6/0 prewaxed
Tail: Ginger Z-lon
Body: Tan poly dubbing
Wing: Natural deer hair
Head: Natural deer hair, butts from wing

SPARKLE CADDIS, olive

Originator: Craig Matthews
Tier: Umpqua Feather Merchants
Hook: TMC 100, Mustad 94845, sizes 14-18
Thread: Olive 6/0 prewaxed
Tail: Golden olive Z-lon
Body: Olive poly dubbing
Wing: Natural deer hair
Head: Natural deer hair, butts from wing

DELTA CADDIS

Originator: Bill Black
Tier: Spirit River Inc
Hook: TMC 100, Mustad 94845, sizes 14-18
Thread: Tan 6/0 prewaxed
Body: Tan fine dubbing
Underwing: White CDC feather
Wing: Light dun fly film
Hackle: Brown and grizzly hackle, mixed

SLOW WATER CADDIS, brown

Originator: René Harrop & Family
Tier: Umpqua Feather Merchants
Hook: TMC 100, Mustad 94845, sizes 12-16
Thread: Brown 6/0 prewaxed
Body: Brown rabbit or poly dubbing
Hackle: Brown hackle, wrapped over thorax area, clipped on the bottom
Wings: Dark brown hen hackle feathers, lacquered

SLOW WATER CADDIS, olive

Originator: René Harrop & Family
Tier: Umpqua Feather Merchants
Hook: TMC 100, Mustad 94845, sizes 12-18
Thread: Olive 6/0 prewaxed
Body: Light olive rabbit or poly dubbing
Hackle: Ginger hackle, wrapped over thorax area, clipped on the bottom
Wings: Light tan hen hackle feathers, lacquered

ARCTOPSYCHE GRANDIS

Hook: TMC 100, Mustad 94842, sizes 10-16
Thread: Olive 6/0 prewaxed
Body: Peacock herl
Underwing: Lemon woodduck fibers
Wing: Natural gray duck quill
Overwing: Black moose body hair
Hackle: Brown and grizzly hackle, mixed

DUN CADDIS

Hook: TMC 100, Mustad 94845, sizes 14-20
Thread: Gray 6/0 prewaxed
Body: 4-6 natural duck secondary wing
   quill fibers
Wing: Two dun hen saddle hackle
   feathers, lacquered
Hackle: Blue dun hackle
Antennae: Feather stems from wings

PENOBSCOT CADDIS

Hook: TMC 100, Mustad 94845, size 14
Thread: Black 6/0 prewaxed
Body: Hare's ear dubbing
Wing: Peacock secondary wing quill
Hackle: Brown hackle
Antennae: Two lemon woodduck fibers

CO'S CADDIS

Originator: Ron Cosgro
Hook: TMC 100, Mustad 94845, sizes 10-20
Thread: Gray 6/0 prewaxed
Body: Beaver fur
Wing: Ringneck pheasant back feather,
   lacquered
Hackle: Brown and grizzly hackle, mixed
Antennae: Two stripped grizzly
   hackle stems

VINCENT SEDGE

Hook: TMC 100, Mustad 94845, sizes 10-12
Thread: Olive 6/0 prewaxed
Body: Dark olive rabbit dubbing
Wing: Mottled turkey wing quill, "V" in end
Hackle: Cree hackle

CADDIS FLY DRIES

ARCTOPSYCHE GRANDIS

KING'S RIVER CADDIS

DUN CADDIS

TENTWING CADDIS

PENOBSCOT CADDIS

HENRYVILLE SPECIAL

CO'S CADDIS

FLAT WING CADDIS

VINCENT SEDGE

HEMMINGWAY CADDIS

KING'S RIVER CADDIS

Originator: Wayne Buszek
Tier: Umpqua Feather Merchants
Hook: TMC 100, Mustad 94845, sizes 12-18
Thread: Dark brown 6/0 prewaxed
Body: Tannish-brown rabbit dubbing
Wing: Mottled turkey wing quill, "V" at end
Hackle: Brown hackle

TENTWING CADDIS

Hook: TMC 100, Mustad 94845, sizes 12-20
Thread: Black 6/0 prewaxed
Body: Ringneck pheasant tail
   fibers, wrapped
Hackle: Dark ginger hackle, clipped top
   and bottom
Wing: Mottled turkey wing quill, "V" in end

HENRYVILLE SPECIAL

Originator: Hiram Brobst
Tier: Umpqua Feather Merchants
Hook: TMC 100, Mustad 94845, sizes 12-20
Thread: Black 6/0 prewaxed
Body: Olive rabbit dubbing
Rib: Grizzly hackle, undersized, palmered
Underwing: Lemon woodduck flank fibers
Wing: Natural gray duck quill, tent style
Hackle: Dark ginger hackle

FLAT WING CADDIS

Hook: TMC 100, Mustad 94845, sizes 14-20
Thread: Gray 6/0 prewaxed
Body: Muskrat fur
Rib: Brown hackle, trimmed top
   and bottom
Wing: Mottled turkey wing quill, "V" at end
Hackle: Brown hackle, trimmed on
   the bottom

HEMMINGWAY CADDIS

Originators: René Harrop and
   Jack Hemmingway
Tier: Umpqua Feather Merchants
Hook: TMC 100, Mustad 94845, sizes 12-20
Thread: Olive 6/0 prewaxed
Body: Medium olive rabbit dubbing
Rib: Medium blue dun hackle, undersized,
   palmered
Underwing: Lemon woodduck flank fibers
Wing: Natural gray duck quill, rounded
   at end
Thorax: Peacock herl
Hackle: Medium blue dun hackle, wound
   over thorax

GODDARD CADDIS

Originator: John Goddard
Tier: Umpqua Feather Merchants
Hook: TMC 100, Mustad 94845, sizes 10-16
Thread: Black 6/0 prewaxed
Body: Natural gray deer hair, spun and clipped to shape
Hackle: Brown hackle
Antennae: Brown hackle stems, stripped

OREGON ORANGE CADDIS

Hook: TMC 5212, Mustad 94831, sizes 8-12
Thread: Black 6/0 prewaxed
Body: Dirty orange rabbit dubbing
Rib: Orange hackle, palmered over body and clipped short
Wing: Deer hair
Hackle: Grizzly hackle

DARK CADDIS

Originator: Polly Rosborough
Hook: TMC 100, Mustad 94845, sizes 6-8
Thread: Black 6/0 prewaxed
Body: Dirty orange rabbit dubbing
Rib: Dark brown hackle, palmered over body
Wing: Dark brown deer hair
Hackle: Dark brown hackle

WHARRY CADDIS

Hook: TMC 100, Mustad 94845, sizes 10-16
Thread: Black 6/0 prewaxed
Tail: Light tan elk hair
Body: Dark brown dubbing
Wing: Light tan elk hair
Hackle: Cree hackle

DESCHUTES CADDIS

Hook: TMC 100, Mustad 94845, sizes 8-12
Thread: Brown 6/0 prewaxed
Tail: Natural gray-brown deer hair, very short
Body: Yellow rabbit dubbing
Wing: Light brown deer hair
Hackle: Dark ginger hackle

CADDIS FLY DRIES

GODDARD CADDIS

TRAVELING SEDGE

OREGON ORANGE CADDIS

MITCH'S SEDGE

DARK CADDIS

SALMON CANDY No. 4

WHARRY CADDIS

CLARK'S DEER HAIR CADDIS

DESCHUTES CADDIS

CREAM SACO CADDIS

TRAVELING SEDGE

Originator: Karl Poulson
Hook: TMC 100, 94845, sizes 8-12
Thread: Black 6/0 prewaxed
Tail: Tan calftail
Rib: Brown hackle, clipped short
Body: Light green dubbing
Wing: Dark deer hair
Hackle: Ginger and grizzly hackle, mixed, clipped on the bottom

MITCH'S SEDGE

Originator: Arthur Mikulak
Hook: TMC 5212, Mustad 94831, sizes 8-12
Thread: Black 6/0 prewaxed
Tail: Elk hair, sparse
Body: Rabbit dubbing of desired color
Mid-Wing: Elk hair
Wing: Elk hair, butt ends form head
Hackle: Brown hackle

SALMON CANDY No. 4

Originator: Lloyd Frese
Hook: TMC 5212, Mustad 94831, size 8
Thread: Black 6/0 prewaxed
Body: Medium olive dubbing
Wing: Deer hair, butt ends form head
Hackle: Brown and grizzly hackle, mixed

CLARK'S DEER HAIR CADDIS

Originator: Lee Clark
Tier: Lee Clark
Hook: TMC 5262, Mustad 9671, sizes 8-14
Thread: Orange 6/0 prewaxed
Body: Flat gold tinsel
Underwing: Orange macrame' yarn, combed
Wing: Deer hair
Hackle: Brown hackle

CREAM SACO CADDIS

Hook: TMC 100, Mustad 94845, sizes 10-16
Thread: Yellow 6/0 prewaxed
Tail: Cream elk hair
Body: Sulfur olive poly dubbing
Shellback: Cream elk hair
Wing: Ginger hackle fibers
Hackle: Ginger hackle

BLACK STONE FEMALE

Originator: Bob Quigley
Hook: TMC 5212, Mustad 94831,
   sizes 12-18
Thread: Black 6/0 prewaxed
Tail: Dyed black deer hair, short
Butt: Fine red wool
Rib: Black neck hackle, palmered
Body: Black rabbit fur, thin
Wing: Black deer hair, leave clipped butts
   to form head and antennae
Hackle: Black hackle

STIMULATOR, black

Originator: Randall Kaufmann
Tier: Umpqua Feather Merchants
Hook: TMC 200R, sizes 6-8
Thread: **Fluorescent** fire orange
   6/0 prewaxed
Tail: Black elk hair
Rib: Fine gold wire and dark blue
   dun hackle
Body: Black, blend of goat (black, purple,
   claret, rust, orange) and black haretron
Wing: Black elk hair
Hackle: Grizzly hackle, wrapped over
   the thorax
Thorax: Fluorescent fire orange antron

CDC LITTLE YELLOW STONE

Tier: Umpqua Feather Merchants
Hook: TMC 100, Mustad 94845, sizes 12-16
Thread: Yellow 6/0 prewaxed
Body: Yellow rabbit dubbing
Wing: Mottled turkey wing quill
Overwing: Cream CDC feather
Legs: Cream CDC feather

LITTLE YELLOW STONE

Originator: Polly Rosborough
Hook: TMC 5212, Mustad 94831,
   sizes 10-12
Thread: Yellow 6/0 prewaxed
Egg Sac: Crimson hackle, clipped short
Tail: Pale yellow grizzly hackle fibers
Rear Hackle: Pale yellow grizzly
   hackle, short
Rib: Yellow thread
Body: Chartreuse rabbit fur
Hackle: Pale yellow grizzly hackle

CLARK'S LITTLE YELLOW STONE

Originator: Lee Clark
Tier: Lee Clark
Hook: TMC 5263, Mustad 9672, size 14
Thread: Yellow 6/0 prewaxed
Body: Flat gold tinsel
Underwing: Gold macramé yarn, combed
Wing: Deer hair
Hackle: Dyed yellow grizzly hackle

STONE FLY DRIES

BLACK STONE FEMALE

IMPROVED GOLDEN STONE

STIMULATOR, black

CLARK'S STONEFLY

CDC LITTLE YELLOW STONE

BIRD'S STONE

LITTLE YELLOW STONE

STIMULATOR, golden

CLARK'S LITTLE YELLOW STONE

LITTLE BROWN STONE

IMPROVED GOLDEN STONE

Tier: Umpqua Feather Merchants
Hook: TMC 200R, Mustad 9672, sizes 6-10
Thread: Black 6/0 prewaxed
Tail: Bleached deer hair
Rib: Cream hackle
Body: Cream wool yarn
Wing: Natural elk hair
Hackle: Cream saddle hackle

CLARK'S STONEFLY

Originator: Lee Clark
Tier: Lee Clark
Hook: TMC 5263, Mustad 9672, sizes 8-10
Thread: Orange 6/0 prewaxed
Body: Flat gold tinsel
Underwing: Rust and gold macramé yarn,
   combed and mixed
Wing: Deer hair
Hackle: Brown saddle hackle

BIRD'S STONE

Originator: Cal Bird
Hook: TMC 5212, Mustad 94831, sizes 4-8
Thread: Orange 6/0 prewaxed
Tail: Dark moose mane, 2 strands
Rib: Furnace saddle hackle, trimmed
Body: Orange floss
Wing: Natural brown bucktail
Hackle: Furnace saddle hackle, clipped top
   and bottom
Antennae: Dark moose mane, 2 strands

STIMULATOR, golden

Originator: Randall Kaufmann
Tier: Umpqua Feather Merchants
Hook: TMC 200R, sizes 6-10
Thread: **Fluorescent** fire orange
   6/0 prewaxed
Tail: Golden-brown elk hair
Rib: Fine gold wire and blue dun hackle
Body: Golden blend of goat (gold, ginger,
   amber, yellow) and golden brown
   haretron
Wing: Golden-brown elk hair
Hackle: Furnace hackle, wrapped over
   the thorax
Thorax: Fluorescent fire orange
   antron dubbing

LITTLE BROWN STONE

Originator: Polly Rosborough
Hook: TMC 5212, Mustad 94831,
   sizes 12-14
Thread: Brown 6/0 prewaxed
Tail: Ringneck pheasant body feather
Rib: Brown thread, 6 turns
Body: Seal brown synthetic yarn
Wing: One dark grizzly hackle tip,
   flat overbody
Hackle: Grizzly hackle

IMPROVED SOFA PILLOW

Originator: Pat and Sig Barnes
Tier: Umpqua Feather Merchants
Hook: TMC 5263, Mustad 9672, sizes 4-10
Thread: Black 6/0 prewaxed
Tail: Natural elk hair
Rib: Brown hackle, undersized
Body: Orange wool yarn
Wing: Natural elk hair
Hackle: Brown saddle hackles

HENRY'S FORK SALMON FLY

Originator: Mike Lawson
Tier: Umpqua Feather Merchants
Hook: TMC 5263, Mustad 94831, sizes 6-8
Thread: Orange 3/0 monocord
Tail: Dark moose body hair
Rib: Brown hackle, clipped
Body: Orange sparkle yarn
Wing: Natural dark elk hair
Head: Dark moose body hair, tips
  form collar

EGG LAYING *PTERONARCYS*

Originator: John Hazel
Tier: John Hazel
Hook: TMC 200R, sizes 4-8
Thread: Black 6/0 prewaxed
Tail: Brown goose biots
Egg sac: Black goat dubbing, dubbed ball
  on the thread
Rib: Fine copper wire
Body: Orange goat dubbing
Body hackle: Dyed orange grizzly saddle
  hackle, clipped
Wing: Moose body hair
Thorax hackle: Dyed orange grizzly saddle
  hackle, clipped flat on the bottom, even
  with body hackle
Antennae: Brown goose biots

EGG LAYING *CALINEURIA*

Originator: John Hazel
Tier: John Hazel
Hook: TMC 200R, sizes 6-10
Thread: Yellow 6/0 prewaxed
Tail: Brown goose biots
Egg Sac: Black goat dubbing, dubbed ball
  on the thread
Rib: Fine copper wire
Body: Yellow goat dubbing
Body hackle: Ginger saddle hackle, clipped
Wing: Elk mane
Thorax hackle: Ginger saddle hackle,
  clipped on the bottom, even with body
  hackle
Antennae: Brown goose biots

LANGTRY SPECIAL

Hook: TMC 5263, Mustad 9672, sizes 6-10
Thread: Orange 6/0 prewaxed
Tail: Tan elk hair
Rib: Brown hackle, undersized
Body: Cream rabbit fur
Wing: Tan elk hair
Head: Orange goat fur
Hackle: Brown hackle

STONE FLY DRIES

IMPROVED SOFA PILLOW

SOFA PILLOW

HENRY'S FORK SALMON FLY

FLUTTERING STONE

EGG LAYING *PTERONARCYS*

WHIT'S ADULT STONE

EGG LAYING *CALINEURIA*

MOOSE HAIR STONE

LANGTRY SPECIAL

S.O.B. CREEK

SOFA PILLOW

Originator: Pat and Sig Barnes
Hook: TMC 5263, Mustad 9672, sizes 4-10
Thread: Brown 6/0 prewaxed
Tail: Red goose quill sections
Body: Red floss, thin
Wing: Red fox squirrel tail
Hackle: Brown saddle hackle

FLUTTERING STONE

Tier: Umpqua Feather Merchants
Hook: TMC 5212, Mustad 9671, sizes 4-8
Thread: Orange 6/0 prewaxed
Body: Orange poly pro yarn, woven and
  extended
Wing: Natural light elk hair
Overwing: Dark elk hair, short
Hackle: Brown saddle hackles
Antennae: Stripped brown hackle stems

WHIT'S ADULT STONE

Originator: Dave Whitlock
Tier: Umpqua Feather Merchants
Hook: TMC 7989, Mustad 90240, sizes 4-8
Thread: Orange 3/0 monocord
Tail: Two strands of clear monofilament
Rib: Brown saddle hackle
Body: Dyed orange deer hair, doubled over
  to form extended body
Wing: Natural elk hair
Head and Collar: Dyed brown deer hair
Antennae: Two strands of clear
  monofilament

MOOSE HAIR STONE

Originator: Bill McMillan
Hook: TMC 5263, Mustad 9672, size 6
Thread: Orange 6/0 prewaxed
Tail: Moose body hair, tied in to make
  overbody and head
Body: Bright red-orange goat dubbing
Wing: Moose body hair, flared butt ends to
  make head

S.O.B. CREEK

Originator: Scott Dawkins
Tier: Scott Dawkins
Hook: TMC 2312, sizes 6-8
Thread: Orange 3/0 monocord
Body: 1/2" wide orange fly foam, colored
  with a brown waterproof marker
Wing: Zing (Taiwanese packing tape), or
  other synthetic
Legs: Black rubber hackle
Thorax: Gray rabbit dubbing
Wingcase: Orange fly foam, colored with a
  brown waterproof marker
Antennae: Black rubber hackle

Chapter 2

Midges, Variants, and Spiders

❖

Terrestrials

❖

BLACK MIDGE PUPA

Hook: TMC 102Y, Mustad 94838,
    sizes 12-16
Thread: Black 6/0 prewaxed
Butt: Black ostrich herl
Body: Black floss
Feelers: Black hackle fibers

MIDGE PUPA

    Originator: Polly Rosborough
Hook: TMC 101, Mustad 94859, sizes 12-14
Thread: Tan 6/0 prewaxed
Butt: 3 black ostrich herl, twisted
Hackle: Grizzly neck hackle, short
Rib: Tan 3/0 thread
Body: Tan rabbit dubbing

TUNKWANAMID

    Originator: Tom Murray
Hook: TMC 101, Mustad 94859, sizes 10-16
Thread: Black 6/0 prewaxed
Rib: Fine silver wire
Body: Peacock herl, poor grade
Thorax: Gray ostrich herl

GRAY MIDGE NYMPH

Hook: TMC 101, Mustad 94859, sizes 16-24
Thread: Gray 6/0 prewaxed
Body: Dark muskrat fur
Thorax: Peacock herl

EMERGING PUPA

    Originator: Dave Whitlock
Hook: TMC 101, Mustad 94842, sizes 16-28
Thread: Black 6/0 prewaxed
Tail: Gray ostrich herl tips
Rib: Fine gold wire
Body: Natural dark deer hair
Thorax: Gray ostrich herl, wrapped over
    deer hair

MIDGES, VARIANTS, SPIDERS

BLACK
MIDGE PUPA

BLACK HERL
MIDGE

MIDGE PUPA

MOSQUITO
LARVA

TUNKWANAMID

E T PUPA

GRAY MIDGE
NYMPH

Y D C

EMERGING
PUPA

CDC MIDGE
PUPA

BLACK HERL MIDGE

Hook: TMC 101, Mustad 94859, sizes 20-28
Thread: Black 6/0 prewaxed
Tail: Black hackle fibers
Body: Black ostrich herl

MOSQUITO LARVA

Hook: TMC 100, Mustad 94845, sizes 14-18
Thread: Gray 6/0 prewaxed
Tail: Grizzly hackle fibers
Body: Stripped grizzly hackle stem
Thorax: Grizzly saddle hackle, clipped
Feelers: Grizzly hackle fibers

E T PUPA

    Originator: Jeff Edvalds
Hook: TMC 5212, Mustad 94831,
    sizes 10-16
Thread: Black 6/0 prewaxed
Rib: Fine silver wire
Body: Dark pheasant tail fibers
Thorax: Natural gray filoplume
Wingcase: Dark dun deer hair
Head: White ostrich herl

Y D C

    Originator: Wayne Yoshida
Hook: TMC 5263, Mustad 9672, sizes 10-12
Thread: Black 6/0 prewaxed
Rib: White 3/0 thread
Body: Black poly pro yarn, thin
Wingcase: Pheasant rump fibers
Thorax: White ostrich herl

CDC MIDGE PUPA

    Originator: René Harrop & Family
    Tier: René Harrop
Hook: TMC 5230, Mustad 94833,
    sizes 14-20
Thread: Black 6/0 prewaxed
Body: Stripped black ostrich herl
Wingcase: White CDC feather, colored gray
    with a waterproof marker
Thorax: Black rabbit dubbing
Head Tuft: White CDC feather, butt
    from wingcase

PEACOCK CHIRONOMID

Hook: TMC 5212, Mustad 94831, sizes 10-16
Thread: White 6/0 prewaxed
Rib: Fine copper wire
Body: Stripped peacock herl
Thorax: Peacock herl
Head: White ostrich herl

CHAN'S CHIRONOMID

Originator: Brian Chan
Hook: TMC 5262, Mustad 9671, sizes 6-16
Thread: Brown 6/0 prewaxed
Tail: Guinea hackle fibers
Rib: Fine gold wire
Body: Pheasant tail fibers
Thorax: Peacock herl
Gills: White antron yarn
Wingcase: Mottled turkey wing quill

T D C

Originator: Richard Thompson
Hook: TMC 5262, Mustad 9671, sizes 6-12
Thread: Black 6/0 prewaxed
Rib: Fine flat silver tinsel
Body: Black rabbit dubbing, tapered
Thorax: Black rabbit fur, 1 1/2 times body
Head: White ostrich herl

RISING MIDGE PUPA

Originator: Dave Whitlock
Hook: TMC 101, Mustad 94842, sizes 16-28
Thread: Gray 6/0 prewaxed
Tail: 2 gray ostrich herl tips, short
Body: Beaver belly underfur
Thorax: Gray ostrich herl, over the body

PUBLIC ENEMY NO. 1

Originator: Don Roberts
Hook: TMC 5262, Mustad 9672, sizes 12-16
Thread: Black 6/0 prewaxed
Tail: Grizzly hackle fibers, short
Body: Stripped grizzly hackle stem
Thorax: Black ostrich herl
Throat: Soft gray deer hair
Wings: Grizzly hen hackle tips

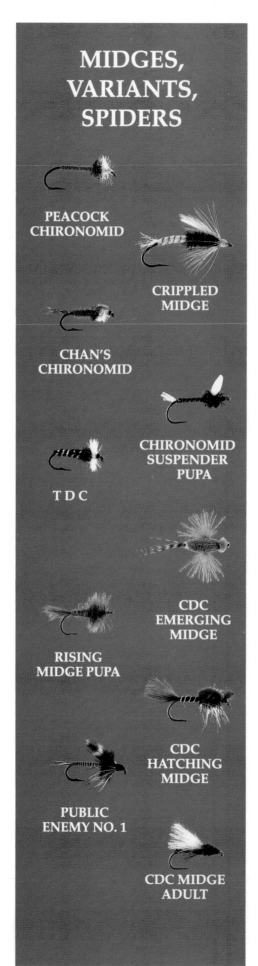

MIDGES, VARIANTS, SPIDERS

PEACOCK CHIRONOMID

CRIPPLED MIDGE

CHAN'S CHIRONOMID

CHIRONOMID SUSPENDER PUPA

T D C

CDC EMERGING MIDGE

RISING MIDGE PUPA

CDC HATCHING MIDGE

PUBLIC ENEMY NO. 1

CDC MIDGE ADULT

CRIPPLED MIDGE

Originator: Greg Carrier
Tier: Greg Carrier
Hook: TMC 200, sizes 12-18
Thread: White 6/0 prewaxed
Tail: Clear antron strands
Rib: Fine copper wire
Body: Rear 1/2; clear antron, front 1/2; peacock herl
Wing: Two white or cream hackle tips
Hackle: White hackle, two to three wraps

CHIRONOMID SUSPENDER PUPA

Originator: Doug Jorgensen
Tier: Doug Jorgensen
Hook: TMC 101, Mustad 94859, sizes 12-20
Thread: Black 6/0 prewaxed
Tail: Closed cell packing foam
Rib: Fine gold wire
Body: Closed cell packing foam, colored with a waterproof marker
Thorax: Peacock herl
Bubble: Closed cell packing foam

CDC EMERGING MIDGE

Originator: René Harrop & Family
Tier: René Harrop
Hook: TMC 5230, Mustad 94833, sizes 14-20
Thread: Olive 6/0 prewaxed
Tail: Teal Flank
Shellback: Gray evazote
Body: Olive poly dubbing
Legs: Gray dun CDC feathers
Head: Gray evazote, butt from shellback

CDC HATCHING MIDGE

Originator: Randall Kaufmann
Tier: Umpqua Feather Merchants
Hook: TMC 100, Mustad 94845, sizes 14-20
Thread: Black 6/0 prewaxed
Tail: Dark dun CDC feather
Rib: White thread
Body: Black thread
Wingcase: Dark dun CDC feather
Thorax: Peacock herl
Hackle: Grizzly hackle
Head: Butts from wingcase

CDC MIDGE ADULT

Originator: René Harrop & Family
Tier: René Harrop
Hook: TMC 5230, Mustad 94833, sizes 14-20
Thread: Black 6/0 prewaxed
Body: Stripped black ostrich herl
Wing: White CDC feather
Legs: Black CDC feathers
Thorax: Black rabbit dubbing

GRAY FOX VARIANT

Hook: TMC 100, Mustad 94845, sizes 10-16
Thread: Yellow 6/0 prewaxed
Tail: Golden ginger hackle fibers
Body: Stripped ginger hackle stem
Hackle: Golden ginger, dark ginger, and grizzly hackle mixed.

HAIR SPIDER

Originator: Al Troth
Hook: Mustad 9523, size 12
Thread: Yellow 3/0 monocord
Tail: Natural deer hair
Body: Yellow tying thread
Hackle: Natural deer hair, spun

BADGER SPIDER

Hook: Mustad 9523, sizes 10-18
Thread: Black 6/0 prewaxed
Tail: Badger hackle fibers
Hackle: Badger hackle, oversized

DUN VARIANT

Hook: TMC 100, Mustad 94845, sizes 10-18
Thread: Olive 6/0 prewaxed
Tail: Dark blue dun hackle fibers
Body: Stripped brown hackle stem
Hackle: Dark blue dun hackle

CLARET SMUT

Hook: TMC 101, Mustad 94859, sizes 18-28
Thread: Claret 6/0 prewaxed
Tail: Brown hackle fibers
Body: Claret silk floss
Hackle: Brown hackle

MIDGES, VARIANTS, SPIDERS

GRAY FOX VARIANT

CREAM MIDGE

HAIR SPIDER

FISHERMAN'S CURSE

BADGER SPIDER

BLACK MIDGE

DUN VARIANT

GRIFFITH'S GNAT

CLARET SMUT

CDC CLUSTER MIDGE

CREAM MIDGE

Hook: TMC 101, Mustad 94859, sizes 18-28
Thread: White 6/0 prewaxed
Tail: Cream hackle fibers
Body: Cream rabbit dubbing
Hackle: Cream hackle

FISHERMAN'S CURSE

Hook: TMC 101, Mustad 94859, sizes 18-28
Thread: Black 6/0 prewaxed
Tail: Blackish-gray dun hackle fibers
Body: 2-3 pheasant tail fibers
Hackle: Blackish-gray dun hackle

BLACK MIDGE

Hook: TMC 101, Mustad 94859, sizes 20-26
Thread: Black 6/0 prewaxed
Tail: Black hackle fibers
Body: Black rabbit dubbing
Hackle: Black neck hackle

GRIFFITH'S GNAT

Originator: George Griffith
Hook: TMC 101, Mustad 94859, sizes 18-28
Thread: Olive 6/0 prewaxed
Rib: Fine gold wire
Body: Peacock herl
Hackle: Grizzly hackle, palmered over the body

CDC CLUSTER MIDGE

Originator: René Harrop & Family
Tier: René Harrop
Hook: TMC 100, Mustad 94845, sizes 16-20
Thread: Olive 6/0 prewaxed
Body: Peacock herl
Hackle: Grizzly hackle, palmered over the body
Wing: White CDC feather

HENRY'S FORK HOPPER

Originator: Mike Lawson
Tier: Umpqua Feather Merchants
Hook: TMC 5212, Mustad 94831, sizes 8-12
Thread: Yellow 6/0 prewaxed
Body: White deer body hair
Rib: Yellow thread
Underwing: Dyed yellow elk hair
Wing: Brown speckled hen saddle
  feather, lacquered
Head: Elk hair, tied forward then pulled
  back to form collar, bullet style

JACKLIN'S HOPPER

Originator: Bob Jacklin
Tier: Umpqua Feather Merchants
Hook: TMC 5212, Mustad 94831, sizes 6-14
Thread: Yellow 6/0 prewaxed
Tail: Red deer hair
Butt: Fluorescent green fuzzy wool
Body: Fluorescent green fuzzy wool
Hackle: Brown hackle, clipped
Wing: Natural gray goose quill
Collar: Natural light elk hair, tips from head
Head: Natural light elk hair, bullet style

JOE'S HOPPER

Tier: Umpqua Feather Merchants
Hook: TMC 5212, Mustad 94831, sizes 6-14
Thread: Black 6/0 prewaxed
Tail: Red hackle fibers
Butt: Yellow poly foam
Body: Yellow wool yarn
Rib: Brown hackle, clipped
Wings: Mottled turkey wing quill
Hackle: Brown and grizzly hackle, mixed

PARACHUTE HOPPER

Originator: Ed Schroeder
Tier: Umpqua Feather Merchants
Hook: TMC 5212, Mustad 94831, sizes 8-14
Thread: Tan 6/0 prewaxed
Hackle Post: White calf body hair
Body: Tan rabbit fur
Wing: Mottled turkey wing quill
Legs: Ringneck pheasant tail
  fibers, knotted
Hackle: Grizzly hackle

AUSSI HOPPER

Originator: Bruce Whalen
Hook: TMC 5212, Mustad 9671, sizes 8-14
Thread: Yellow 6/0 prewaxed
Body: Yellow deer hair with natural latex
  wrapped over the top
Wings: Whole golden pheasant tippets
Overwing: Deer hair tips from head
Head: Natural deer hair

TERRESTRIALS

HENRY'S FORK HOPPER

RUBBER LEGS HENRY'S FORK HOPPER

JACKLIN'S HOPPER

MacHOPPER

JOE'S HOPPER

PHEASANT LEG HOPPER

PARACHUTE HOPPER

DAVE'S HOPPER

AUSSI HOPPER

CLARKS HOPPER

RUBBER LEGS HENRY'S FORK HOPPER

Originator: Mike Lawson
Umpqua Feather Merchants
Hook: TMC 5212, Mustad 94831, sizes 8-12
Thread: Yellow 6/0 prewaxed
Body: White deer hair
Rib: Yellow thread
Underwing: Dyed yellow elk hair
Wing: Brown speckled hen saddle
  feather, lacquered
Head: Elk hair, tied forward then pulled
  back to form collar, bullet style
Legs: Cream round rubber hackle, knotted

MacHOPPER

Originator: Al Troth
Tier: Umpqua Feather Merchants
Hook: TMC 5263, Mustad 79580, size 8
Thread: Yellow 6/0 prewaxed
Body: Yellow braided macramé cord,
  3/8" extended
Underwing: pearl-yellow Krystal Flash
Wing: Dark mottled fly film
Legs: Yellow rubber hackle, knotted
Head &Collar: Olive-yellow dyed deer hair,
  bullet style

PHEASANT LEG HOPPER

Tier: John Hazel
Hook: TMC 300, Mustad 79580, sizes 6-10
Thread: Black 6/0 prewaxed
Rib: Fine copper wire
Body: Pale yellow rabbit dubbing
Underwing: Yellow deer hair
Wing: Mottled turkey quill
Legs: Knotted pheasant tail fibers, long
Collar: Natural dark deer hair
Head: Natural dark deer hair, spun
  and clipped

DAVE'S HOPPER

Originator: Dave Whitlock
Tier: Umpqua Feather Merchants
Hook: TMC 5212, Mustad 94831, sizes 4-12
Thread: Gray 6/0 prewaxed
Tail: Red deer hair, and small loop of
  yellow yarn
Body: Yellow wool yarn
Hackle: Brown hackle, palmered over the
  body and clipped
Underwing: Yellow calftail
Wing: Turkey wing quill, lacquered
Legs: Dyed yellow grizzly hackle stems,
  clipped and knotted
Collar: Natural light tan deer hair, spun
Head: Natural light tan deer hair, spun
  and clipped

CLARKS HOPPER

Originator: Lee Clark
Tier: Lee Clark
Hook: TMC 5263, Mustad 9672, sizes 8-12
Thread: Yellow 6/0 prewaxed
Tail: Red macramé yarn
Body: Flat gold tinsel
Underwing: Gold macramé yarn, combed
Wing: Deer hair
Hackle: Brown saddle hackle

WALNUT CATERPILLAR

Hook: TMC 300, Mustad 79580, sizes 6-8
Thread: Black 6/0 prewaxed
Butt: Black chenille
Tail: Black stripped goose fibers
Rib: Black hackle, clipped close
Stripes: Black chenille, on each side
Body: Yellow chenille
Head: Red chenille

LETORT CRICKET

Originator: Ed Shenk
Hook: TMC 5212, Mustad 94831, sizes 12-16
Thread: Black 6/0 prewaxed
Body: Black rabbit fur
Wing: Black goose quill
Overwing: Black deer hair
Head: Black deer hair, spun and clipped

HAIR CRICKET

Originator: Al Troth
Hook: TMC 5212, Mustad 94831, sizes 6-16
Thread: Black 6/0 prewaxed
Body: Black elk hair, tied toward rear and pulled forward
Rib: Black thread
Underwing: Black goose quill
Overwing: Black elk hair, butt ends form head
Legs: Black stripped goose

CICADA

Originator: George Harvey
Hook: TMC 100, Mustad 94845, sizes 4-6
Thread: Black 3/0 monocord
Body: Natural brown deer hair, spun and clipped
Wings: 4 blue dun hackle tips, tied in at thorax

DRY WOOLLY WORM

Hook: TMC 5212, Mustad 94831, sizes 8-12
Thread: Olive 6/0 prewaxed
Body: Olive rabbit fur
Hackle: Grizzly hackle, reverse palmered through body, V clipped on the bottom

TERRESTRIALS

WALNUT CATERPILLAR
LETORT HOPPER
LETORT CRICKET
MEADOW GRASSHOPPER
HAIR CRICKET
GREEN CICADA
CICADA
ELK HOPPER
DRY WOOLLY WORM
SPRUCE MOTH

LETORT HOPPER

Originator: Ed Shenk
Hook: TMC 5212, Mustad 94831, sizes 8-16
Thread: Gray 6/0 prewaxed
Body: Yellow rabbit fur
Wing: Mottled turkey wing quill
Overwing: Natural deer hair
Head: Natural deer hair, spun and clipped

MEADOW GRASSHOPPER

Originator: Polly Rosborough
Hook: TMC 5212, Mustad 94831, sizes 8-10
Thread: Gray 6/0 prewaxed
Body: Pale cream yarn
Rib: Ginger hackle, palmered over the body and clipped
Underwing: Yellow bucktail, sparse
Overwing: Mottled turkey wing quill
Hackle: Ginger and grizzly hackle, mixed

GREEN CICADA

Tier: Umpqua Feather Merchants
Hook: TMC 5212, Mustad 94831, sizes 6-12
Thread: Green 6/0 prewaxed
Tail: Natural deer hair
Butt: Lime green wool yarn
Body: Lime green wool yarn
Hackle: Medium dun hackle, clipped
Legs: Dyed olive grizzly hackle stems, clipped and knotted
Collar: Dyed green deer hair, spun
Head: Dyed green deer hair, spun and clipped

ELK HOPPER

Originator: John Bailey
Tier: Umpqua Feather Merchants
Hook: TMC 5212, Mustad 94831, sizes 6-12
Thread: Black 6/0 prewaxed
Tail: Red hackle fibers
Butt: Yellow wool yarn
Body: Yellow wool yarn
Rib: Brown hackle, palmered over body, clipped short
Wing: Natural elk hair, slightly flared
Hackle: Brown and grizzly hackle, mixed

SPRUCE MOTH

Hook: TMC 5212, Mustad 94831, size 10
Thread: Black 6/0 prewaxed
Tail: Golden pheasant tippets
Body: Tan wool yarn, thin
Hackle: Ginger hackle
Wing: Natural light tan deer hair, leave butts to form head

BLACK BEETLE

Hook: TMC 100, Mustad 94845, sizes 14-20
Thread: Black 6/0 prewaxed
Shellback: Dyed black deer hair, clipped to
form legs and head
Body: Black wool yarn

FOAM BEETLE

Hook: TMC 900BL, Mustad 94845,
sizes 8-14
Thread: Black 6/0 prewaxed
Shellback: Black evazote
Body: Black rabbit dubbing
Legs: Black rubber hackle
Thorax: Red yarn, small spot
Head: Black evazote, butt from shellback

DAVE'S JAPANESE BEETLE

Originator: Dave Whitlock
Tier: Umpqua Feather Merchants
Hook: TMC 100, Mustad 94845, sizes 10-14
Thread: Yellow 6/0 prewaxed
Body: Flat gold tinsel
Abdomen: Light gold deer hair
Legs: Light gold deer hair
Indicator: Fl. orange deer hair
Thorax: Light gold deer hair
Antennae: Light gold deer hair
Markings: Black waterproof marker

BEETLE

Hook: TMC 100, Mustad 94845, sizes 14-20
Thread: Black 6/0 prewaxed
Shellback: Gray goose quill
Body: Peacock herl
Hackle: Black hackle, palmered through
body, clipped on the bottom

INCHWORM

Hook: TMC 5212, Mustad 94831, size14
Thread: Green 3/0 monocord
Body: Green deer hair, tied toward the rear
and pulled forward
Rib: Green thread
Head: Peacock herl

TERRESTRIALS

BLACK
BEETLE

CDC
FLYING ANT

FOAM BEETLE

DAVE'S
JAPANESE
BEETLE

BROWN
FLYING
ANT

BEETLE

AUTUMN
ANT

CARPENTER
ANT

INCHWORM

DEER
HAIR
BEE

CDC FLYING ANT

Originator: Ken Shimazaki
Tier: Umpqua Feather Merchants
Hook: TMC 100, Mustad 94845, sizes 10-16
Thread: Brown 6/0 prewaxed
Tag: Brown thread
Abdomen: Reddish tan rabbit dubbing
Wings: Light dun CDC feathers
Hackle: Brown hackle
Head Shellback: White CDC feather, tips to
form overwing
Head: Reddish tan rabbit dubbing

BROWN FLYING ANT

Tier: Umpqua Feather Merchants
Hook: TMC 100, Mustad 94845, sizes 14-18
Thread: Brown 6/0 prewaxed
Abdomen: Medium brown rabbit fur, form a
hump
Wing: Two blue dun hackle tips
Hackle: Brown hackle
Thorax: Medium brown rabbit fur, form a
hump

AUTUMN ANT

Originator: Lloyd Byerly
Hook: TMC 100, Mustad 94845, sizes 14-16
Thread: Black 6/0 prewaxed
Tail: Black hackle fibers
Body: Black rabbit fur, two distinctive humps
Wings: Two furnace hackle tips
Hackle: Black hackle

CARPENTER ANT

Originator: Dave Whitlock
Tier: Umpqua Feather Merchants
Hook: TMC 100, Mustad 94845, sizes 10-16
Thread: Black 6/0 prewaxed
Abdomen: Black deer hair
Legs: Black deer hair
Indicator: Fluorescent orange glo bug yarn
Thorax: Black deer hair
Antennae: Black deer hair

DEER HAIR BEE

Hook: TMC 100, Mustad 94845, sizes 8-12
Thread: Black 6/0 prewaxed
Body: Alternating black and yellow deer
hair, spun and clipped
Wing: Natural deer hair tips, tied in
at thorax

BLACK DEER HAIR ANT

Originator: Chauncy K. Lively
Hook: TMC 100, Mustad 94845, sizes 10-14
Thread: Black 6/0 prewaxed
Butt: Black deer hair, pulled forward to form hump
Legs: Black deer hair, butt ends
Thorax: Black deer hair, pulled forward to form hump

CDC ANT

Originator: René Harrop & Family
Tier: René Harrop
Hook: TMC 100, Mustad 94845, sizes 14-16
Thread: Black 6/0 prewaxed
Shellback: Black CDC feather, over both humps
Abdomen: Black rabbit dubbing
Legs: Black CDC feathers
Thorax: Black rabbit dubbing

CARPENTER ANT

Hook: TMC 100, Mustad 94845, sizes 12-16
Thread: Black 6/0 prewaxed
Body: Black deer hair
Legs: Black deer hair, tips from body

BLACK FUR ANT

Hook: TMC 100, Mustad 94845, sizes 14-20
Thread: Black 6/0 prewaxed
Abdomen: Black rabbit fur, form a hump
Hackle: Black hackle
Thorax: Black rabbit fur, form a hump

BLACK CDC ANT

Hook: TMC 100, Mustad 94845, sizes 14-20
Thread: Black 6/0 prewaxed
Body: Black rabbit dubbing, form a hump
Hackle: Dark dun CDC feather, wrapped
Thorax: Black rabbit dubbing, form a hump

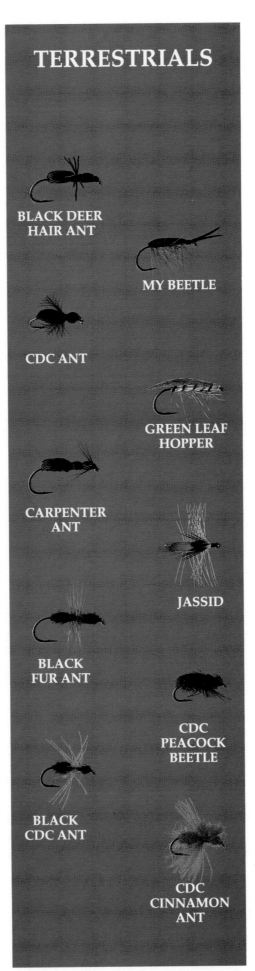

TERRESTRIALS

BLACK DEER HAIR ANT

MY BEETLE

CDC ANT

GREEN LEAF HOPPER

CARPENTER ANT

JASSID

BLACK FUR ANT

CDC PEACOCK BEETLE

BLACK CDC ANT

CDC CINNAMON ANT

MY BEETLE

Originator: Dave Engerbretson
Hook: TMC 100, Mustad 94845, sizes 16-24
Thread: Black 6/0 prewaxed
Shellback: Black duck quill
Body: Black thread
Hackle: Black hackle, palmered over the body, clipped on top
Antennae: Black duck quill, left from shellback

GREEN LEAF HOPPER

Hook: TMC 100, Mustad 94845, sizes 16-22
Thread: White 6/0 prewaxed
Body: White thread
Hackle: Insect green hackle, palmered over body, clipped top and bottom
Wing: Insect green mallard flank, lacquered

JASSID

Originator: Vince Marinaro
Hook: TMC 101, Mustad 94859, sizes 16-24
Thread: Black 6/0 prewaxed
Body: Black thread
Hackle: Ginger hackle, palmered over the body, clipped top and bottom
Wing: Single jungle cock eye

CDC PEACOCK BEETLE

Originator: René Harrop & Family
Tier: René Harrop
Hook: TMC 100, Mustad 94845, sizes 14-16
Thread: Black 6/0 prewaxed
Shellback: Black CDC feather
Body: Peacock herl
Legs: Black CDC feathers
Head: Butts from shellback

CDC CINNAMON ANT

Hook: TMC 100, Mustad 94845, sizes 14-18
Thread: Brown 6/0 prewaxed
Body: Rust rabbit dubbing, form a hump
Hackle: Dark dun CDC feather, wrapped
Indicator: Fluorescent orange tow yarn
Thorax: Rust rabbit dubbing

Chapter 3
Wet Flies
❖
Soft Hackle Flies
❖

IRON BLUE DUN

Hook: TMC 3761, Mustad 3906, sizes 10-16
Thread: Black 6/0 prewaxed
Tail: Furnace hackle fibers
Butt: Red floss
Body: Muskrat fur
Hackle: Furnace hen hackle
Wing: Natural dark duck wing quill

BLUE DUN

Tier: Umpqua Feather Merchants
Hook: TMC 3761, Mustad 3906, sizes 10-16
Thread: Gray 6/0 prewaxed
Tail: Medium blue dun hackle fibers
Body: Muskrat fur
Hackle: Medium blue dun hen hackle
Wing: Natural gray duck quill

GRAY HACKLE PEACOCK

Tier: John Kistler
Hook: TMC 3761, Mustad 3906, sizes 10-14
Thread: Black 6/0 prewaxed
Tail: Red hackle fibers
Body: Peacock herl
Hackle: Grizzly hen hackle

BLUE QUILL

Hook: TMC 3769, Mustad 3906, sizes 12-16
Thread: Black 6/0 prewaxed
Tail: Medium blue dun hackle fibers
Rib: Fine gold wire
Body: Stripped peacock herl
Hackle: Medium blue dun hen hackle
Wing: Natural gray duck quill

AMERICAN MARCH BROWN

Hook: TMC 3761, Mustad 3906, sizes 10-14
Thread: Black 6/0 prewaxed
Tail: Dark ginger hackle fibers
Rib: Yellow thread
Body: Grayish-tan rabbit dubbing
Hackle: Dark ginger hen hackle
Wing: Mottled turkey wing quill

WET FLIES

IRON BLUE DUN

WICKHAM'S FANCY

BLUE DUN

YELLOW DUN

GRAY HACKLE PEACOCK

OLIVE QUILL

BLUE QUILL

LIGHT CAHILL

AMERICAN MARCH BROWN

PALE EVENING DUN

WICKHAM'S FANCY

Hook: TMC 3761, Mustad 3906, sizes 10-16
Thread: Black 6/0 prewaxed
Rib: Fine gold wire
Body: Flat gold tinsel
Hackle: Golden ginger hackle, palmered over body
Wing: Natural gray duck wing quill

YELLOW DUN

Originator: Doc Phillips
Hook: TMC 3761, Mustad 3906, sizes 4-10
Thread: Black 6/0 prewaxed
Tail: Barred woodduck flank fibers
Rib: Fine oval gold tinsel
Body: Fleshy pink rabbit dubbing
Hackle: Dark ginger hen hackle
Wing: Lemon woodduck flank fibers

OLIVE QUILL

Hook: TMC 3761, Mustad 3906, sizes 10-16
Thread: Olive 6/0 prewaxed
Tail: Olive hackle fibers
Rib: Fine gold wire
Body: Stripped peacock herl
Hackle: Olive hen hackle
Wing: Lemon woodduck flank fibers

LIGHT CAHILL

Tier: Umpqua Feather Merchants
Hook: TMC 3761, Mustad 3906, sizes 10-16
Thread: Cream 6/0 prewaxed
Tail: Ginger hackle fibers
Body: Cream rabbit dubbing
Hackle: Ginger hen hackle
Wing: Lemon woodduck flank fibers

PALE EVENING DUN

Hook: TMC 3761, Mustad 3906, sizes 14-18
Thread: Pale yellow 6/0 prewaxed
Tail: Light dun hackle fibers
Body: Pale yellow rabbit dubbing
Hackle: Pale dun hen hackle
Wing: Natural light gray duck wing quill

TIMBERLINE EMERGER, gray

Originator: Randall Kaufmann
Tier: Umpqua Feather Merchants
Hook: TMC 3761, Mustad 3906, sizes 10-16
Thread: Gray 6/0 prewaxed
Tail: Natural grizzly marabou
Rib: Copper wire
Body: Gray haretron dubbing
Hackle: Brown hen hackle
Wing: Hen grizzly hackle tips

TIMBERLINE EMERGER, olive

Originator: Randall Kaufmann
Tier: Umpqua Feather Merchants
Hook: TMC 3761, Mustad 3906, sizes 10-16
Thread: Olive 6/0 prewaxed
Tail: Olive grizzly marabou
Rib: Copper wire
Body: Olive haretron
Hackle: Two turns of dyed olive grizzly
hen hackle
Wings: Two grizzly hen hackle tips

BLACK GNAT

Tier: Umpqua Feather Merchants
Hook: TMC 3761, Mustad 3906, sizes 10-14
Thread: Black 6/0 prewaxed
Tail: Black hackle fibers
Body: Black rabbit dubbing
Hackle: Black hen hackle
Wings: Natural gray duck quill

LEADWING COACHMAN

Tier: Umpqua Feather Merchants
Hook: TMC 3761, Mustad 3906, sizes 6-16
Thread: Black 6/0 prewaxed
Tip: Fine flat gold tinsel
Body: Peacock herl
Hackle: Brown hen hackle
Wing: Natural gray duck quill

ALDER

Hook: TMC 3761, Mustad 3906, sizes 10-14
Thread: Black 6/0 prewaxed
Tag: Fine flat gold tinsel
Body: Peacock herl
Hackle: Black hen hackle
Wing: Mottled turkey wing quill

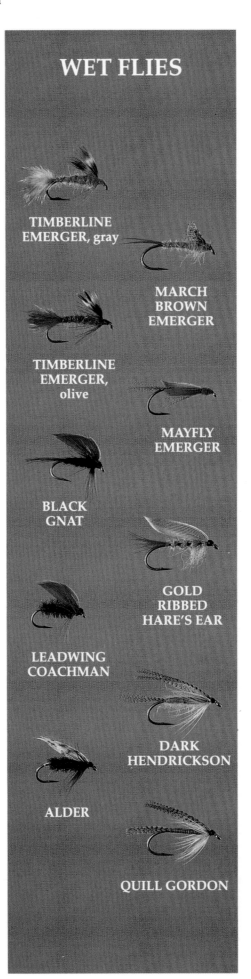

WET FLIES

TIMBERLINE
EMERGER, gray

MARCH
BROWN
EMERGER

TIMBERLINE
EMERGER,
olive

MAYFLY
EMERGER

BLACK
GNAT

GOLD
RIBBED
HARE'S EAR

LEADWING
COACHMAN

DARK
HENDRICKSON

ALDER

QUILL GORDON

MARCH BROWN EMERGER

Originator: Al Troth
Hook: TMC 3769, Mustad 3906B,
sizes 10-12
Thread: Brown 6/0 prewaxed
Tail: Three ringneck pheasant tail fibers
Rib: Gold thread, rib body only
Body: Hare's ear fur
Thorax: Hare's ear fur
Collar: Hare's ear fur, well picked out
Wingcase: Brown partridge hackle
fibers, short
Head: Hare's ear fur

MAYFLY EMERGER

Hook: TMC 100, Mustad 94845, sizes 12-20
Thread: 6/0 prewaxed, to match natural
Tail: Lemon woodduck flank fibers
Abdomen: Rabbit dubbing, to
match natural
Rib: Fine gold wire
Throat: Lemon woodduck flank fibers
Wings: Natural gray duck quill
Thorax: Rabbit dubbing, to match natural

GOLD RIBBED HARE'S EAR

Hook: TMC 3761, Mustad 3906, sizes 6-16
Thread: Black 6/0 prewaxed
Tail: Brown hackle fibers
Rib: Flat gold tinsel
Body: Hare's ear fur, picked out at thorax
Wing: Natural gray duck quill

DARK HENDRICKSON

Tier: John Kistler
Hook: TMC 3761, Mustad 3906, sizes 10-16
Thread: Black 6/0 prewaxed
Tail: Lemon woodduck flank fibers
Body: Muskrat fur
Hackle: Medium blue dun hen hackle
Wing: Lemon woodduck flank fibers

QUILL GORDON

Tier: John Kistler
Hook: TMC 3761, Mustad 3906, sizes 10-14
Thread: Black 6/0 prewaxed
Tail: Lemon woodduck flank fibers
Body: Stripped peacock quill
Hackle: Medium blue dun hen hackle
Wing: Lemon woodduck flank fibers

GINGER QUILL

Tier: John Kistler
Hook: TMC 3761, Mustad 3906, sizes 10-16
Thread: Gray 6/0 prewaxed
Tail: Golden ginger hackle fibers
Body: Stripped peacock quill
Hackle: Golden ginger hen hackle
Wing: Natural gray duck quill

BLACK QUILL

Tier: John Kistler
Hook: TMC 3761, Mustad 3906, sizes 10-16
Thread: Black 6/0 prewaxed
Tail: Black hackle fibers
Body: Stripped peacock quill
Hackle: Black hen hackle
Wings: Natural gray duck quill

GREENWELL'S GLORY

Tier: John Kistler
Hook: TMC 3761, Mustad 3906, sizes 10-16
Thread: Black 6/0 prewaxed
Tail: Golden ginger hackle fibers
Rib: Fine oval gold tinsel
Body: Medium olive floss
Hackle: Golden ginger hen hackle
Wing: Natural gray duck quill

COWDUNG

Tier: John Kistler
Hook: TMC 3761, Mustad 3906, sizes 10-16
Thread: Black 6/0 prewaxed
Tag: Fine flat gold tinsel
Body: Dark olive floss
Hackle: Brown hen hackle
Wing: Cinnamon turkey wing quill

WHITE MILLER

Hook: TMC 3761, Mustad 3906, sizes 10-16
Thread: White 6/0 prewaxed
Rib: Fine flat silver tinsel
Body: White floss
Hackle: White hen hackle
Wing: White duck wing quill

WET FLIES

GINGER QUILL
BLUE WING OLIVE
BLACK QUILL
MARCH BROWN
GREENWELL'S GLORY
LIGHT HENDRICKSON
COWDUNG
DARK CAHILL
WHITE MILLER
BROWN HACKLE PEACOCK

BLUE WING OLIVE

Tier: John Kistler
Hook: TMC 3761, Mustad 3906, sizes 14-18
Thread: Olive 6/0 prewaxed
Tail: Dark dun hackle fibers
Body: Medium olive rabbit dubbing
Hackle: Dark blue dun hen hackle
Wing: Natural gray duck quill

MARCH BROWN

Hook: TMC 3761, Mustad 3906, sizes 10-16
Thread: Tan 6/0 prewaxed
Tail: Three ringneck pheasant tail fibers
Body: Hare's ear fur
Hackle: Brown hen hackle, sparse
Wing: Natural gray duck quill

LIGHT HENDRICKSON

Tier: John Kistler
Hook: TMC 3761, Mustad 3906, sizes 12-16
Thread: Gray 6/0 prewaxed
Tail: Lemon woodduck flank fibers
Body: Fawn colored red fox fur
Hackle: Medium bronze dun hen hackle
Wing: Lemon woodduck flank fibers

DARK CAHILL

Tier: John Kistler
Hook: TMC 3761, Mustad 3906, sizes 10-16
Thread: Black 6/0 prewaxed
Tail: Lemon woodduck flank fibers
Body: Muskrat fur
Hackle: Dark ginger hen hackle
Wing: Lemon woodduck flank fibers

BROWN HACKLE PEACOCK

Tier: John Kistler
Hook: TMC 3761, Mustad 3906, sizes 10-16
Thread: Black 6/0 prewaxed
Tail: Red floss or wool, short
Body: Peacock herl
Hackle: Brown hen hackle

COACHMAN

Originator: Tom Bosworth
Tier: Umpqua Feather Merchants
Hook: TMC 3761, Mustad 3906, sizes 6-16
Thread: Black 6/0 prewaxed
Tag: Fine flat gold tinsel
Body: Peacock herl
Hackle: Brown hen hackle
Wing: White duck quill

ROYAL COACHMAN

Tier: Umpqua Feather Merchants
Hook: TMC 3769, Mustad 3906B,
sizes 10-16
Thread: Black 6/0 prewaxed
Tail: Golden pheasant tippet fibers
Rib: Fine gold wire
Butt: Peacock herl
Body: Red floss
Shoulder: Peacock herl
Hackle: Dark brown hen hackle
Wing: White duck wing quill

McGINTY

Tier: Umpqua Feather Merchants
Hook: TMC 5262, Mustad 9671, sizes 6-16
Thread: Black 6/0 prewaxed
Tail: Teal flank fibers and red hackle fibers
Body: Black and yellow wool yarn,
alternating
Hackle: Dark brown hen hackle
Wing: White tipped mallard wing quill

ALEXANDRA

Hook: TMC 3769, Mustad 3906B,
sizes 10-16
Thread: Black 6/0 prewaxed
Tail: Dyed red duck wing quill
Body: Flat silver tinsel
Hackle: Black hen hackle
Wing: Peacock sword fibers, with dyed red
duck quill, thin strips on each side

GRIZZLY KING

Hook: TMC 3769, Mustad 3906B,
sizes 10-14
Thread: Black 6/0 prewaxed
Tail: Dyed red duck quill
Rib: Fine flat gold tinsel
Body: Bright green floss
Hackle: Grizzly hen hackle
Wing: Mallard flank fibers

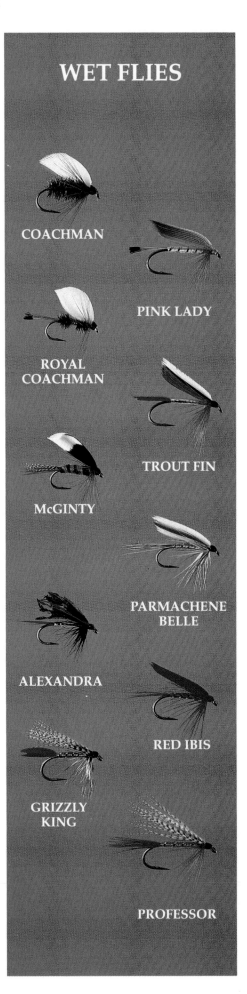

WET FLIES

COACHMAN

PINK LADY

ROYAL COACHMAN

TROUT FIN

McGINTY

PARMACHENE BELLE

ALEXANDRA

RED IBIS

GRIZZLY KING

PROFESSOR

PINK LADY

Hook: TMC 3761, Mustad 3906, sizes 10-16
Thread: Gray 6/0 prewaxed
Tail: Golden pheasant tippet fibers
Rib: Fine flat gold tinsel
Body: Pink floss
Hackle: Golden ginger hen hackle
Wing: Natural gray duck wing quill

TROUT FIN

Hook: TMC 3761, Mustad 3906, sizes 8-16
Thread: Black 6/0 prewaxed
Tail: Dyed red duck wing quill
Body: Flat silver tinsel
Hackle: Light ginger hen hackle
Wing: Married duck wing quill, white over
black (thin) over red

PARMACHENE BELLE

Hook: TMC 3761, Mustad 3906, sizes 10-16
Thread: Black 6/0 prewaxed
Tail: Red and white hackle fibers, mixed
Rib: Fine flat gold tinsel
Body: Yellow floss
Hackle: Red and white hen hackle, mixed
Wing: Married sections of dyed duck quills,
white than red than white

RED IBIS

Hook: TMC 3761, Mustad 3906, sizes 12-16
Thread: Red 6/0 prewaxed
Tail: Red hackle fibers
Rib: Fine flat gold tinsel
Body: Red floss
Hackle: Red hen hackle
Wing: Dyed red duck wing quill

PROFESSOR

Hook: TMC 3761, Mustad 3906, sizes 10-16
Thread: Black 6/0 prewaxed
Tail: Red hackle fibers
Rib: Fine flat gold tinsel
Body: Yellow floss
Hackle: Brown hen hackle
Wing: Mallard flank fibers

DOC SPRATLEY

Originator: Dick Prankard
Hook: TMC 5263, Mustad 9672, size 8
Thread: Black 6/0 prewaxed
Tail: Guinea hackle fibers
Rib: Fine flat silver tinsel
Body: Black wool
Hackle: Grizzly hen hackle
Wing: Ringneck pheasant tail fibers
Head: Peacock herl

BRINDLE BUG

Hook: TMC 5262, Mustad 9671, sizes 6-12
Thread: Black 6/0 prewaxed
Tail: Brown hackle fibers
Body: Black and yellow variegated chenille
Hackle: Brown hen hackle

ZULU

Hook: TMC 3769, Mustad 3906B,
  sizes 10-16
Thread: Black 6/0 prewaxed
Tail: Red wool, short
Rib: Fine gold wire
Body: Peacock herl
Hackle: Black hackle, palmered over body

PICKET PIN

Tier: Umpqua Feather Merchants
Hook: TMC 5263, Mustad 9672, sizes 8-12
Thread: Black 6/0 prewaxed
Tail: Brown hackle fibers
Body: Peacock herl
Hackle: Brown hackle, palmered over body
Wing: Gray squirrel tail
Head: Peacock herl

MORSE'S ALDER FLY

Hook: TMC 3761, Mustad 3906, sizes 8-16
Thread: Black 6/0 prewaxed
Body: Dyed black squirrel tail, wrapped
Shellback: Dyed black squirrel tail,
  four segments
Wing: Dyed black squirrel tail

WET FLIES

DOC
SPRATLEY

DOWNWING
ADAMS

BRINDLE
BUG

WESTERN
COACHMAN

ZULU

MORMON GIRL

PICKET PIN

EARLY BROWN
STONE

MORSE'S
ALDER FLY

GRAY SPIDER

DOWNWING ADAMS

Hook: TMC 3769, Mustad 3906, sizes 10-16
Thread: Black 6/0 prewaxed
Tail: Rabbit fur guard hairs
Body: Muskrat fur
Wings: Grizzly hen hackle tips
Hackle: Brown and grizzly hen
  hackle, mixed

WESTERN COACHMAN

Hook: TMC 3761, Mustad 3906, sizes 6-14
Thread: Black 6/0 prewaxed
Tail: Golden pheasant tippet fibers
Rib: Fine gold wire
Body: Peacock herl
Hackle: Dark brown hen hackle
Wing: White deer hair

MORMON GIRL

Tier: John Kistler
Hook: TMC 5262, Mustad 9671, sizes 10-16
Thread: Gray 6/0 prewaxed
Tag: Red floss
Body: Yellow floss
Hackle: Grizzly hackle, palmered over body
Wing: Mallard flank fibers

EARLY BROWN STONE

Originator: Preston Jennings
Hook: TMC 5262, Mustad 9671, size 14
Thread: Orange 6/0 prewaxed
Tail: Two ringneck pheasant tail fibers
Body: Reddish-brown seal fur
Hackle: Rusty dun hen hackle
Wings: Rusty dun hackle tips, tied flat
  over back

GRAY SPIDER

Originator: Al Knudson
Hook: TMC 3769, Mustad 3906B, sizes 6-14
Thread: Gray 6/0 prewaxed
Tail: Mallard flank fibers
Rib: Gold silk thread
Body: Yellow chenille
Hackle: Mallard flank over grizzly hackle

CAREY SPECIAL, brown

Hook: TMC 300, Mustad 79580, sizes 4-12
Thread: Black 6/0 prewaxed
Tail: Ringneck pheasant breast fibers
Rib: Fine copper wire
Body: Brown chenille
Hackle: Ringneck pheasant rump

CAREY SPECIAL, olive

Hook: TMC 300, Mustad 79580, sizes 4-12
Thread: Black 6/0 prewaxed
Tail: Ringneck pheasant back fibers
Rib: Copper wire
Body: Dark olive chenille
Hackle: Ringneck pheasant back

CAREY SPECIAL, peacock

Hook: TMC 5262, Mustad 79580, sizes 4-12
Thread: Olive 6/0 prewaxed
Tail: Ringneck pheasant back fibers
Rib: Fine gold wire
Body: Peacock herl
Hackle: Ringneck pheasant back feather

WOOLLY WORM

Hook: TMC 300, Mustad 79580, sizes 2-12
Thread: Black 6/0 prewaxed
Tail: Red hackle fibers
Rib: Fine silver wire
Body: Black chenille
Hackle: Grizzly hackle, palmered over body

BROWN BOMBER

Hook: TMC 300, Mustad 79580, sizes 4-12
Thread: Black 6/0 prewaxed
Tail: Red hackle fibers
Body: Black chenille
Hackle: Three brown hackles, tied in aft,
  middle, front

WET FLIES

CAREY SPECIAL, brown

HORNBERG

CAREY SPECIAL, olive

BORDENS SPECIAL

CAREY SPECIAL, peacock

GOLDEN STONE WET

WOOLLY WORM

DARK WET STONE

BROWN BOMBER

DAVE'S WOOLLY WORM

HORNBERG

Hook: TMC 5263, Mustad 9672, sizes 6-10
Thread: Black 6/0 prewaxed
Body: Flat silver tinsel
Underwing: Dyed yellow calftail
Wing: Two whole mallard flank feathers,
  tied one on each side
Cheeks: Jungle cock eyes
Hackle: Brown and grizzly hackle, mixed

BORDENS SPECIAL

Originator: Robert Borden
Hook: TMC 5263, Mustad 9672, sizes 6-12
Thread: Fluorescent red 6/0 prewaxed
Tail: Fluorescent red and yellow hackle
  fibers, mixed
Rib: Fine flat silver tinsel
Body: Fluorescent pink rabbit dubbing
Hackle: Fluorescent red and yellow
  hackle, mixed
Wing: White calftail
Topping: Pearl Krystal Flash

GOLDEN STONE WET

Originator: Polly Rosborough
Hook: TMC 5263, Mustad 9672, sizes 4-8
Thread: Gold 6/0 prewaxed
Tail: Dyed gold mallard flank
Rib: Antique gold thread
Body: Antique gold wool
Hackle: Antique gold hen hackle, dyed gold
  mallard flank in front
Wing: Dyed gold bucktail

DARK WET STONE

Originator: Polly Rosborough
Hook: TMC 5263, Mustad 9672, sizes 2-8
Thread: Black 6/0 prewaxed
Tail: Brown turkey body feather fibers
Rib: Gray "A" thread
Body: Tangerine orange wool
Hackle: Dark furnace hen hackle,
  undersized
Wing: Dark brown bucktail
Head: Long, band of hot orange floss at
  wing base

DAVE'S WOOLLY WORM

Originator: Dave Whitlock
Hook: TMC 5212, Mustad 94831, sizes 6-10
Thread: Black 6/0 prewaxed
Tail: Red wool, short
Rib: Fine gold wire
Body: Yellow chenille
Shellback: Peacock herl
Hackle: Grizzly hackle, palmered over body

GROUSE AND ORANGE

Tier: John Kistler
Hook: TMC 3769, Mustad 3906, sizes 10-16
Thread: Orange 6/0 prewaxed
Body: Orange silk floss
Hackle: Grouse body hackle

ORANGE FISH HAWK

Hook: TMC 3769, Mustad 3906, sizes 10-14
Thread: Black 6/0 prewaxed
Tag: Fine flat gold tinsel
Rib: Fine flat gold tinsel
Body: Orange silk floss
Hackle: Light badger hen hackle

FEBRUARY RED SOFT HACKLE

Hook: TMC 3761, Mustad 9671, sizes 12-16
Thread: Maroon red 6/0 prewaxed
Body: Dark red silk floss
Hackle: Brown partridge hackle

YORKSHIRE WET

Hook: TMC 3769, Mustad 3906, sizes 10-16
Thread: Black 6/0 prewaxed
Body: Purple silk floss
Thorax: Dark hare's ear fur
Hackle: Moorhen wing feather

LEISENRING DARK OLIVE

Hook: TMC 3769, Mustad 3906, sizes 12-16
Thread: Olive 6/0 prewaxed
Body: Olive and brown seal fur, mixed
Hackle: Gray chukar body feather

SOFT HACKLE FLIES

GROUSE AND ORANGE

ORANGE FISH HAWK

FEBRUARY RED SOFT HACKLE

YORKSHIRE WET

LEISENRING DARK OLIVE

BAETIS SOFT HACKLE

MARCH BROWN FLYMPH

PHEASANT TAIL

COPPER AND PARTRIDGE

PARTRIDGE AND GREEN

BAETIS SOFT HACKLE

Hook: TMC 3761, Mustad 9671, sizes 14-20
Thread: Gray 6/0 prewaxed
Tail: Blue dun hackle fibers
Body: Gray seal fur
Hackle: Blue dun hen hackle

MARCH BROWN FLYMPH

Hook: Partridge D5B, sizes 14-16
Thread: Red 6/0 prewaxed
Tail: 2-3 pheasant tail fibers
Body: Dark hare's ear dubbing
Hackle: Furnace or brown hen hackle

PHEASANT TAIL

Tier: John Kistler
Hook: TMC 3769, Mustad 3906, sizes 10-16
Thread: Olive 6/0 prewaxed
Tail: 2-3 pheasant tail fibers
Rib: Fine copper wire, reversed
Body: 4-5 long pheasant tail fibers
Hackle: Brown partridge hackle

COPPER AND PARTRIDGE

Originator: Bill McMillan
Hook: TMC 3769, Mustad 7948A, sizes 8-16
Thread: Brown 6/0 prewaxed
Body: Grayish-brown antron dubbing
Hackle: Brown partridge hackle, tie tip of
  feather back over the top as short
  wing stub

PARTRIDGE AND GREEN

Tier: John Kistler
Hook: TMC 3769, Mustad 3906, sizes 10-16
Thread: Green 6/0 prewaxed
Body: Green silk floss
Thorax: Hare's ear fur
Hackle: Gray partridge hackle

LEISENRING BLACK GNAT

Hook: TMC 3769, Mustad 3906, sizes 12-18
Thread: Red 6/0 prewaxed
Body: 2-3 fibers from a crows wing secondary, wrapped
Hackle: Purplish-black starling shoulder feather

STARLING AND HERL

Hook: TMC 3769, Mustad 3906, sizes 10-16
Thread: Olive 6/0 prewaxed
Body: Peacock herl
Hackle: Starling wing covert feather

RED HACKLE

Hook: TMC 3769, Mustad 3906, sizes 12-14
Thread: Red 6/0 prewaxed
Rib: Fine flat gold tinsel
Body: Bronze peacock herl
Hackle: Furnace hen hackle

SNIPE AND PURPLE

Hook: TMC 3769, Mustad 3906, sizes 10-16
Thread: Black 6/0 prewaxed
Body: Purple silk floss
Hackle: Snipe wing covert feather

PARTRIDGE AND ORANGE

Tier: John Kistler
Hook: TMC 3769, Mustad 3906, sizes 10-16
Thread: Orange 6/0 prewaxed
Body: Orange silk floss
Thorax: Hare's ear fur
Hackle: Gray partridge hackle

SOFT-HACKLE WET FLIES

LEISENRING BLACK GNAT

TUP'S INDISPENSABLE

STARLING AND HERL

FLUORESCENT GREEN

RED HACKLE

MARCH BROWN SPIDER

SNIPE AND PURPLE

SIBERIAN OUTPOST

PARTRIDGE AND ORANGE

IRON BLUE WINGLESS

TUP'S INDISPENSABLE

Hook: TMC 3769, Mustad 3906, sizes 10-16
Thread: Yellow 6/0 prewaxed
Tail: Blue dun hen hackle fibers
Body: Yellow silk floss
Thorax: Light pink rabbit dubbing
Hackle: Blue dun hen hackle

FLUORESCENT GREEN

Hook: TMC 3769, Mustad 3906, sizes 6-14
Thread: Bright green 6/0 prewaxed
Body: Fluorescent green floss
Thorax: Hare's ear dubbing
Hackle: Gray partridge hackle

MARCH BROWN SPIDER

Tier: John Kistler
Hook: TMC 3769, Mustad 3906, sizes 10-16
Thread: Orange 6/0 prewaxed
Rib: Fine flat silver tinsel
Body: Hare's mask fur
Hackle: Brown partridge hackle

SIBERIAN OUTPOST

Hook: TMC 3769, Mustad 3906, sizes 10-16
Thread: Light tan 6/0 prewaxed
Tail: Brown partridge hackle fibers
Rib: Fine gold wire
Body: Light brown mink fur
Hackle: Brown partridge hackle

IRON BLUE WINGLESS

Hook: TMC 3769, Mustad 3906, sizes 12-18
Thread: Red 6/0 prewaxed
Tail: Honey dun hen hackle
Body: Dark mole fur, very thin at tail
Hackle: Honey dun hen hackle

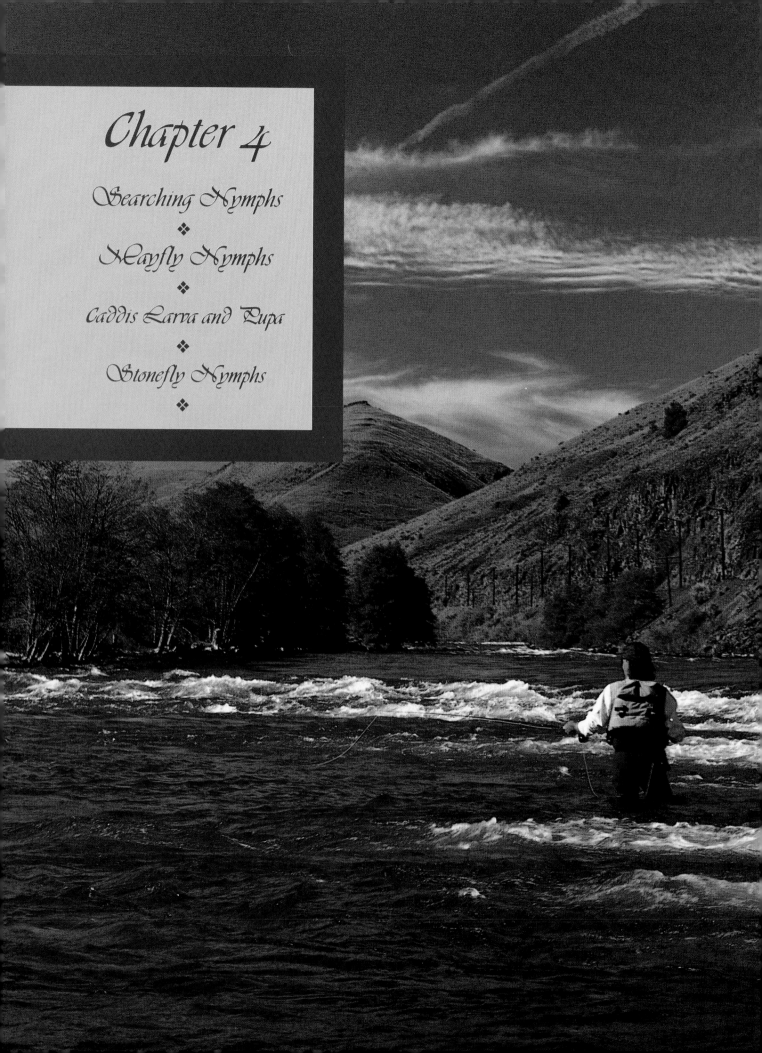

Chapter 4

Searching Nymphs

❖

Mayfly Nymphs

❖

Caddis Larva and Pupa

❖

Stonefly Nymphs

❖

DDD

Originator: Dick Thrasher
Hook: TMC 5263, Mustad 9672,
   sizes 8-12, wt.
Thread: Black 6/0 prewaxed
Tail: Ringneck pheasant tail fibers
Body: Peacock herl
Wingcase: Pheasant tail fibers
Thorax: Dark olive chenille
Legs: Pheasant tail fibers
Head: Peacock herl

HALFBACK

Hook: TMC 5263, Mustad 9672,
   sizes 8-14, wt.
Thread: Olive 6/0 prewaxed
Tail: Brown hackle fibers
Body: Peacock herl
Wingcase: Dyed brown mallard flank
   fibers, short
Legs: Brown hackle fibers

LEIB'S BUG

Originator: Don Leib
Tier: Umpqua Feather Merchants
Hook: TMC 5262, Mustad 9671, sizes
   8-14, wt.
Thread: Black 6/0 prewaxed
Tail: Brown stripped goose, forked
Rib: Oval gold tinsel
Body: Peacock herl
Hackle: Furnace hackle, palmered
   through body
Legs: Brown stripped goose fibers, one on
   each side

SCHOEDER'S CARROT NYMPH

Originator: Ed Schroeder
Tier: Umpqua Feather Merchants
Hook: TMC 3769, Mustad 3906B, sizes
   10-14, wt.
Thread: Orange 6/0 prewaxed
Tail: Grouse hackle fibers
Back: Peacock herl
Rib: Fine copper wire
Body: Orange floss
Wingcase: Pearl Flashabou
Thorax: Peacock herl
Hackle: Brown hackle

RENEGADE NYMPH

Hook: TMC 5252, Mustad 9671, sizes
   8-14, wt.
Thread: Brown 6/0 prewaxed
Tip: Fine flat gold tinsel
Shellback: Ringneck pheasant tail fibers
Butt: White hen hackle
Body: Peacock herl
Hackle: Brown hen hackle

SEARCHING NYMPHS

DDD

MAGGOT

HALFBACK

MARTINEZ NYMPH

LEIB'S BUG

MONO EYED HARE'S EAR

SCHOEDER'S CARROT NYMPH

NEAR ENOUGH

RENEGADE NYMPH

BLONDE BURLAP

MAGGOT

Hook: TMC 5262, Mustad 9671, sizes
   10-16, wt.
Thread: Black 6/0 prewaxed
Shellback: Ringneck pheasant tail fibers
Rib: Copper wire
Body: Pale yellow rabbit dubbing
Hackle: Brown hackle, sparse

MARTINEZ NYMPH

Originator: Don Martinez
Hook: TMC 5262, Mustad 9671, sizes
   8-12, wt.
Thread: Black 6/0 prewaxed
Tail: Guinea body feather fibers
Rib: Silver wire
Body: Black rabbit dubbing
Wingcase: Green raffia
Thorax: Black rabbit dubbing
Legs: Gray partridge hackle

MONO EYED HARE'S EAR

Hook: TMC 3761, Mustad 3906B, sizes
   6-12, wt.
Thread: Brown 6/0 prewaxed
Tail: Hare's ear guard fibers
Rib: Fine flat tinsel
Body: Hare's ear dubbing
Wingcase: Dark turkey tail
Eyes: Mono nymph eyes
Thorax: Hare's ear dubbing

NEAR ENOUGH

Originator: Polly Rosborough
Hook: TMC 5263, Mustad 9672, sizes 8-14
Thread: Tan 6/0 prewaxed
Tail: Dyed tan mallard flank fibers
Body: Gray fox fur
Legs: Dyed tan mallard flank fibers
Wingcase: Dyed tan mallard flank fibers,
   clipped short

BLONDE BURLAP

Originator: Polly Rosborough
Hook: TMC 5263, Mustad 9672, sizes 2-10
Thread: Tan 6/0 prewaxed
Tail: Soft honey dun hen hackle
   fibers, short
Body: Light tan burlap
Legs: Soft honey dun hen hackle

CRANE FLY

Originator: Ernest Schwiebert
Hook: TMC 2302, Mustad 9672, sizes 6-12, wt.
Thread: Gray 6/0 prewaxed
Body: Light gray rabbit dubbing
Thorax: Dark gray rabbit dubbing
Horns: Muskrat guard hairs

BRASSIE

Originator: Gene Lynch
Tier: Bill Beardsley
Hook: TMC 5262, Mustad 9671, sizes 10-18
Thread: Black 6/0 prewaxed
Body: Copper wire
Thorax: Gray muskrat fur, with guard hairs

DUN VARIANT

Hook: TMC 5263, Mustad 9672, size 10, wt.
Thread: Olive 6/0 prewaxed
Tail: Peacock herl, short
Body: Claret and black goat fur, mixed
Hackle: Brown partridge hackle

IDA MAY

Originator: Charles Brooks
Hook: TMC 5262, Mustad 9671, sizes 8-10, wt.
Thread: Black 6/0 prewaxed
Tail: Grizzly hen hackle fibers dyed dark green
Rib: Peacock herl and fine gold wire
Body: Black rabbit dubbing
Hackle: Grizzly hen hackle dyed dark green

LEADWING COACHMAN

Hook: TMC 5262, Mustad 9671, sizes 10-12, wt.
Thread: Black 6/0 prewaxed
Tail: One brown hackle tip
Body: Peacock herl
Throat: Brown hackle fibers
Wingcase: Brown mallard shoulder feather, short

SEARCHING NYMPHS

CRANE FLY

COOPER BUG

BRASSIE

CARROT NYMPH

DUN VARIANT

CRYSTAL BACK SQUIRREL NYMPH

IDA MAY

GOLD RIBBED HARE'S EAR

LEADWING COACHMAN

FLASHBACK PHEASANT TAIL

COOPER BUG

Originator: Jack Cooper
Hook: TMC 3761, Mustad 3906B, sizes 12-16, wt.
Thread: Black 6/0 prewaxed
Tail: Natural deer hair
Shellback: Deer hair, butts from tail
Body: Black chenille
Head: Deer hair, butts from shellback

CARROT NYMPH

Originator: Rube Cross
Hook: TMC 5262, Mustad 9671, sizes 12-18, wt.
Thread: Orange 6/0 prewaxed
Tail: Black hackle fibers
Body: Orange rabbit dubbing
Thorax: Black rabbit dubbing
Legs: Black hen hackle

CRYSTAL BACK SQUIRREL NYMPH

Originator: Bill Black
Tier: Spirit River Inc
Hook: TMC 2302, Mustad 9671, sizes 6-12, wt.
Thread: Olive 6/0 prewaxed
Tail: Olive marabou
Rib: Olive Krystal Flash
Body: Olive squirrel dubbing
Wingcase: Olive Krystal Flash, on underside
Thorax: Olive squirrel dubbing
Legs: Olive Krystal Flash
Eyes: Plain lead eyes
Head: Olive hare's ear dubbing

GOLD RIBBED HARE'S EAR

Tier: Umpqua Feather Merchants
Hook: TMC 2302, Mustad 3906B, sizes 8-16, wt.
Thread: Black 6/0 prewaxed
Tail: Hare's mask guard hairs
Rib: Fine oval gold tinsel
Body: Hare's ear dubbing
Wingcase: Mottled turkey quill
Thorax: Hare's ear dubbing

FLASHBACK PHEASANT TAIL

Hook: TMC 2302, Mustad 9671, sizes 8-18, wt.
Thread: Black 6/0 prewaxed
Tail: Ringneck pheasant tail fibers
Shellback: Pearl Flashabou
Rib: Fine copper wire
Body: Ringneck pheasant tail fibers, wrapped
Wingcase: Pearl Flashabou
Thorax: Peacock herl
Legs: Ringneck pheasant tail fibers
Head: Copper wire

BURLAP

Hook: TMC 5263, Mustad 9672, sizes
4-10, wt.
Thread: Gray 6/0 prewaxed
Tail: Blacktail deer hair
Body: Burlap
Hackle: Grizzly hen hackle

BIRD'S NEST

Originator: Cal Bird
Hook: TMC 2302, Mustad 9671, sizes
10-16, wt.
Thread: Brown 6/0 prewaxed
Tail: Lemon woodduck flank
Rib: Copper wire
Body: Olive hare's ear dubbing
Hackle: Lemon woodduck flank
Thorax: Olive hare's ear dubbing

CASUAL DRESS

Originator: Polly Rosborough
Hook: TMC 5263, Mustad 79580, sizes 4-10
Thread: Black 6/0 prewaxed
Tail: Muskrat fur, with guard hairs, short
Body: Muskrat fur, noodle style
Thorax: Muskrat fur, with guard hairs
Head: Black ostrich herl

BEAVERPELT

Originator: Don E. Earnest
Hook: TMC 5263, Mustad 9672, sizes
6-8, wt.
Thread: Black 6/0 prewaxed
Tail: Ringneck pheasant rump fibers
Body: Dark beaver underfur
Hackle: Ringneck pheasant rump

PRINCE NYMPH

Originator: Doug Prince
Hook: TMC 5263, Mustad 9672, sizes
4-10, wt.
Thread: Black 6/0 prewaxed
Tail: Brown stripped goose, forked
Rib: Fine flat gold tinsel
Body: Peacock herl
Hackle: Brown hackle
Wings: White stripped goose

SEARCHING NYMPHS

BURLAP

BIGHOLE DEMON

BIRD'S NEST

SAN JUAN WORM, maroon

CASUAL DRESS

SAN JUAN WORM, red

BEAVERPELT

TELLICO NYMPH

PRINCE NYMPH

SMOKEY ALDER LARVA

BIGHOLE DEMON

Hook: TMC 5262, Mustad 9671, sizes
2-10, wt.
Thread: Black 6/0 prewaxed
Tail: Badger hackle fibers
Body: Flat silver tinsel
Thorax: Black chenille
Hackle: Badger hackle, palmered
through thorax

SAN JUAN WORM, maroon

Tier: Umpqua Feather Merchants
Hook: TMC 2457. size 10
Thread: Fluorescent Red 6/0 prewaxed
Body: Maroon vernille, extended with
ends burned

SAN JUAN WORM, red

Tier: Umpqua Feather Merchants
Hook: TMC 2457, size 10
Thread: Fluorescent red 6/0 prewaxed
Body: Fluorescent red vernille, extended
with ends burned

TELLICO NYMPH

Hook: TMC 5262, Mustad 9671, sizes
12-16, wt.
Thread: Black 6/0 prewaxed
Tail: Guinea body fibers
Shellback: Ringneck pheasant tail fibers
Rib: Peacock herl
Body: Yellow floss
Hackle: Furnace hackle, sparse

SMOKEY ALDER LARVA

Originator: George L. Herter
Hook: TMC 5262, Mustad 9671, sizes
10-14, wt.
Thread: Yellow 6/0 prewaxed
Tail: Ginger hackle tip, clipped short
Body: Dark brown wool
Thorax: Yellow wool
Rib: White hackle and yellow thread,
clipped short
Hackle: Yellow hackle, clipped top
and bottom

BEAVER

Hook: TMC 5262, Mustad 9671, sizes 10-14, wt.
Thread: Gray 6/0 prewaxed
Tail: Gray partridge hackle fibers
Rib: Fine gold wire
Body: Beaver underfur
Legs: Gray partridge hackle, beard style

BROWN BOMBER

Hook: TMC 3761, Mustad 3906B, sizes 8-14, wt.
Thread: Black 6/0 prewaxed
Rib: Fine flat gold tinsel
Body: Beaver fur
Hackle: Brown partridge hackle

FLEDERMAUS

Originator: Jack Schneider
Tier: Bill Beardsley
Hook: TMC 5262, Mustad 9671, sizes 6-10, wt.
Thread: Black 6/0 prewaxed
Body: Muskrat fur
Wing: Gray squirrel tail, short

BURKE

Originator: Ed Burke
Hook: TMC 3761, Mustad 3906B, sizes 6-12, wt.
Thread: Black 6/0 prewaxed
Tag: Fine flat gold tinsel
Tail: Black hackle fibers
Rib: Fine flat gold tinsel
Body: Black rabbit dubbing
Wingcase: Hen ringneck pheasant wing quill
Thorax: Black rabbit dubbing
Legs: Black hackle

ZUG BUG

Originator: Cliff Zug
Tier: Umpqua Feather Merchants
Hook: TMC 2302, Mustad 3906B, sizes 8-16, wt.
Thread: Black 6/0 prewaxed
Tail: Peacock sword fibers, short
Body: Peacock herl
Legs: Brown hackle fibers
Wingcase: Lemon wooduck flank, clipped short

SEARCHING NYMPHS

BEAVER

BREADCRUST

BROWN BOMBER

BLADE'S OLIVE NYMPH

FLEDERMAUS

RED SQUIRREL NYMPH

BURKE

SAND FLY

ZUG BUG

GINGER QUILL

BREADCRUST

Hook: TMC 3761, Mustad 3906B, sizes 8-14, wt.
Thread: Black 6/0 prewaxed
Rib: Stripped ruffed grouse tail quill, and fine copper wire
Body: Burnt orange rabbit dubbing
Hackle: Grizzly hen hackle

BLADE'S OLIVE NYMPH

Originator: Bill Blades
Hook: TMC 2302, Mustad 9671, sizes 8-14, wt.
Thread: Black 6/0 prewaxed
Tail: Blue dun hackle fibers
Rib: Fine flat gold tinsel
Body: Olive rabbit dubbing
Wingcase: Orange floss
Thorax: Olive rabbit dubbing
Legs: Honey badger hackle

RED SQUIRREL NYMPH

Originator: Dave Whitlock
Tier: Umpqua Feather Merchants
Hook: TMC 5263, Mustad 9672, sizes 6-10, wt.
Thread: Black 6/0 prewaxed
Tail: Hare's mask guard hair
Body: Red squirrel belly fur
Rib: Fine oval gold tinsel
Thorax: Black antron dubbing
Hackle: Grouse hackle

SAND FLY

Originator: Herb Butler
Hook: TMC 3761, Mustad 3906B, sizes 8-14, wt.
Thread: Black 6/0 prewaxed
Tail: White marabou, short
Rib: Yellow thread
Body: Brown rabbit dubbing
Hackle: Ginger hen hackle

GINGER QUILL

Hook: TMC 3761, Mustad 3906B, sizes 10-16, wt.
Thread: Tan 6/0 prewaxed
Tail: Ginger hackle fibers
Rib: Fine gold wire, reversed
Body: Stripped peacock quill, over tan floss
Legs: Ginger hackle fibers

RAGGLE BOMB

Hook: TMC 5262, Mustad 9671, sizes 8-14, wt.
Thread: Black 6/0 prewaxed
Underbody: Dark olive wool, tapered
Rib: Fine gold wire
Body: Peacock herl
Hackle: Brown hackle, palmered through body, two turns at head

RIFFLE DEVIL

Originator: Charles Brooks
Hook: TMC 5263, Mustad 9672, sizes 4-6, wt.
Thread: Black 6/0 prewaxed
Body: Large olive chenille
Hackle: Brown hackle, palmered over the body

SIMULATOR, peacock

Originator: Randall Kaufmann
Tier: Umpqua Feather Merchants
Hook: TMC 5263, Mustad 9575, sizes 2-12, wt.
Thread: Maroon 6/0 prewaxed
Tail: Brown stripped goose, forked
Rib: Fine copper wire
Body: Peacock herl
Hackle: Furnace hackle, palmered through body and clipped at angle

SIMULATOR, brown

Originator: Randall Kaufmann
Tier: Umpqua Feather Merchants
Hook: TMC 300, Mustad 9575, sizes 2-12, wt.
Thread: Brown 6/0 prewaxed
Tail: Brown stripped goose, forked
Rib: Fine copper wire
Body: 50% brown haretron and 50% goat (claret, amber, orange, rust, black, brown, blue, ginger, purple)
Hackle: Brown hackle, palmered through body and clipped at angle

HELLGRAMMITE

Originator: Randall Kaufmann
Tier: Umpqua Feather Merchants
Hook: TMC 5263, Mustad 79580, sizes 2-8, wt.
Thread: Brown 6/0 prewaxed
Tail: Brown stripped goose fibers, forked
Shellback: Ringneck pheasant tail fibers
Rib: Fine copper wire
Body: Brown antron dubbing, picked out on the sides
Wingcase: Ringneck pheasant tail fibers
Thorax: Brown antron dubbing, Picked out on the sides
Legs: Speckled hen saddle, pulled over thorax
Antennae: Brown stripped goose, forked

SEARCHING NYMPHS

RAGGLE BOMB

HENRY'S LAKE NYMPH

RIFFLE DEVIL

GRAY NYMPH

SIMULATOR, peacock

STOVE PIPE

SIMULATOR, brown

PRINCE HELLGRAMMITE

HELLGRAMMITE

GIRDLE BUG

HENRY'S LAKE NYMPH

Hook: TMC 5263, Mustad 9672, size 8, wt.
Thread: Black 6/0 prewaxed
Tail: Gray squirrel tail
Shellback: Gray squirrel tail
Body: Yellow chenille
Antennae: Gray squirrel tail, natural tips from shellback

GRAY NYMPH

Tier: Umpqua Feather Merchants
Hook: TMC 5252, Mustad 9671, sizes 6-14, wt.
Thread: Gray 6/0 prewaxed
Tail: Grizzly hackle fibers
Body: Gray muskrat fur
Hackle: Grizzly hen hackle

STOVE PIPE

Hook: TMC 5263, Mustad 9672, sizes 6-10, wt.
Thread: Orange 6/0 prewaxed
Tail: Golden pheasant tippets
Body: Dark olive chenille
Legs: Brown hackle fibers
Wing: Teal flank feather

PRINCE HELLGRAMMITE

Originator: Doug Prince
Hook: TMC 5263, Mustad 9672, sizes 6-10, wt.
Thread: Black 6/0 prewaxed
Tail: Black stripped goose, forked
Rib: Black ostrich herl
Body: Black floss
Wingcase: Black goose quill
Thorax: Black rabbit dubbing, with a strand of red wool pulled across the bottom
Legs: Black hackle, palmered through thorax
Wings: Black stripped goose, two strands

GIRDLE BUG

Tier: Bill Beardsley
Hook: TMC 5263, Mustad 9672, sizes 6-10, wt.
Thread: Black 6/0 prewaxed
Tail: Black rubber hackle, forked
Body: Black chenille
Legs: Black rubber hackle

GENIE MAY

Originator: Charles Brooks
Hook: TMC 5262, 9671, size 6, wt.
Thread: Brown 6/0 prewaxed
Tail: Dyed orange grizzly hackle fibers
Rib: Dark purple wool and gray ostrich
Overrib: Fine gold wire, reversed
Body: Dark brown mohlon
Hackle: Dyed orange grizzly hackle

KAUFMANN'S HARE'S EAR, black

Originator: Randall Kaufmann
Tier: Umpqua Feather Merchants
Hook: TMC 3761, Mustad 9671, sizes 6-16, wt.
Thread: Black 6/0 prewaxed
Tail: Black rabbit guard hair
Rib: Fine copper wire
Body: Black rabbit dubbing
Wingcase: Peacock herl
Thorax: Black rabbit dubbing

FILOPLUME MAYFLY, olive

Originator: Randall Kaufmann
Tier: Umpqua Feather Merchants
Hook: TMC 200R, Mustad 3906B, sizes 12-16, wt.
Thread: Olive 6/0 prewaxed
Tail: Olive marabou
Rib: Fine copper wire
Body: Olive marabou
Wingcase: Peacock sword herl
Thorax: Olive filoplume, wrapped

FILOPLUME MAYFLY, black

Originator: Randall Kaufmann
Tier: Umpqua Feather Merchants
Hook: TMC 200R, Mustad 3906B, sizes 12-16, wt.
Thread: Black 6/0 prewaxed
Tail: Black marabou
Rib: Fine copper wire
Body: Black marabou, wrapped
Wingcase: Peacock sword herl
Thorax: Black filoplume, wrapped

FILOPLUME MAYFLY, brown

Originator: Randall Kaufmann
Tier: Umpqua Feather Merchants
Hook: TMC 200R, Mustad 3906B, sizes 12-16, wt.
Thread: Brown 6/0 prewaxed
Tail: Brown marabou
Rib: Fine copper wire
Body: Brown marabou, wrapped
Wingcase: Peacock sword herl
Thorax: Brown filoplume, wrapped

MAYFLY NYMPHS

GENIE MAY

KAUFMANN'S HARE'S EAR, brown

KAUFMANN'S HARE'S EAR, black

KAUFMANN'S HARE'S EAR, olive

FILOPLUME MAYFLY, olive

BLACK'S LITE BRITE HARE'S EAR

FILOPLUME MAYFLY, black

BLACK DRAKE

FILOPLUME MAYFLY, brown

BIG YELLOW MAY

KAUFMANN'S HARE'S EAR, brown

Originator: Randall Kaufmann
Tier: Umpqua Feather Merchants
Hook: TMC 3761, Mustad 9671, sizes 6-16, wt.
Thread: Brown 6/0 prewaxed
Tail: Brown rabbit guard hair
Rib: Fine copper wire
Body: Brown rabbit dubbing
Wingcase: Peacock herl
Thorax: Brown rabbit dubbing

KAUFMANN'S HARE'S EAR, olive

Originator: Randall Kaufmann
Tier: Umpqua Feather Merchants
Hook: TMC 3671, Mustad 9671, sizes 6-16, wt.
Thread: Olive 6/0 prewaxed
Tail: Olive rabbit guard hair
Rib: Fine copper wire
Body: Olive rabbit dubbing
Wingcase: Peacock herl
Thorax: Olive rabbit dubbing

BLACK'S LITE BRITE HARE'S EAR

Originator: Bill Black
Tier: Spirit River Inc
Hook: TMC 200R, sizes 6-12, wt.
Thread: Gray 6/0 prewaxed
Tail: White lite brite
Rib: Fine flat gold tinsel
Body: White lite brite
Wingcase: Dark turkey tail
Eyes: Mono nymph eyes
Thorax: White lite brite

BLACK DRAKE

Originator: Polly Rosborough
Hook: TMC 5263, Mustad 38941, size 10
Thread: Gray 6/0 prewaxed
Tail: Guinea hackle fibers
Body: Beaver belly fur, with guard hairs
Wingcase: Black ostrich herl, short
Legs: Guinea hackle fibers

BIG YELLOW MAY

Originator: Polly Rosborough
Hook: TMC 5263, Mustad 38941, sizes 6-8
Thread: Yellow 6/0 prewaxed
Tail: Lemon woodduck flank fibers
Rib: Yellow thread
Shellback: Lemon woodduck flank fibers
Body: Yellow wool
Legs: Lemon woodduck flank fibers
Wingcase: Lemon woodduck flank fibers

VELMA MAY

Originator: Charles Brooks
Hook: TMC 5263, Mustad 9672, size 10, wt.
Thread: Olive 6/0 prewaxed
Tail: Dark green grizzly hackle fibers
Rib: Purple wool and gray ostrich herl
Body: Mottled brown wool
Overrib: Fine gold wire
Hackle: Dark green grizzly hackle

FLASHABOU NYMPH

Originator: Ed Schroeder
Tier: Umpqua Feather Merchants
Hook: TMC 2302, Mustad 3906B, sizes 10-18, wt.
Thread: Black 6/0 prewaxed
Tail: Ringneck pheasant tail fibers
Body: Pearl Flashabou, wrapped
Wingcase: Pearl Flashabou
Thorax: Black rabbit and goat dubbing, well picked out

LAWSON'S BROWN DRAKE

Originator: Mike Lawson
Tier: Umpqua Feather Merchants
Hook: TMC 2302, Mustad 3906B, size 10, wt.
Thread: Brown 6/0 prewaxed
Tail: Dark mottled brown hen hackle fibers
Rib: Fine copper wire
Gills: Grayish-brown ostrich herl
Body: Blended tannish-brown rabbit dubbing and clear antron dubbing
Wingcase: Mottled turkey wing quill
Thorax: Same as body
Hackle: Brown partridge hackle

LAWSON'S GREEN DRAKE

Originator: Mike Lawson
Tier: Umpqua Feather Merchants
Hook: TMC 5262, Mustad 9671, sizes 10-12, wt.
Thread: Black 6/0 prewaxed
Tail: Brown partridge hackle fibers
Rib: Fine gold wire
Body: Blended 50% natural hare's ear fur, 25% gold and 25% olive dyed hare's ear fur
Wingcase: White tipped turkey tail section
Thorax: Same as body
Legs: Brown partridge hackle fibers

FEATHER DUSTER

Hook: TMC 5262, Mustad 9671, sizes 8-12, wt.
Thread: Brown 6/0 prewaxed
Tail: Lemon woodduck flank fibers
Rib: Fine gold wire
Body: Brown ostrich herl, wrapped
Wingcase: Brown partridge hackle
Thorax: Brown ostrich herl, wrapped
Legs: Brown partridge hackle fibers

MAYFLY NYMPHS

VELMA MAY

GREEN DRAKE EMERGER

FLASHABOU NYMPH

WIGGLE GREEN DRAKE

LAWSON'S BROWN DRAKE

WIGGLE GRAY DRAKE

LAWSON'S GREEN DRAKE

GREEN DRAKE CDC EMERGER

FEATHER DUSTER

HARROP GREEN DRAKE EMERGER

GREEN DRAKE EMERGER

Originator: Mike Lawson
Tier: Umpqua Feather Merchants
Hook: TMC 5262, Mustad 9671, sizes 8-12
Thread: Olive 6/0 prewaxed
Tail: Lemon woodduck flank fibers
Rib: Yellow silk thread
Body: Olive haretron
Hackle: Dyed olive grizzly hen hackle

WIGGLE GREEN DRAKE

Originator: Fred Arbona
Tier: Umpqua Feather Merchants
Hook: TMC 5262, Mustad 9671, size 12
Thread: Olive 6/0 prewaxed
Tail: Three dark moose hairs
Body: Olive ostrich herl, wrapped over moose to form extended body
Wingcase: Gray goose wing quill
Thorax: Olive ostrich herl
Planer: Thick clear plastic

WIGGLE GRAY DRAKE

Originator: Fred Arbona
Tier: Umpqua Feather Merchants
Hook: TMC 5262, Mustad 9671, size 12
Thread: Gray 6/0 prewaxed
Tail: Three dark moose hairs
Body: Gray ostrich herl, wrapped over moose to form extended body
Wingcase: Gray goose wing quill
Thorax: Gray ostrich herl, wrapped
Planer: Thick clear plastic

GREEN DRAKE CDC EMERGER

Hook: TMC 5212, Mustad 94831, sizes 10-14
Thread: Olive 6/0 prewaxed
Tail: Olive marabou
Body: Olive marabou, wrapped
Wing: White CDC feather
Head: Olive fine dubbing

HARROP GREEN DRAKE EMERGER

Originator: René Harrop
Hook: TMC 101, Mustad 94842, sizes 10-12
Thread: Black 6/0 prewaxed
Tail: 4-5 lemon woodduck flank fibers
Body: Dyed bright olive-yellow goose wing quill, wrapped
Thorax: Dark olive seal fur
Hackle: Three turns of dyed bright olive-yellow grizzly hackle, with two turns of dark dun hen hackle in front

A. P. PEACOCK AND PHEASANT NYMPH

Originator: Andre Puyans
Tier: Umpqua Feather Merchants
Hook: TMC 5262, Mustad 9671, sizes 10-14, wt.
Thread: Black 6/0 prewaxed
Tail: Dark ringneck pheasant tail fibers
Rib: Fine copper wire
Body: Bronze peacock herl
Wingcase: Dark ringneck pheasant tail fibers
Thorax: Bronze peacock herl
Legs: Dark ringneck pheasant tail fibers

A. P. OLIVE NYMPH

Originator: Andre Puyans
Tier: Umpqua Feather Merchants
Hook: TMC 2302, Mustad 3906B, sizes 10-18, wt.
Thread: Olive 6/0 prewaxed
Tail: Woodduck flank fibers
Rib: Fine copper wire
Body: Dyed olive beaver fur
Wingcase: Mallard flank
Thorax: Dyed olive beaver fur
Legs: Mallard flank
Head: Dyed olive beaver fur

HARROP CAPTIVE DUN

Originator: René Harrop & Family
Tier: Umpqua Feather Merchants
Hook: TMC 5230, Mustad 94833, sizes 12-18
Thread: Olive 6/0 prewaxed
Tail: Brown marabou
Shellback: Natural gray goose quill
Body: Dark olive poly dubbing
Legs: Natural gray deer hair

BROWN FLOATING NYMPH

Hook: TMC 100, Mustad 94845, sizes 12-18
Thread: Brown 6/0 prewaxed
Tail: Brown hackle fibers
Rib: Dark brown thread
Body: Dark brown super fine dubbing
Legs: Brown hackle fibers
Wingcase: Black poly dubbing, shaped into a ball and placed on top
Head: Dark Brown super fine dubbing

A. P. BEAVER NYMPH

Originator: Andre Puyans
Tier: Umpqua Feather Merchants
Hook: TMC 2302, Mustad 3906B, sizes 10-16, wt.
Thread: Black 6/0 prewaxed
Tail: Dark moose hair
Rib: Fine copper wire
Body: Beaver fur
Wingcase: Dark moose hair
Thorax: Same as body
Legs: Dark moose body, butt ends
Head: Same as body

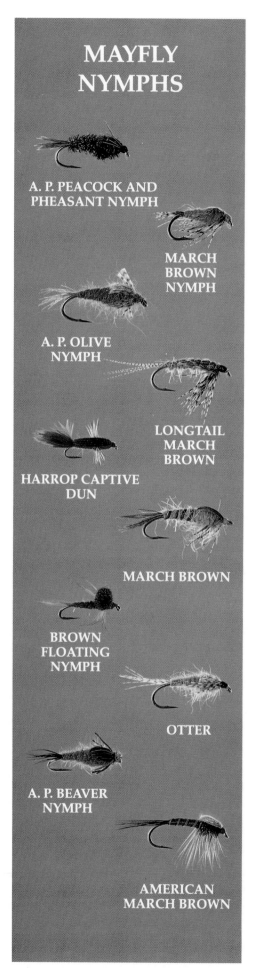

MAYFLY NYMPHS

A. P. PEACOCK AND PHEASANT NYMPH

MARCH BROWN NYMPH

A. P. OLIVE NYMPH

LONGTAIL MARCH BROWN

HARROP CAPTIVE DUN

MARCH BROWN

BROWN FLOATING NYMPH

OTTER

A. P. BEAVER NYMPH

AMERICAN MARCH BROWN

MARCH BROWN NYMPH

Originator: Randle Scott Stetzer
Hook: TMC 3769, Mustad 3906, sizes 12-16, wt.
Thread: Tan 6/0 prewaxed
Tail: Brown partridge hackle fibers
Rib: Fine copper wire
Body: Tan rabbit dubbing
Wingcase: Clear antron fibers
Thorax: Tan rabbit dubbing
Legs: Brown partridge hackl

LONGTAIL MARCH BROWN

Hook: TMC 2302, Mustad 3906B, sizes 8-14, wt.
Thread: Black 6/0 prewaxed
Tail: Lemon wodduck flank fibers, long
Shellback: Mottled brown turkey wing quill
Rib: Yellow thread
Body: Hare's ear fur
Hackle: Brown partridge hackle

MARCH BROWN

Originator: Al Troth
Tier: Umpqua Feather Merchants
Hook: TMC 200, Mustad 9671, sizes 12-18, wt.
Thread: Yellow 6/0 prewaxed
Tail: Ringneck pheasant tail fibers
Rib: Dark brown thread
Body: Blended 2/3 red fox fur, 1/3 amber goat fur
Wingcase: Dark mottled turkey wing quill
Thorax: Same as body
Legs: Brown partridge hackle fibers

OTTER

Hook: TMC 2302, Mustad 3906B, sizes 10-16, wt.
Thread: Black 6/0 prewaxed
Tail: Gray mallard flank fibers
Body: Otter fur
Wingcase: Gray mallard flank fibers
Thorax: Otter fur
Legs: Gray mallard flank fibers

AMERICAN MARCH BROWN

Hook: TMC 2302, Mustad 9671, sizes 10-14, wt..
Thread: Brown 6/0 prewaxed
Tail: Dark moose mane fibers
Rib: Stripped peacock herl
Body: Brown floss
Wingcase: Natural gray duck quill
Thorax: Peacock herl
Hackle: Brown hackle, wrapped over thorax

CATE'S TURKEY

Originator: Jerry Cate
Tier: Umpqua Feather Merchants
Hook: TMC 2302, Mustad 3906B, sizes
   12-18, wt.
Thread: Black 6/0 prewaxed
Tail: Lemon woodduck flank fibers
Rib: Fine gold wire
Body: Turkey tail fibers, wrapped
Thorax: Peacock herl
Legs: Lemon woodduck flank fibers

PHEASANT TAIL

Originator: Al Troth
Tier: Umpqua Feather Merchants
Hook: TMC 2302, Mustad 3906B, sizes
   10-18, wt.
Thread: Brown 6/0 prewaxed
Tail: Ringneck pheasant tail fibers
Rib: Fine copper wire
Body: Ringneck pheasant tail
   fibers, wrapped
Wingcase: Ringneck pheasant tail fibers
Thorax: Peacock herl
Legs: Ringneck pheasant tail fibers, tips
   from wingcase
Head: Fine copper wire

SKIP NYMPH LIGHT

Originator: Skip Morris
Tier: Skip Morris
Hook: TMC 5262, Mustad 9671, sizes
   8-20, wt.
Thread: Brown 6/0 prewaxed
Tail: Ringneck pheasant tail fibers
Shellback: Ringneck pheasant fibers, dark
   side up.
Rib: Fine copper wire
Body: Natural hare's ear dubbing
Wingcase: Ringneck pheasant tail fibers,
   dark side up
Thorax: Natural hare's ear dubbing

SKIP NYMPH DARK

Originator: Skip Morris
Tier: Skip Morris
Hook: TMC 5262, Mustad 9671, sizes
   8-20, wt.
Thread: Brown 6/0 prewaxed
Tail: Ringneck pheasant tail fibers
Shellback: Ringneck pheasant tail, dark
   side up
Rib: Fine copper wire
Body: Dark brown hare's ear dubbing
Wingcase: Ringneck pheasant tail fibers,
   dark side up
Thorax: Dark brown hare's ear dubbing

BLACK MAYFLY NYMPH

Hook: TMC 2302, 3906B, sizes 10-14, wt.
Thread: Black 6/0 prewaxed
Tail: Black hackle fibers
Rib: Gray thread
Body: Black floss
Wingcase: Dyed black duck wing quill
Thorax: Black rabbit dubbing
Hackle: Black hackle, wrapped over thorax

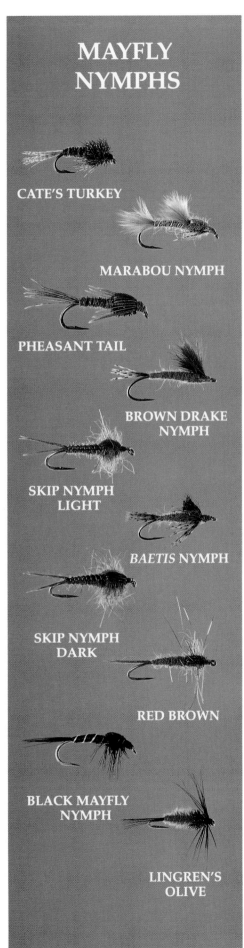

MAYFLY NYMPHS

CATE'S TURKEY

MARABOU NYMPH

PHEASANT TAIL

BROWN DRAKE NYMPH

SKIP NYMPH LIGHT

BAETIS NYMPH

SKIP NYMPH DARK

RED BROWN

BLACK MAYFLY NYMPH

LINGREN'S OLIVE

MARABOU NYMPH

Hook: TMC 2302, Mustad 3906B, sizes
   6-14, wt.
Thread: Gray 6/0 prewaxed
Tail: Gray marabou, short
Rib: Fine oval silver tinsel, 3 turns
Body: Gray rabbit dubbing
Wing: Gray marabou
Wingcase: Gray Z-lon
Thorax: Gray rabbit dubbing
Legs: Speckled guinea hackle fibers

BROWN DRAKE NYMPH

Originator: Doug Swisher and
   Carl Richards
Hook: TMC 5263, Mustad 9672, sizes
   10-12, wt.
Thread: Tan 6/0 prewaxed
Tail: Light tan partridge hackle fibers
Body: Medium brown rabbit dubbing
Wingcase: Dark brown ostrich herl, short
Legs: Light tan partridge hackle fibers

BAETIS NYMPH

Originator: Doug Swisher and Carl
   Richards
Hook: TMC 200, Mustad 3906B, sizes
   12-22, wt.
Thread: Olive 6/0 prewaxed
Tail: Dyed olive mallard flank fibers
Body: Medium olive rabbit dubbing
Wingcase: Black ostrich herl, short
Legs: Dyed olive mallard flank

RED BROWN

Originator: Gary Borger
Hook: TMC 200, Mustad 3906, sizes 8-18, wt.
Thread: Brown 6/0 prewaxed
Tail: Ringneck pheasant tail fibers
Body: Rusty brown rabbit dubbing
Wingcase: Peacock herl
Thorax: Rusty brown rabbit dubbing, with
   hare's ear guard hairs mixed in, well
   picked out and clipped on the bottom

LINGREN'S OLIVE

Originator: Ira Lingren
Hook: TMC 5262, Mustad 9671, sizes
   14-18, wt.
Thread: Black 6/0 prewaxed
Tail: Black hackle fibers
Rib: Fine gold wire
Body: Olive marabou, wrapped
Thorax: Peacock herl
Hackle: Black hackle, clipped top
   and bottom

BLACK QUILL

Hook: TMC 2302, Mustad 9671, sizes
    10-14, wt.
Thread: Black 6/0 prewaxed
Tail: Medium dun hackle fibers
Body: Stripped peacock quill
Wingcase: Dark mallard wing quill
Thorax: Muskrat fur
Hackle: Medium blue dun hen hackle

WESTERN BLUE QUILL NYMPH

Originator: Ernest Schwiebert
Hook: TMC 5263, Mustad 9671, sizes
    14-16, wt.
Thread: Gray 6/0 prewaxed
Tail: Dark lemon woodduck flank fibers
Rib: Fine gold wire
Gills: Pale gray marabou
Body: Grayish-brown rabbit dubbing
Wingcase: Dark grayish-brown duck quill
Thorax: Grayish-brown rabbit dubbing
Hackle: Dark grayish-brown hen hackle

ATHERTON DARK

Originator: John Atherton
Hook: TMC 5262, Mustad 9671, sizes
    10-16, wt.
Thread: Maroon 6/0 prewaxed
Tail: Furnace hackle fibers
Rib: Fine oval gold tinsel
Body: 50% muskrat fur and 50% claret
    seal or goat fur
Wingcase: Dyed blue goose wing quill fibers
Thorax: Same as body
Hackle: Furnace hackle, clipped top
    and bottom

ATHERTON MEDIUM

Originator: John Atherton
Hook: TMC 5262, Mustad 9671, sizes
    10-16, wt.
Thread: Brown 6/0 prewaxed
Tail: Brown partridge hackle fibers
Rib: Fine oval gold tinsel
Body: Hare's ear fur
Wingcase: Dyed blue goose wing quill fibers
Thorax: Hare's ear fur
Hackle: Brown partridge hackle

ATHERTON LIGHT

Originator: John Atherton
Hook: TMC 5262, Mustad 9671, sizes
    12-18, wt.
Thread: Yellow 6/0 prewaxed
Tail: Lemon woodduck flank fibers
Rib: Fine oval gold tinsel
Body: Cream seal fur or goat dubbing
Hackle: Gray partridge hackle
Wingcase: Two tiny Jungle cock eyes, tied
    flat on top

MAYFLY NYMPHS

BLACK QUILL

QUILL GORDON

WESTERN BLUE QUILL NYMPH

CATSKILL *CANADENSIS*

ATHERTON DARK

CATSKILL HENDRICKSON

ATHERTON MEDIUM

CATSKILL MARCH BROWN

ATHERTON LIGHT

BLUE QUILL NYMPH

QUILL GORDON

Hook: TMC 2302, Mustad 3906B, sizes
    10-14, wt.
Thread: Olive 6/0 prewaxed
Tail: Two ringneck pheasant tail fibers
Rib: Brown thread
Body: Beaver belly fur
Wingcase: Mottled turkey wing quill
Thorax: Beaver belly fur
Legs: Brown partridge hackle fibers

CATSKILL *CANADENSIS*

Hook: TMC 5262, Mustad 9671, sizes
    12-14, wt.
Thread: Orange 6/0 prewaxed
Tail: Ringneck pheasant tail fibers
Rib: Brown silk floss
Body: Amber rabbit dubbing
Wingcase: Ringneck pheasant tail fibers
Thorax: Amber rabbit dubbing
Legs: Brown partridge hackle

CATSKILL HENDRICKSON

Hook: TMC 2302, Mustad 3906B, sizes
    12-16, wt.
Thread: Olive 6/0 prewaxed
Tail: Lemon woodduck flank fibers
Rib: Fine gold wire
Body: Grayish brown rabbit dubbing
Wingcase: Natural gray goose quill
Thorax: Grayish brown rabbit dubbing
Legs: Brown partridge hackle

CATSKILL MARCH BROWN

Hook: TMC 2302, Mustad 3906B,
    size 12, wt.
Thread: Orange 6/0 prewaxed
Tail: Ringneck pheasant tail fibers
Rib: Brown silk thread
Body: Amber goat fur
Wingcase: Ringneck pheasant tail fibers
Thorax: Amber goat fur
Legs: Brown partridge hackle, tied full

BLUE QUILL NYMPH

Hook: TMC 2302, Mustad 3906B, sizes
    12-18, wt.
Thread: Black 6/0 prewaxed
Tail: Ringneck pheasant tail fibers
Body: Amber rabbit dubbing
Wingcase: Black goose wing quill fibers
Thorax: Amber rabbit dubbing
Legs: Ginger hen hackle fibers

TIMBERLINE

Originator: Randall Kaufmann
Tier: Umpqua Feather Merchants
Hook: TMC 2302, Mustad 3906B, sizes 12-18, wt.
Thread: Tan 6/0 prewaxed
Tail: Ringneck pheasant tail fibers
Rib: Fine copper wire
Body: Blended 50% beaver fur and 50% gray goat fur or hare's ear
Wingcase: Ringneck pheasant tail fibers
Thorax: Same as body
Legs: Ringneck pheasant tail fibers, tips from wingcase

PARALEPTOPHLEBIA NYMPH

Originator: Randle Scott Stetzer
Hook: TMC 2302, Mustad 9671, sizes 12-18, wt.
Thread: Tan 6/0 prewaxed
Tail: Brown hen hackle fibers
Rib: Fine copper wire
Gills: Dark brown ostrich herl, laid along each side
Body: Rusty tan rabbit dubbing
Wingcase: Dark ringneck pheasant tail fibers
Thorax: Rusty tan rabbit dubbing

DARK *LEPTOPHLEBIA* NYMPH

Hook: TMC 5262, Mustad 9671, sizes 12-18, wt.
Thread: Brown 6/0 prewaxed
Tail: Three ringneck pheasant tail fibers
Rib: Brown hackle, palmered over body, clipped close on the sides and off on top and bottom
Body: Beaver fur
Wingcase: Bronze mallard flank fibers
Thorax: Beaver fur
Legs: Dark brown hen hackle

CALLIBAETIS NYMPH

Originator: Jim Cope
Tier: Jim Cope
Hook: TMC 2302, Mustad 3906B, sizes 12-16, wt.
Thread: Black 6/0 prewaxed
Tail: Dark mottled deer hair
Rib: Fine copper wire
Body: Gray black rabbit dubbing
Collar: Dark mottled deer hair

KRYSTAL FLASH *BAETIS*

Hook: TMC 100, Mustad 94845, sizes 14-18
Thread: Black 6/0 prewaxed
Body: Four strands of dyed black Krystal Flash, twisted
Wing: Dark dun hen hackle fibers
Head: Butts from wing

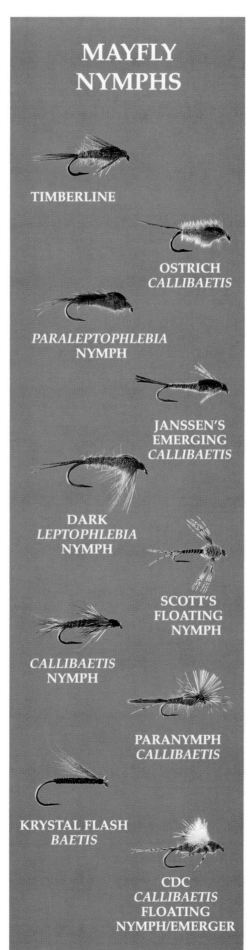

MAYFLY NYMPHS

TIMBERLINE

OSTRICH *CALLIBAETIS*

PARALEPTOPHLEBIA NYMPH

JANSSEN'S EMERGING *CALLIBAETIS*

DARK *LEPTOPHLEBIA* NYMPH

SCOTT'S FLOATING NYMPH

CALLIBAETIS NYMPH

PARANYMPH *CALLIBAETIS*

KRYSTAL FLASH *BAETIS*

CDC *CALLIBAETIS* FLOATING NYMPH/EMERGER

OSTRICH *CALLIBAETIS*

Originator: Fred Arbona
Tier: Umpqua Feather Merchants
Hook: TMC 100, Mustad 94845, sizes 12-16, wt.
Thread: Gray 6/0 prewaxed
Tail: Grouse hackle fibers
Rib: Gray thread
Body: Gray ostrich herl, wrapped
Wingcase: Gray duck quill
Thorax: Gray ostrich herl

JANSSEN'S EMERGING *CALLIBAETIS*

Originator: Hal Janssen
Tier: Umpqua Feather Merchants
Hook: TMC 5262, Mustad 9671, sizes 12-16
Thread: Gray 6/0 prewaxed
Tail: Dyed gray Amherst pheasant tippets
Underbody: Gray rabbit dubbing
Overbody: Clear plastic strip, wrapped
Wingcase: Dark duck quill, lacquered
Thorax: Same as body
Legs: Woodduck flank fibers

SCOTT'S FLOATING NYMPH

Originator: Scott Dawkins
Tier: Scott Dawkins
Hook: TMC 200, Mustad 94845, sizes 10-18
Thread: Olive 6/0 prewaxed
Tail: Gray partridge hackle fibers
Abdomen: Stripped peacock quill, from near eye
Wingcase: Gray evazote
Thorax: Olive dun rabbit dubbing
Legs: Gray partridge hackle

PARANYMPH *CALLIBAETIS*

Originator: Bob Quigley
Tier: Umpqua Feather Merchants
Hook: TMC 100, Mustad 94845, sizes 12-16
Thread: Gray 6/0 prewaxed
Tail: Mottled brown hen hackle fibers
Rib: Fine copper wire
Body: Gray muskrat dubbing
Wingcase: Natural deer hair
Thorax: Gray muskrat dubbing
Post: Natural deer hair, butts from wingcase
Hackle: Grizzly hackle, parachute style

CDC *CALLIBAETIS* FLOATING NYMPH/EMERGER

Originator: René Harrop & Family
Tier: René Harrop
Hook: TMC 5230, Mustad 94833, sizes 12-16
Thread: Tan 6/0 prewaxed
Tail: Woodduck flank fibers
Rib: Fine copper wire
Body: Tan rabbit dubbing
Legs: Brown partridge hackle fibers
Wing: White CDC feathers, short
Thorax: Tan rabbit dubbing

OSTRICH PALE MORNING DUN

Originator: Fred Arbona
Tier: Umpqua Feather Merchants
Hook: TMC 100, Mustad 94845, sizes 14-18, wt.
Thread: Brown 6/0 prewaxed
Tail: Brown partridge hackle fibers
Rib: Brown thread
Body: Brown ostrich herl, wrapped
Wingcase: Gray duck quill
Thorax: Brown ostrich herl

LIGHT CAHILL

Hook: TMC 2302, Mustad 3906B, sizes 10-18, wt.
Thread: Cream 6/0 prewaxed
Tail: Lemon woodduck flank fibers
Body: Buff red fox fur
Wingcase: Lemon woodduck flank fibers
Thorax: Buff red fox fur
Legs: Lemon woodduck flank fibers

PMD FLOATING NYMPH

Tier: Umpqua Feather Merchants
Hook: TMC 100, Mustad 94845, sizes 12-20
Thread: 6/0 prewaxed to match body
Tail: Ginger hackle fibers, or to match body
Rib: Silk thread, to match or slightly contrast body
Body: Antron dubbing, to match natural
Wingcase: Dark dun poly dubbing, shaped into a ball and placed on top of thorax area
Legs: Ginger hackle fibers

SRI CDC EMERGER, rust/brown

Originator: Bill Black
Tier: Spirit River Inc
Hook: TMC 2487, sizes 14-20
Thread: Brown 6/0 prewaxed
Tail: Ringneck pheasant tail fibers
Rib: Black Krystal Flash
Body: Dark brown super fine dubbing
Wingcase: Brown CDC feather, humped
Thorax: Dark brown super fine dubbing
Legs: Brown CDC fibers
Head: Dark brown super fine dubbing

SRI CDC EMERGER, sulphur

Originator: Bill Black
Tier: Spirit River Inc
Hook: TMC 2487, sizes 14-20
Thread: Cream 6/0 prewaxed
Tail: Lemon woodduck flank fibers
Rib: Pearl Krystal Flash
Body: Cream super fine dubbing
Wingcase: Pale yellow CDC feather, humped
Thorax: Cream super fine dubbing
Legs: Pale yellow CDC fibers
Head: Cream super fine dubbing

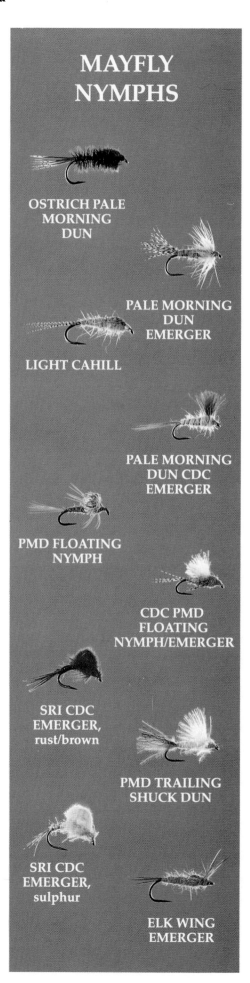

MAYFLY NYMPHS

OSTRICH PALE MORNING DUN

PALE MORNING DUN EMERGER

LIGHT CAHILL

PALE MORNING DUN CDC EMERGER

PMD FLOATING NYMPH

CDC PMD FLOATING NYMPH/EMERGER

SRI CDC EMERGER, rust/brown

PMD TRAILING SHUCK DUN

SRI CDC EMERGER, sulphur

ELK WING EMERGER

PALE MORNING DUN EMERGER

Originator: Mike Lawson
Tier: Umpqua Feather Merchants
Hook: TMC 100, Mustad 94845, sizes 14-18
Thread: Pale yellow 6/0 prewaxed
Tail: Teal flank fibers
Rib: Fine gold wire
Body: Pale yellow rabbit dubbing
Hackle: Light blue dun hen hackle

PALE MORNING DUN CDC EMERGER

Hook: TMC 100, Mustad 94845, sizes 14-18
Thread: Cream 6/0 prewaxed
Tail: Medium dun hackle fibers
Rib: Fine copper wire
Body: Fine tan dubbing
Wing: Dark dun CDC feather

CDC PMD FLOATING NYMPH/EMERGER

Originator: René Harrop & Family
Tier: René Harrop
Hook: TMC 5230, Mustad 94833, sizes 16-18
Thread: Yellow 6/0 prewaxed
Tail: Woodduck flank fibers
Rib: Fine gold wire
Body: Yellow rabbit dubbing
Legs: Woodduck flank fibers
Wing: White CDC feathers, short
Thorax: Yellow rabbit dubbing

PMD TRAILING SHUCK DUN

Originator: Bill Black
Tier: Spirit River Inc
Hook: TMC 100, Mustad 94845, sizes 14-18
Thread: Cream 6/0 prewaxed
Tail: Pale olive CDC feather with olive Z-lon over the top
Body: Cream super fine dubbing
Wing: White CDC feather, flared on top half of fly
Head: Cream super fine dubbing

ELK WING EMERGER

Hook: TMC 101, Mustad 94859, sizes 12-20
Thread: Tan 6/0 prewaxed
Tail: Ringneck pheasant tail fibers
Rib: Brown thread
Body: Tan rabbit dubbing
Wingcase: Elk hair, tied to extend over head for wing
Thorax: Tan antron dubbing
Head: Tan antron dubbing

BLUE WING OLIVE CDC FLOAT-ING NYMPH

Hook: TMC 100, Mustad 94845, sizes 16-20
Thread: Olive 6/0 prewaxed
Tail: Dark blue dun hackle tips
Rib: Fine gold wire
Body: Fine olive dubbing
Wingcase: Dark dun CDC feather, humped

HARROP SURFACE EMERGER

Originator: René Harrop
Tier: Umpqua Feather Merchants
Hook: TMC 100, Mustad 94845, sizes 12-20
Thread: Brown 6/0 prewaxed
Tail: Lemon wooduck flank fibers
Rib: Brown thread
Body: Rust rabbit dubbing
Wing: Rusty brown duck quill, clipped short
Legs: Light brown hackle fibers
Head: Rusty rabbit dubbing

CAENIS NYMPH

Hook: TMC 101, Mustad 94859, sizes 18-26, wt.
Thread: Brown 6/0 prewaxed
Tail: Three dark ringneck pheasant tail fibers
Rib: Tan thread
Body: Grayish-tan rabbit dubbing
Wingcase: Black ostrich herl, short

BLUE WING OLIVE

Hook: TMC 2302, Mustad 3906B, sizes 14-18, wt.
Thread: Olive 6/0 prewaxed
Tail: Lemon wooduck flank fibers
Rib: Brown silk thread
Body: Medium olive rabbit dubbing
Wingcase: Goose wing quill fibers
Thorax: Medium olive rabbit dubbing
Legs: Brown partridge hackle

OSTRICH BLUE WING OLIVE

Originator: Fred Arbona
Tier: Umpqua Feather Merchants
Hook: TMC 100, Mustad 3906B, sizes 12-18, wt.
Thread: Olive 6/0 prewaxed
Tail: Brown partridge hackle fibers
Body: Olive ostrich herl, wrapped
Wingcase: Natural dark gray duck quill
Thorax: Olive ostrich herl

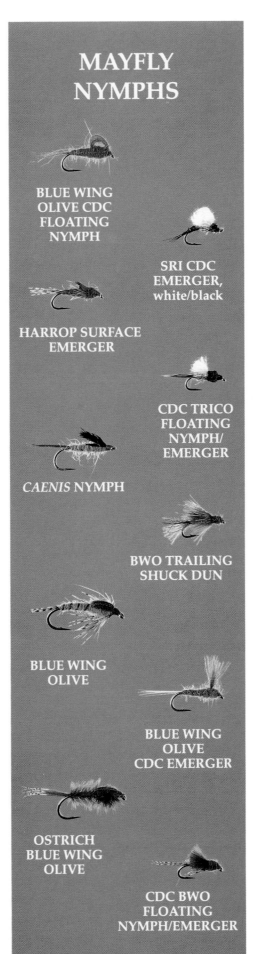

MAYFLY NYMPHS

BLUE WING OLIVE CDC FLOATING NYMPH

SRI CDC EMERGER, white/black

HARROP SURFACE EMERGER

CDC TRICO FLOATING NYMPH/ EMERGER

CAENIS NYMPH

BWO TRAILING SHUCK DUN

BLUE WING OLIVE

BLUE WING OLIVE CDC EMERGER

OSTRICH BLUE WING OLIVE

CDC BWO FLOATING NYMPH/EMERGER

SRI CDC EMERGER, white/black

Originator: Bill Black
Tier: Spirit River Inc
Hook: TMC 2457, sizes 18-20
Thread: Black 6/0 prewaxed
Tail: Black hackle fibers
Rib: Dyed black Krystal Flash
Body: Black super fine dubbing
Wingcase: White CDC feather, humped
Thorax: Black super fine dubbing
Legs: White CDC fibers
Head: Black super fine dubbing.

CDC TRICO FLOATING NYMPH/EMERGER

Originator: René Harrop & Family
Tier: René Harrop
Hook: TMC 5230, Mustad 94833, sizes 20-24
Thread: Black 6/0 prewaxed
Tail: Brown partridge hackle fibers
Rib: Fine silver wire
Body: Light olive rabbit dubbing
Legs: Brown partridge hackle fibers
Wing: White CDC feathers, short
Thorax: Black rabbit dubbing

BWO TRAILING SHUCK DUN

Originator: Bill Black
Tier: Spirit River Inc
Hook: TMC 100, Mustad 94845, sizes 16-20
Thread: Olive 6/0 prewaxed
Tail: Olive CDC feather with olive Z-lon over the top
Body: Olive super fine dubbing
Wing: Dark dun CDC feather, flared on the top half of the fly
Topping: Brown partridge hackle fibers
Head: Dark brown super fine dubbing

BLUE WING OLIVE CDC EMERGER

Hook: TMC 100, Mustad 94845, sizes 16-20
Thread: Olive 6/0 prewaxed
Tail: Light blue dun hackle fibers
Rib: Fine gold wire
Body: Fine olive dubbing
Wing: Dark dun CDC feather

CDC BWO FLOATING NYMPH/EMERGER

Originator: René Harrop & Family
Tier: René Harrop
Hook: TMC 5230, Mustad 94833, sizes 18-20
Thread: Olive 6/0 prewaxed
Tail: Teal flank fibers
Rib: Fine gold wire
Body: Olive rabbit dubbing
Legs: Brown partridge hackle fibers
Wing: Dark dun CDC feathers, short
Thorax: Olive rabbit dubbing

SWANNUNDAZE CADDIS

Hook: TMC 200R, Mustad 9671, sizes
10-16, wt.
Thread: Brown 6/0 prewaxed
Body: Fine amber swannundaze
Head: Dark brown rabbit dubbing,
picked out

LITTLE GREEN ROCK WORM

Originator: Polly Rosborough
Tier: John Kistler
Hook: TMC 5262, Mustad 9671, size 8
Thread: Black 6/0 prewaxed
Rib: Copper wire
Body: Bright green antron yarn
Legs: Dyed green guinea hackle fibers
Head: Black ostrich herl

RHYACOPHILA CADDIS

Originator: Randall Kaufmann
Hook: TMC 200, Mustad 9671, sizes
12-20, wt.
Thread: Black 6/0 prewaxed
Rib: Fine green wire
Body: Creamy green antron dubbing
Head: 75% creamy green antron dubbing,
25% black haretron

RANDALL'S CADDIS, olive

Originator: Randall Kaufmann
Tier: Umpqua Feather Merchants
Hook: TMC 200R, sizes 10-16, wt.
Thread: Black 6/0 prewaxed
Rib: Fine copper wire
Body: Olive antron yarn, twisted into rope
Head: Black haretron, well picked out

OLIVE CADDIS MIDGE NYMPH

Originator: Ed Koch
Tier: John Kistler
Hook: TMC 3769, Mustad 7948A,
sizes 16-24
Thread: Black 6/0 prewaxed
Body: Olive rabbit dubbing
Head: Peacock herl

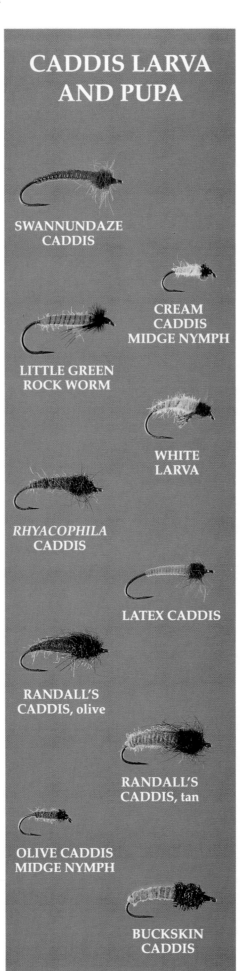

CADDIS LARVA AND PUPA

SWANNUNDAZE CADDIS

CREAM CADDIS MIDGE NYMPH

LITTLE GREEN ROCK WORM

WHITE LARVA

RHYACOPHILA CADDIS

LATEX CADDIS

RANDALL'S CADDIS, olive

RANDALL'S CADDIS, tan

OLIVE CADDIS MIDGE NYMPH

BUCKSKIN CADDIS

CREAM CADDIS MIDGE NYMPH

Originator: Ed Koch
Tier: John Kistler
Hook: TMC 3769, Mustad 7948A,
sizes 16-24
Thread: Brown 6/0 prewaxed
Body: Cream fox fur
Head: Peacock herl

WHITE LARVA

Hook: TMC 2487, sizes 10-18, wt.
Thread: Brown 6/0 prewaxed
Rib: Fine gold wire
Body: Dirty white rabbit dubbing
Legs: Brown partridge hackle fibers
Head: Dark brown rabbit dubbing

LATEX CADDIS

Hook: TMC 200R, Mustad 3906B, sizes
10-16, wt.
Thread: Brown 6/0 prewaxed
Underbody: Brown thread
Body: Latex strip, colored with waterproof
marker to match natural
Thorax: Dark brown rabbit dubbing, picked
out on bottom

RANDALL'S CADDIS, tan

Originator: Randall Kaufmann
Tier: Umpqua Feather Merchants
Hook: TMC 200R, sizes 10-16, wt.
Thread: Black 6/0 prewaxed
Body: Tan antron yarn, twisted into rope
Head: Black haretron, well picked out

BUCKSKIN CADDIS

Tier: Umpqua Feather Merchants
Hook: TMC 200R, sizes 10-14, wt.
Thread: Black 6/0 prewaxed
Body: Tan stripped deer hide
Head: Peacock herl

HERL NYMPH

Tier: John Kistler
Hook: TMC 5262, Mustad 9671, sizes 10-16, wt.
Thread: Black 6/0 prewaxed
Body: Peacock herl
Thorax: Black ostrich herl
Legs: Black hackle fibers

SRI CADDIS PUPA

Originator: Bill Black
Tier: Spirit River Inc
Hook: TMC 2457 sizes 10-16, wt.
Body: Tan camel dubbing
Wings: Clear fly film
Throat: Gray marabou
Eyes: Mono nymph eyes
Head: Peacock herl

SRI CADDIS LARVA

Originator: Bill Black
Tier: Spirit River Inc
Hook: TMC 2457, sizes 10-16, wt.
Thread: Olive 6/0 prewaxed
Body: Medium green antron dubbing
Eyes: Mono nymph eyes
Head: Peacock herl

GILL-RIBBED LARVA

Originator: Larry Solomon
Hook: TMC 2487, sizes 14-20, wt.
Thread: Black 6/0 prewaxed
Rib: Peacock herl
Body: Bright green floss
Head: Peacock herl

TRUEBLOOD'S CADDIS

Originator: Ted Trueblood
Hook: TMC 3769, Mustad 7957BX, sizes 8-12, wt.
Thread: Black 6/0 prewaxed
Tail: Green floss, short
Shellback: Peacock herl fibers
Rib: Fine oval silver tinsel
Body: Green floss, tapered
Legs: Mallard flank fibers

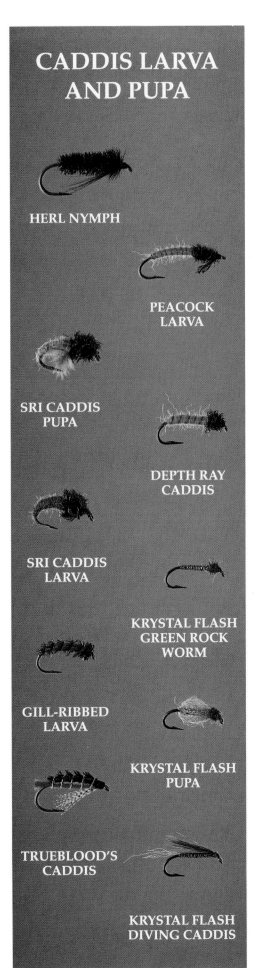

CADDIS LARVA AND PUPA

HERL NYMPH

PEACOCK LARVA

SRI CADDIS PUPA

DEPTH RAY CADDIS

SRI CADDIS LARVA

KRYSTAL FLASH GREEN ROCK WORM

GILL-RIBBED LARVA

KRYSTAL FLASH PUPA

TRUEBLOOD'S CADDIS

KRYSTAL FLASH DIVING CADDIS

PEACOCK LARVA

Originator: Greg Carrier
Tier: Greg Carrier
Hook: TMC 200, sizes 12-16, wt.
Thread: Black 6/0 prewaxed
Rib: Fine copper wire, through body and thorax
Body: Bright green crewel yarn, or depth ray wool
Thorax: Peacock herl
Legs: Two strands of peacock herl, tied down at each side

DEPTH RAY CADDIS

Originator: Greg Carrier
Tier: Greg Carrier
Hook: TMC 3761, Mustad 3906B, sizes 12-16, wt.
Thread: Black 6/0 prewaxed
Rib: Fine copper wire
Body: Fluorescent green wool
Head: Peacock herl

KRYSTAL FLASH GREEN ROCK WORM

Originator: Rick Hafele
Tier: Jim Schollmeyer
Hook: TMC 3761, Mustad 3906B, sizes 12-16
Thread: Brown 6/0 prewaxed
Body: Peacock green Krystal Flash, twisted and wrapped
Head: Brown rabbit dubbing, picked out

KRYSTAL FLASH PUPA

Tier: Jim Schollmeyer
Hook: TMC 3761, Mustad 3906B, sizes 12-18
Thread: Brown 6/0 prewaxed
Underbody: Peacock green Krystal Flash, twisted and wrapped
Body: Light tan antron yarn
Head: Brown rabbit dubbing

KRYSTAL FLASH DIVING CADDIS

Tier: Jim Schollmeyer
Hook: TMC 3769, Mustad 3906, sizes 12-16
Thread: Olive 6/0 prewaxed
Tail: Clear antron fibers
Body: Peacock green Krystal Flash, twisted and wrapped
Wing: Dark dun hen hackle fibers

LAFONTAINE'S CADDIS LARVA

Originator: Gary LaFontaine
Tier: Umpqua Feather Merchants
Hook: TMC 200, sizes 10-16, wt.
Thread: Black 6/0 prewaxed
Rib: Stripped brown hackle stem
Body: Bright green antron dubbing
Thorax: Brown antron dubbing
Legs: Brown grouse hackle fibers

LAFONTAINE CASED CADDIS

Originator: Gary LaFontaine
Hook: TMC 100, Mustad 94845, sizes 8-14, wt.
Thread: Brown 6/0 prewaxed
Body: Dark brown and gray grouse hackles, wrapped together and clipped
Thorax: Pale yellow rabbit dubbing
Legs: Dark brown and gray grouse hackle fibers

DIVING CADDIS, tan

Originator: Gary LaFontaine
Tier: Umpqua Feather Merchants
Hook: TMC 3761, Mustad 3906B, sizes 12-16
Thread: Black 6/0 prewaxed
Body: Tannish brown antron dubbing
Underwing: Grouse hackle fibers
Overwing: Clear antron fibers
Hackle: Brown neck hackle, sparse.

DIVING CADDIS, gray

Originator: Gary LaFontaine
Tier: Umpqua Feather Merchants
Hook: TMC 3761, Mustad 3906B, sizes 12-16
Thread: Black 6/0 prewaxed
Body: Medium gray antron dubbing
Underwing: Grouse hackle fibers
Overwing: Clear antron fibers
Hackle: Bronze dun neck hackle, sparse

DIVING CADDIS, bright green

Originator: Gary LaFontaine
Tier: Umpqua Feather Merchants
Hook: TMC 3769, Mustad 3906B, sizes 12-16
Thread: Black 6/0 prewaxed
Body: Bright olive green antron dubbing
Underwing: Grouse hackle fibers
Overwing: Clear antron fibers
Hackle: Brown neck hackle, sparse

CADDIS LARVA AND PUPA

LAFONTAINE'S CADDIS LARVA

DEEP SPARKLE PUPA, green

LAFONTAINE CASED CADDIS

DEEP SPARKLE PUPA, gray

DIVING CADDIS, tan

EMERGENT SPARKLE PUPA, gray

DIVING CADDIS, gray

EMERGENT SPARKLE PUPA, green

DIVING CADDIS, bright green

EMERGENT SPARKLE PUPA, ginger

DEEP SPARKLE PUPA, green

Originator: Gary LaFontaine
Tier: Umpqua Feather Merchants
Hook: TMC 100, Mustad 94845, sizes 12-18, wt.
Thread: Black 6/0 prewaxed
Underbody: 1/3 olive antron dubbing, 2/3 bright antron dubbing
Overbody: Medium olive antron yarn
Legs: Grouse hackle fibers
Head: Brown rabbit fur

DEEP SPARKLE PUPA, gray

Originator: Gary LaFontaine
Tier: Umpqua Feather Merchants
Hook: TMC 100, Mustad 94845, sizes 12-18, wt.
Thread: Black 6/0 prewaxed
Underbody: Gray antron dubbing
Overbody: Gray antron yarn
Legs: Mallard flank fibers
Head: Gray rabbit dubbing

EMERGENT SPARKLE PUPA, gray

Originator: Gary LaFontaine
Tier: Umpqua Feather Merchants
Hook: TMC 100, Mustad 94845, sizes 12-18
Thread: Black 6/0 prewaxed
Underbody: 1/2 gray muskrat fur, 1/2 dark brown antron dubbing
Overbody: Gray antron yarn
Wing: Dark gray deer hair
Head: Dark gray rabbit dubbing

EMERGENT SPARKLE PUPA, green

Originator: Gary LaFontaine
Tier: Umpqua Feather Merchants
Hook: TMC 100, Mustad 94845, sizes 12-18
Thread: Black 6/0 prewaxed
Underbody: Green antron dubbing and cream fur, mixed
Overbody: Green antron yarn
Wing: Dark gray deer hair
Head: Brown rabbit dubbing

EMERGENT SPARKLE PUPA, ginger

Originator: Gary LaFontaine
Tier: Umpqua Feather Merchants
Hook: TMC 100, Mustad 94845, sizes 12-18
Thread: Black 6/0 prewaxed
Underbody: 1/2 gold antron dubbing, 1/2 brown rabbit dubbing
Overbody: Gold antron yarn
Wing: Dark speckled deer hair
Head: Brown rabbit dubbing

CDC CADDIS EMERGER, cream

Originator: René Harrop & Family
Tier: René Harrop
Hook: TMC 100, Mustad 94845, sizes 12-18
Thread: Brown 6/0 prewaxed
Tail: Gold Z-lon
Rib: Fine gold wire
Body: Gold antron dubbing
Antennae: Two woodduck flank fibers
Wing: Cream CDC feathers
Legs: Brown partridge hackle
Head: Brown antron dubbing

AMERICAN GRANNOM

Originator: Ernest Schwiebert
Hook: TMC 3769, Mustad 3906,
  sizes 10-14
Thread: Dark brown 6/0 prewaxed
Rib: Fine oval gold tinsel
Body: Brown rabbit dubbing
Thorax: Deep chocolate brown
  rabbit dubbing
Wings: Natural gray duck wing quill
Antennae: Two bronze mallard flank fibers
Hackle: Brown partridge hackle
Head: Brown rabbit dubbing

SPECKLED SEDGE

Hook: TMC 3761, Mustad 3906B,
  sizes 12-16
Thread: Brown 6/0 prewaxed
Rib: Reddish-brown Australian opossum fur,
  thinly but firmly spun on to the thread
Body: Light brown mink fur
Wings: Natural gray duck quill
Legs: Brown partridge hackle fibers
Head: Dark brown rabbit dubbing

LITTLE GRAY CADDIS

Originator: Charles Brooks
Hook: TMC 3761, Mustad 3906B,
  sizes 12-18
Thread: Olive 6/0 prewaxed
Eggsack: Fluorescent green yarn, short
Body: Dark gray yarn
Thorax: Gray ostrich herl
Wings: Gray ostrich herl butts
Hackle: Grouse body hackle

DRIFTING CASED CADDIS

Originator: René Harrop
Tier: Umpqua Feather Merchants
Hook: TMC 5262, Mustad 9671,
  sizes 8-18, wt.
Thread: Black 6/0 prewaxed
Body: Mottled turkey wing quill
  fibers, wrapped
Thorax: Green antron dubbing
Legs: Black hackle barbules, stiff
  and clipped
Head: Black antron dubbing

CADDIS LARVA AND PUPA

CDC CADDIS EMERGER, cream

CADDIS FILO PUPA

AMERICAN GRANNOM

FLASHABOU CADDIS

SPECKLED SEDGE

CDC CADDIS EMERGER, olive

LITTLE GRAY CADDIS

TRANSLUCENT CADDIS PUPA

DRIFTING CASED CADDIS

SOLOMON'S CADDIS PUPA

CADDIS FILO PUPA

Originator: John Hazel
Tier: John Hazel
Hook: TMC 2302, Mustad 9671, sizes 10-18
Thread: Brown 6/0 prewaxed
Rib: Green single strand nylon floss
Body: Caddis green haretron
Wing: Clear antron fibers
Thorax: Natural gray filoplume feather
Head: Light brown haretron
Antennae: Two lemon woodduck
  flank fibers

FLASHABOU CADDIS

Originator: Greg Carrier
Tier: Greg Carrier
Hook: TMC 3769, Mustad 3906B,
  sizes 10-18
Thread: Black 6/0 prewaxed
Rib: Fine gold wire
Body: Medium olive rabbit dubbing
Wing: Pearl Flashabou
Head: Dark brown rabbit dubbing, combed
  towards rear

CDC CADDIS EMERGER, olive

Originator: René Harrop & Family
Tier: René Harrop
Hook: TMC 100, Mustad 94845, sizes 12-18
Thread: Olive 6/0 prewaxed
Tail: Olive Z-lon
Rib: Fine copper wire
Body: Olive antron dubbing
Antennae: Two woodduck flank fibers
Wing: Dark dun CDC feathers
Legs: Brown partridge hackle
Head: Dark brown antron dubbing

TRANSLUCENT CADDIS PUPA

Hook: TMC 3761, Mustad 3906B,
  sizes 10-18
Thread: Brown 6/0 prewaxed
Body: Pale green antron dubbing
Wing: Clear 4 mil. plastic, on underside
  of shank
Legs: Deer hair
Antennae: Two mallard flank fibers
Head: Brown rabbit dubbing.

SOLOMON'S CADDIS PUPA

Originator: Larry Solomon
Hook: TMC 5262, Mustad 9671, sizes 12-18
Thread: Dark olive 6/0 prewaxed
Rib: Dark olive thread
Body: Olive rabbit dubbing
Wings: Natural gray duck quill
Legs: Brown partridge hackle fibers
Head: Peacock herl

MUSKRAT

Originator: Polly Rosborough
Tier: John Kistler
Hook: TMC 5263, Mustad 9672, sizes 6-16
Thread: Black 6/0 prewaxed
Body: Muskrat fur
Legs: Speckled guinea hackle fibers
Head: Black ostrich herl

GRAY DREDGEBUG

Hook: TMC 5263, Mustad 9672, sizes 8-12
Thread: Gray 6/0 prewaxed
Body: Light gray haretron
Wing: Teal flank fibers
Legs: Gray partridge hackle fibers
Head: Charcoal gray haretron

SKIMMING CADDIS

Originator: Dave McNeese
Tier: Dave McNeese
Hook: TMC 100, Mustad 94845, sizes 6-18
Thread: Gray 6/0 prewaxed
Body: Light green rabbit dubbing
Downwing: Natural gray duck wing
   quill, lacquered
Wing: Natural deer hair, with two brown
   partridge hackles over the top
Head: Gray rabbit dubbing

LITTLE GREEN CADDIS PUPA

Originator: Charles Brooks
Tier: John Kistler
Hook: TMC 3761, Mustad 3906B,
   sizes 10-16
Thread: Olive 6/0 prewaxed
Egg Sac: Fluorescent green yarn, short
Rib: Fine gold wire
Body: Green yarn
Thorax: Tan ostrich herl
Wings: Two tan ostrich herl fibers
Hackle: Grouse hackle, sparse

BROWN DREDGEBUG

Hook: TMC 5262, Mustad 9672, sizes 8-12
Thread: Black 6/0 prewaxed
Rib: Fine gold wire
Body: Peacock herl
Hackle: Mottled brown hen hackle
Wing: Dyed brown mallard flank
Head: Brown chenille

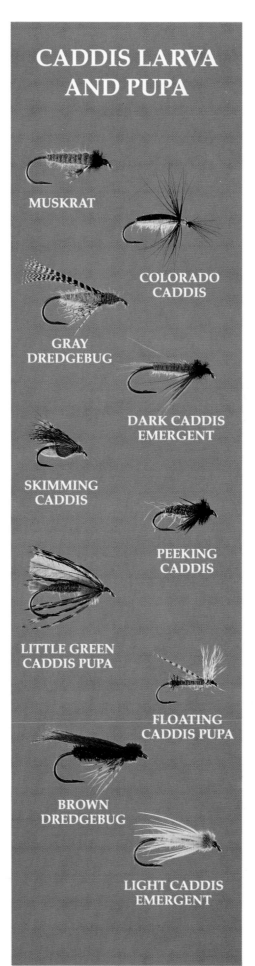

CADDIS LARVA AND PUPA

MUSKRAT

COLORADO CADDIS

GRAY DREDGEBUG

DARK CADDIS EMERGENT

SKIMMING CADDIS

PEEKING CADDIS

LITTLE GREEN CADDIS PUPA

FLOATING CADDIS PUPA

BROWN DREDGEBUG

LIGHT CADDIS EMERGENT

COLORADO CADDIS

Originator: Bob Good
Hook: TMC 5262, Mustad 9671, sizes
   8-12, wt.
Thread: Yellow 6/0 prewaxed
Shellback: Gray goose wing quill
Body: Light yellow rabbit dubbing
Hackle: Black hen hackle
Antennae: 6-10 black hackle fibers

DARK CADDIS EMERGENT

Originator: Polly Rosborough
Tier: John Kistler
Hook: TMC 3761, Mustad 3906B, size 8
Thread: Black 6/0 prewaxed
Rib: Orange thread
Body: Light orange rabbit dubbing
Hackle: Furnace hackle, clipped top and
   bottom
Head: Black ostrich herl

PEEKING CADDIS

Originator: George Anderson
Tier: Umpqua Feather Merchants
Hook: TMC 3761, Mustad 3906B, sizes
   12-16, wt.
Thread: Black 6/0 prewaxed
Rib: Fine oval gold tinsel
Body: Natural hare's ear dubbing
Thorax: Olive rabbit dubbing
Legs: Ringneck pheasant back fibers
Head: Black ostrich herl

FLOATING CADDIS PUPA

Originator: Preben Trop Jacobsen and
   Ken Bostrom
Hook: TMC 100, Mustad 94845, sizes 8-14
Thread: Black 6/0 prewaxed
Butt: Black hackle, clipped short
Body: Gray-brown rabbit dubbing
Antennae: Two lemon woodduck flank
   fibers
Hackle: Grizzly hackle, clipped on
   the bottom

LIGHT CADDIS EMERGENT

Originator: Polly Rosborough
Tier: John Kistler
Hook: TMC 3761, Mustad 3906B, sizes 6-8
Thread: Black 6/0 prewaxed
Rib: Medium yellow thread
Body: Creamy yellow antron yarn
Hackle: Light ginger hackle, clipped top
   and bottom
Head: Tan ostrich herl

DICOSMOECUS CASED CADDIS

Originator: John Hazel
Tier: John Hazel
Hook: TMC 300, Mustad 79580, sizes
  6-10, wt.
Thread: Black 6/0 prewaxed
Rib: Fine copper wire
Body: Peacock herl
Hackle: Furnace saddle hackle, palmered
  over the body, and clipped irregular
Thorax: Cream to pinkish orange rabbit
  dubbing
Head: Black goat dubbing, well picked out

MEDIUM CASED CADDIS

Hook: TMC 300, Mustad 79580, sizes
  8-14, wt.
Thread: Black 6/0 prewaxed
Underbody: Silver tinsel chenille
Body: Muskrat fur
Head: Black ostrich herl

SALMON CANDY No. 1

Originator: Lloyd Frese
Hook: TMC 5262, Mustad 9671, size 8
Thread: Black 6/0 prewaxed
Tail: Deer hair, short and sparse
Body: Medium dark olive wool
Hackle: Brown hackle, one turn
Head: Deer hair, spun and clipped

SALMON CANDY No. 2

Originator: Lloyd Frese
Hook: TMC 5262, Mustad 9671, size 8
Thread: Black 6/0 prewaxed
Tail: Deer hair, short and sparse
Shellback: Deer hair
Body: Medium dark olive wool
Hackle: Brown hackle, palmered over body,
  clipped at an angle
Head: Deer hair, butt ends from shellback

SALMON CANDY No. 3

Originator: Lloyd Frese
Hook: TMC 5262, Mustad 9671, size 8
Thread: Black 6/0 prewaxed
Body: Medium dark olive wool
Wing: Deer hair
Thorax: Deer hair
Hackle: Brown and grizzly hackle mixed
Head: Deer hair, butts from thorax

CADDIS LARVA AND PUPA

DICOSMOECUS CASED CADDIS

SKUNK HAIR CADDIS

MEDIUM CASED CADDIS

CASED CADDIS

SALMON CANDY No. 1

STRAWMAN

SALMON CANDY No. 2

TIED DOWN CADDIS, orange

SALMON CANDY No. 3

TIED DOWN CADDIS, yellow

SKUNK HAIR CADDIS

Originator: Charles Brooks
Tier: John Kistler
Hook: TMC 5262, Mustad 9671, sizes
  6-10, wt.
Thread: Black 6/0 prewaxed
Rib: Fine copper wire
Body: Blackish skunk tail hair, twisted and
  wrapped
Hackle: Black hen hackle, one turn
Head: Black thread, large

CASED CADDIS

Originator: George Bodmer
Tier: John Kistler
Hook: TMC 5262, Mustad 9671, sizes
  10-16, wt.
Thread: Black 6/0 prewaxed
Rib: Copper wire
Underbody: Tapered dark brown yarn
Overbody: Brown and black hackle,
  palmered over underbody than clipped
  short
Head: Black ostrich herl

STRAWMAN

Originator: Paul Young
Tier: John Kistler
Hook: TMC 5262, Mustad 9671, sizes 10-14
Thread: Brown 6/0 prewaxed
Tail: Mallard flank fibers
Body: Deer hair, spun and clipped with a
  taper
Hackle: Light gray partridge hackle

TIED DOWN CADDIS, orange

Hook: TMC 3761, Mustad 3906B, sizes 8-14
Thread: Orange 6/0 prewaxed
Tail: Deer hair
Shellback: Deer hair
Body: Orange wool
Hackle: Brown hackle, palmered over body

TIED DOWN CADDIS, yellow

Tier: Umpqua Feather Merchants
Hook: TMC 3761, Mustad 3906B, sizes 8-14
Thread: Yellow 6/0 prewaxed
Tail: Deer hair
Shellback: Deer hair
Body: Yellow wool
Hackle: Brown hackle, palmered over body

TED'S STONE

Tier: Umpqua Feather Merchants
Hook: TMC 5263, Mustad 9672, sizes
 6-10, wt.
Thread: Black 6/0 prewaxed
Tail: Two reddish brown stripped
 goose fibers
Body: Brown chenille
Wingcase: Brown chenille
Thorax: Orange chenille
Hackle: Black hackle, palmered over thorax

MONTANA STONE

Tier: Umpqua Feather Merchants
Hook: TMC 5263, Mustad 9672, sizes
 6-10, wt.
Thread: Black 6/0 prewaxed
Tail: Black hackle fibers
Body: Black chenille
Wingcase: Black chenille
Thorax: Yellow chenille
Hackle: Black hackle, palmered over thorax

MORRISTONE

Originator: Skip Morris
Tier: Skip Morris
Hook: TMC 300, Mustad 79580, sizes
 6-10, wt.
Thread: Brown 6/0 prewaxed
Tail: Mottled brown hen saddle feather,
 with center clipped to a "V"
Rib: Dark brown larva lace
Body: Dark gray antron yarn
Wingcase: Ringneck pheasant tail fibers
Legs: Mottled brown hen saddle feather
Thorax: Dark gray antron yarn
Head: Dark brown rabbit dubbing

BOX CANYON STONE

Originator: Mims Barker
Hook: TMC 3761, Mustad 3906B, sizes
 2-8, wt.
Thread: Black 6/0 prewaxed
Tail: Dark brown stripped goose fibers
Body: Black yarn, twisted
Wingcase: Brown mottled turkey quill
Thorax: Black yarn
Hackle: Furnace hackle, wrapped
 over thorax

LITTLE YELLOW STONE

Originator: Polly Rosborough
Hook: TMC 300, Mustad 79580, size 10
Thread: Light yellow 6/0 prewaxed
Tail: Dyed chartreuse mallard flank fibers
Rib: Yellow thread
Shellback: Dyed chartreuse mallard flank
Body: Chartreuse wool yarn
Legs: Dyed chartreuse mallard flank fibers,
 ¼ body length
Wingcase: Dyed chartreuse mallard flank
 fibers, ⅓ body length

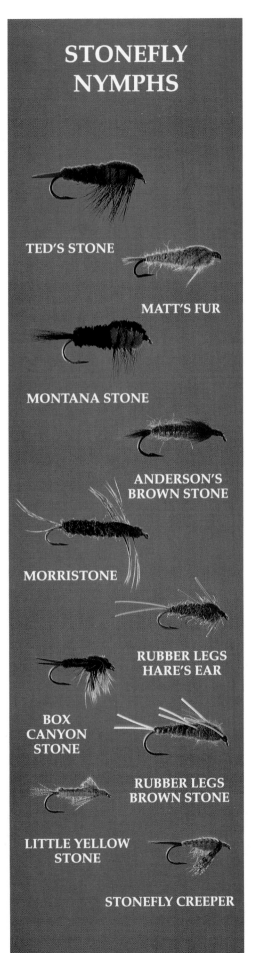

STONEFLY NYMPHS

TED'S STONE

MATT'S FUR

MONTANA STONE

ANDERSON'S BROWN STONE

MORRISTONE

RUBBER LEGS HARE'S EAR

BOX CANYON STONE

RUBBER LEGS BROWN STONE

LITTLE YELLOW STONE

STONEFLY CREEPER

MATT'S FUR

Originator: Matt Lavell
Tier: Umpqua Feather Merchants
Hook: TMC 5263, Mustad 9672, sizes
 6-12, wt.
Thread: Brown 6/0 prewaxed
Tail: Lemon woodduck flank fibers
Rib: Fine oval gold tinsel
Body: Blended, 50% cream seal fur, 50%
 otter fur
Wingcase: Lemon woodduck flank fibers
Thorax: Same as body
Legs: Lemon woodduck flank fibers, ends
 from wingcase

ANDERSON'S BROWN STONE

Originator: George Anderson
Tier: Umpqua Feather Merchants
Hook: TMC 5263, Mustad 9672, sizes
 6-10, wt.
Thread: Brown 6/0 prewaxed
Tail: Brown mink tail fibers
Body: Brown wool yarn and tan
 burlap, woven
Hackle: Brown mink fur with guard
 fibers, spun

RUBBER LEGS HARE'S EAR

Hook: TMC 2302, Mustad 9671, sizes
 8-14, wt.
Thread: Black 6/0 prewaxed
Tail: Cream round rubber hackle
Rib: Oval gold tinsel
Body: Hare's ear dubbing
Wingcase: Dark turkey tail
Legs: Cream round rubber hackle
Thorax: Hare's ear dubbing

RUBBER LEGS BROWN STONE

Originator: George Anderson
Tier: Umpqua Feather Merchants
Hook: TMC 5263, Mustad 9672, sizes
 4-10, wt.
Thread: Gray 6/0 prewaxed
Tail: White rubber hackle
Body: Brown wool yarn and tan burlap,
 woven
Legs: White rubber hackle
Thorax: Dark gray rabbit dubbing

STONEFLY CREEPER

Originator: Art Flick
Hook: TMC 5263, Mustad 9672, sizes
 6-12, wt.
Thread: Yellow 6/0 prewaxed
Tail: Ringneck pheasant tail fibers
Shellback: Lemon woodduck flank fibers
Body: Stripped ginger hackle quill
Thorax: Amber goat fur
Legs: Brown partridge hackle, collar style

EARLY STONE

Tier: Bill Beardsley
Hook: TMC 5262, Mustad 9671, sizes 10-16, wt.
Thread: Black 6/0 prewaxed
Tail: Two dark gray stripped goose fibers
Body: Iron dun rabbit dubbing
Wingcase: Black goose quill
Thorax: Iron dun rabbit dubbing
Legs: Iron blue dun hackle fibers

PEACOCK MATT'S FUR

Originator: Ed Schroeder
Tier: Bill Beardsley
Hook: TMC 5263, Mustad 9672, sizes 8-18, wt.
Thread: Tan 6/0 prewaxed
Tail: Lemon woodduck flank fibers
Rib: Fine oval gold tinsel
Body: Blended, 50% cream seal fur, 50% otter fur
Wingcase: Peacock herl
Thorax: Same as body

EARLY BROWN STONE

Tier: Bill Beardsley
Hook: TMC 5262, Mustad 9671, 10-14, wt.
Thread: Tan 6/0 prewaxed
Tail: Ginger stripped goose
Body: Medium brown rabbit dubbing
Wingcase: Dark brown mottled turkey quill
Thorax: Medium brown rabbit dubbing
Legs: Brown hen hackle fibers

WHIT'S BLACK STONE NYMPH

Originator: Dave Whitlock
Tier: Umpqua Feather Merchants
Hook: TMC 7999, Mustad 36890, sizes 2-8, wt.
Thread: Black 6/0 prewaxed
Tails: Black monofilament
Rib: Fine copper wire
Shellback: Black Swiss straw
Butt: Reddish-brown wool dubbing
Body: Black wool dubbing
Wingcase: Black swiss straw
Legs: Grouse hackle, flat over thorax
Thorax: Reddish-brown wool dubbing
Head: Black wool dubbing
Antennae: Black monofilament

BROOK'S STONE

Originator: Charles Brooks
Tier: Umpqua Feather Merchants
Hook: TMC 5263, Mustad 9672, sizes 4-8, wt.
Thread: Black 6/0 prewaxed
Tail: Black stripped goose fibers
Rib: Copper wire
Body: Black wool yarn
Hackle: Brown and grizzly hackle, stripped one side and wrapped over thorax area together
Gills: White ostrich herl, wrapped with hackle

STONEFLY NYMPHS

EARLY STONE

DARK STONE

PEACOCK MATT'S FUR

BIRD'S STONE NYMPH

EARLY BROWN STONE

WHIT'S GOLDEN STONE NYMPH

WHIT'S BLACK STONE NYMPH

YELLOW STONE NYMPH

BROOK'S STONE

BITCH CREEK

DARK STONE

Originator: Polly Rosborough
Hook: TMC 5263, Mustad 9672, sizes 2-6
Thread: Tan 6/0 prewaxed
Tail: Two dyed brown ringneck pheasant quill
Rib: Gold thread
Shellback: Dyed brown ringneck pheasant quill
Body: Cream badger fur
Legs: Dyed brown ringneck pheasant quill fibers
Wingcase: Dyed brown ringneck pheasant church window back feather

BIRD'S STONE NYMPH

Originator: Cal Bird
Tier: Bill Beardsley
Hook: TMC 5263, Mustad 9672, sizes 4-10, wt.
Thread: Orange 6/0 prewaxed
Tail: Two brown stripped goose fibers
Rib: Orange floss
Body: Reddish-brown rabbit dubbing
Wingcase: Mottled turkey tail
Thorax: Peacock herl
Hackle: Furnace hackle, palmered over thorax

WHIT'S GOLDEN STONE NYMPH

Originator: Dave Whitlock
Tier: Umpqua Feather Merchants
Hook: TMC 7999, Mustad 36890, sizes 4-8, wt.
Thread: Yellow 6/0 prewaxed
Tails: Yellow monofilament
Rib: Yellow floss
Shellback: Light mottled turkey wing quill
Butt: Cream wool dubbing
Body: Yellow wool dubbing
Wingcase: Light mottled turkey wing quill
Legs: Light tan mottled hen hackle, flat over thorax
Thorax: Cream wool dubbing
Head: Yellow wool dubbing
Antennae: Yellow monofilament

YELLOW STONE NYMPH

Originator: Charles Brooks
Hook: TMC 5263, Mustad 9672, size 8, wt.
Thread: Brown 6/0 prewaxed
Tail: Cinnamon turkey quill, forked, three fibers per side
Rib: Antique gold yarn, one strand, and fine gold wire
Body: Yellowish-brown yarn
Hackle: Grizzly and dyed brown grizzly hackle, wound over thorax area
Gills: Light gray ostrich herl, wrapped with hackle

BITCH CREEK

Tier: Umpqua Feather Merchants
Hook: TMC 5263, Mustad 9672, sizes 2-10, wt.
Thread: Black 6/0 prewaxed
Tails: White rubber hackle
Body: Black and orange chenille, woven
Rib: Fine gold wire, over thorax
Thorax: Black Chenille
Hackle: Brown hackle, palmered over thorax area
Antennae: White rubber hackle

LARGE BLACK STONE

Hook: TMC 300, Mustad 79580, sizes 2-8, wt.
Thread: Black 6/0 prewaxed
Tail: Black stripped goose
Rib: Flat gold tinsel
Body: Black rabbit dubbing
Wingcase: Peacock herl
Thorax: Same as body
Legs: Black hackle over the thorax, dense and clipped

RUBBER LEGS KAUFMANN'S STONE

Originator; Randall Kaufmann
Tier: Umpqua Feather Merchants
Hook: TMC 5263, Mustad 79580, sizes 2-12, wt.
Thread: Black 6/0 prewaxed
Tail: Black stripped goose fibers
Rib: Fine black swannundaze
Body: Blended, 50% black rabbit dubbing, 50% claret, amber, orange, rust, black, brown, blue, purple, ginger goat fur
Legs: Black rubber hackle
Wingcase: Three separate sections of lacquered dark turkey tail, clipped to shape
Thorax: Same as body
Head: Same as body
Antennae: Black stripped goose fibers.

PHEASANT BACK STONE

Hook: TMC 300, Mustad 9575, sizes 2-6, wt.
Thread: Black 6/0 prewaxed
Tail: Brown stripped goose
Rib: Thin brown swannundaze
Body: Brown goat dubbing
Wingcase: Marked pheasant back feather
Thorax: Brown goat dubbing
Hackle: Marked pheasant back feather
Antennae: Brown stripped goose

CARRIER'S STONE

Originator: Greg Carrier
Tier: Greg Carrier
Hook: TMC 300, Mustad 9575, sizes 2-8, wt.
Thread: Black 6/0 prewaxed
Tail: Black stripped goose
Rib: Fine brown swannundaze
Body: Blended, black, brown and amber goat dubbing
Wingcase: Dark turkey tail
Legs: Mottled dark brown hen hackle, laid flat under the wingcase
Thorax: Gray wool yarn and brown ostrich herl
Head: Blended, black, brown, and amber goat dubbing
Antennae: Black stripped goose

KAUFMANN'S BLACK STONE

Originator: Randall Kaufmann
Tier: Umpqua Feather Merchants
Hook: TMC 300, Mustad 9575, sizes 2-12, wt.
Thread: Black 6/0 prewaxed
Tail: Two black stripped goose fibers
Rib: Black swannundaze
Body: Blended, 50% black rabbit dubbing, 50% claret, amber, orange, rust, black, brown, blue, purple, ginger goat fur
Wingcase: Three separate sections of lacquered dark turkey tail, clipped to shape
Thorax: Same as body
Head: Same as body
Antennae: Two black stripped goose fibers

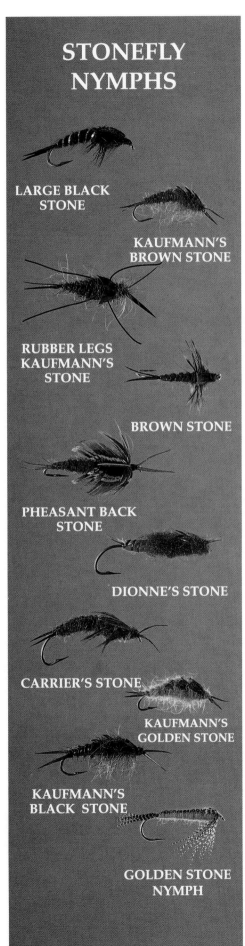

STONEFLY NYMPHS

LARGE BLACK STONE

KAUFMANN'S BROWN STONE

RUBBER LEGS KAUFMANN'S STONE

BROWN STONE

PHEASANT BACK STONE

DIONNE'S STONE

CARRIER'S STONE

KAUFMANN'S GOLDEN STONE

KAUFMANN'S BLACK STONE

GOLDEN STONE NYMPH

KAUFMANN'S BROWN STONE

Originator: Randall Kaufmann
Tier: Umpqua Feather Merchants
Hook: TMC 300, Mustad 9575, sizes 2-12, wt.
Thread: Brown 6/0 prewaxed
Tail: Two brown stripped goose fibers
Rib: Brown swannundaze
Body: Blended, 50% brown rabbit dubbing, 50% claret, amber, orange, rust, black, brown, blue, purple, ginger goat fur
Wingcase: Three separate sections of lacquered dark turkey tail, clipped to shape
Thorax: Same as body
Head: Same as body
Antennae: Two brown stripped goose fibers

BROWN STONE

Tier: Bill Beardsley
Hook: TMC 300, Mustad 79580, sizes 4-8, wt.
Thread: Brown 6/0 prewaxed
Tail: Dark brown stripped goose
Rib: Brown swannundaze
Body: Blended dark brown rabbit dubbing and brown seal fur
Wingcase: Dark brown mottled turkey quill
Thorax: Yellowish-brown rabbit dubbing
Hackle: Brown hackle, wrapped over thorax, clipped on the bottom
Head: Blended dark brown rabbit dubbing and brown seal fur

DIONNE'S STONE

Originator: Jim Dionne
Tier: Jim Dionne
Hook: TMC 300, Mustad 79580, sizes 2-8, wt.
Thread: Brown 6/0 prewaxed
Tail: Orange stripped goose
Rib: Thin brown swannundaze
Shellback: Gray goose quill
Body: Orange poly pro yarn
Thorax: Dark brown antron dubbing
Wingcases: Dark turkey tail, three plates, "V" clipped
Head: Same as the thorax
Antennae: Orange stripped goose

KAUFMANN'S GOLDEN STONE

Originator: Randall Kaufmann
Tier: Umpqua Feather Merchants
Hook: TMC 300, Mustad 9575, sizes 2-12, wt.
Thread: Gold 6/0 prewaxed
Tail: Two ginger stripped goose fibers
Rib: Pale ginger swannundaze
Body: Blended, 50% golden brown rabbit dubbing, 50% claret, amber, orange, rust, black, brown, blue, purple, ginger goat fur
Wingcase: Three separate sections of lacquered mottled turkey wing quill, clipped to shape
Thorax: Same as body
Head: Same as body
Antennae: Two ginger stripped goose fibers

GOLDEN STONE NYMPH

Originator: Polly Rosborough
Tier: Bill Beardsley
Hook: TMC 5263, Mustad 9672, sizes 4-6, wt.
Thread: Gold 6/0 prewaxed
Tail: Teal flank fibers
Rib: Gold thread
Shellback: Teal flank fibers
Body: Antique gold yarn
Legs: Teal flank fibers
Wingcase: Teal flank

Chapter 5

Damsels, Dragons,
Crustaceans and Leeches

❖

NYERGES NYMPH

Originator: Gil Nyerges
Hook: TMC 5263, Mustad 9672, size 10, wt.
Thread: Brown 6/0 prewaxed
Tail: Brown hackle fibers
Body: Dark olive chenille
Hackle: Brown hackle, palmered through
body, clipped top and sides

TRUEBLOOD'S OTTER

Originator: Ted Trueblood
Tier: Umpqua Feather Merchants
Hook: TMC 3769, Mustad 3906, sizes
8-16, wt.
Thread: Tan 6/0 prewaxed
Tail: Brown partridge hackle fibers
Body: Otter fur mixed with a small amount
of natural seal fur
Throat: Brown partridge hackle fibers

CLAUSER'S CRAYFISH

Originator: Bob Clauser
Tier: Umpqua Feather Merchants
Hook: TMC 2302, sizes 4-8, wt.
Thread: White 6/0 prewaxed
Tail: Ringneck pheasant tail, two bunches,
one long one short
Shellback: Brown pheasant wing quill
Body: Gray antron yarn
Wings: Brown webby saddle hackle, from
under shellback
Hackle: White hackle, over the thorax area
Head: Brown pheasant wing quill, butt
from shellback

WATER BOATMAN

Originator: Everett Caryl, Sr
Hook: TMC 3761, Mustad 3906B, size
10, wt.
Thread: Black 6/0 prewaxed
Tail: Brown partridge hackle fibers, short
and sparse
Shellback: Metallic blue drake mallard
secondary wing fibers
Body: Reddish-tan red fox fur, tapered
Paddles: Natural gray stripped goose

CORIXID

Tier: Bill Beardsley
Hook: TMC 3761, Mustad 3906B, sizes
16-20
Thread: Dark olive 6/0 prewaxed
Body: Dark olive rabbit dubbing, loose

DAMSELS, DRAGONS, CRUSTACEANS AND LEECHES

NYERGES NYMPH

GAMMARUS-HYALELLA SCUD, tan

TRUEBLOOD'S OTTER

BIGHORN SCUD

CLAUSER'S CRAYFISH

PINK SHRIMP

WATER BOATMAN

OSTRICH SCUD

CORIXID

GAMMARUS-HYALELLA SCUD, olive

GAMMARUS-HYALELLA SCUD, tan

Originator: Randall Kaufmann
Tier: Umpqua Feather Merchants
Hook: TMC 200R, sizes 10-18, wt.
Thread: Tan 6/0 prewaxed
Tail: Ginger hackle fibers
Rib: Clear monofilament
Shellback: Heavy clear plastic
Body: Mixed, tan haretron and goat, picked
out on bottom
Antennae: Ginger hackle fibers

BIGHORN SCUD

Tier: Umpqua Feather Merchants
Hook: TMC 3761, Mustad 3906B, sizes
8-16, wt.
Thread: Orange 6/0 prewaxed
Tail: Ringneck pheasant tail fibers
Rib: Copper wire
Shellback: Clear plastic
Body: Orange antron dubbing, picked out
on underside

PINK SHRIMP

Hook: TMC 2457, sizes 12-18, wt.
Thread: Pink 6/0 prewaxed
Tail: Fluorescent pink hackle fibers
Rib: Clear monofilament
Shellback: One strand of pearl Flashabou,
with clear plastic over
Body: Fluorescent pink antron dubbing,
well picked out
Antennae: Fluorescent pink hackle fibers

OSTRICH SCUD

Originator: Fred Arbona
Tier: Umpqua Feather Merchants
Hook: TMC 20o, Mustad 37160, sizes 12-18
Thread: Olive 6/0 prewaxed
Rib: Clear Monofilament
Shellback: Clear plastic
Body: Olive ostrich herl

GAMMARUS-HYALELLA SCUD, olive

Originator: Randall Kaufmann
Tier: Umpqua Feather Merchants
Hook: TMC 200R, sizes 10-18, wt.
Thread: Brown 6/0 prewaxed
Tail: Olive hackle fibers
Rib: Clear monofilament
Shellback: Heavy clear plastic
Body: Mixed, olive haretron and goat,
picked out on bottom
Antennae: Olive hackle fibers

GIANT DAMSEL

Originator: Jim Cope
Tier: Jim Cope
Hook: TMC 300, Mustad 79580, sizes 6-10, wt.
Thread: Black 6/0 prewaxed
Tail: Dyed Olive grizzly hackle
Body: Olive and black variegated wool yarn
Hackle: Dyed olive grizzly hackle
Head: Light olive chenille

DAMSELFLY NYMPH

Originator: Marshall Escola
Tier: Bill Beardsley
Hook: TMC 5263, Mustad 9672, sizes 8-16, wt.
Thread: Brown 6/0 prewaxed
Tail: Dyed green grizzly hackle tip
Body: Variegated green yarn
Hackle: Dyed green grizzly hen hackle
Wingcase: Knot of variegated green yarn

FILOPLUME DAMSEL

Originator: Gene Armstrong
Hook: TMC 5263, Mustad 9672, sizes 10-14
Thread: Olive 6/0 prewaxed
Tail: Olive marabou
Body: Olive marabou
Rib: Fine silver wire
Thorax: Dyed olive filoplume feathers
Hackle: Silver badger hackle, through thorax
Head: Peacock herl

WINGCASE DAMSEL

Originator: Jim Cope
Tier: Jim Cope
Hook: TMC 200R, sizes 8-12
Thread: Olive 6/0 prewaxed
Tail: Dyed green guinea hackle fibers
Rib: Fine flat gold tinsel
Body: Olive hare's ear dubbing
Wingcase: Peacock herl
Thorax: Olive hare's ear dubbing, well picked out
Legs: Dyed green guinea hackle fibers

MARABOU DAMSEL

Originator: Randall Kaufmann
Tier: Umpqua Feather Merchants
Hook: TMC 200, Mustad 9672, sizes 8-12
Thread: Olive 6/0 prewaxed
Tail: Olive marabou, short
Rib: Fine copper wire
Body: Olive marabou, wrapped
Wing: Olive marabou, short

DAMSELS, DRAGONS, CRUSTACEANS AND LEECHES

GIANT DAMSEL

DOUG'S DAMSEL

DAMSELFLY NYMPH

JIM'S DAMSEL

FILOPLUME DAMSEL

EYED DAMSEL

WINGCASE DAMSEL

JANSSEN'S DAMSEL

MARABOU DAMSEL

MISS TAKE

DOUG'S DAMSEL

Originator: Doug Jorgensen
Tier: Doug Jorgensen
Hook: TMC 101, Mustad 94859, size 12
Thread: Olive 6/0 prewaxed
Tail: Olive marabou, shank length
Body: Olive rabbit dubbing
Wingcase: Olive duck quill, shiny side down
Legs: Olive marabou
Eyes: Mono nymph eyes
Thorax: Olive rabbit dubbing

JIM'S DAMSEL

Originator: Jim Schollmeyer
Tier: Jim Schollmeyer
Hook: TMC 5263, Mustad 9672, sizes 8-12
Thread: Olive 6/0 prewaxed
Tail: Olive marabou and olive Krystal Flash
Rib: Olive Krystal Flash
Body: Olive marabou, wrapped
Legs: Green Ringneck pheasant back fibers
Eyes: Olive green craft beads
Head: Olive marabou, wrapped

EYED DAMSEL

Originator: Jim Cope
Tier: Jim Cope
Hook: TMC 300, Mustad 79580, sizes 8-12
Thread: Olive 6/0 prewaxed
Tail: Dyed olive mallard flank
Body: Olive rabbit dubbing, with clear flat mono
Wingcase: Ringneck pheasant tail fibers, folded
Legs: Dyed olive mallard flank
Eyes: Green craft beads
Head: Olive rabbit dubbing

JANSSEN'S DAMSEL

Originator: Hal Janssen
Tier: Umpqua Feather Merchants
Hook: TMC 5263, Mustad 9672, sizes 8-12
Thread: Olive 6/0 prewaxed
Tail: Brownish-olive marabou
Abdomen: 40% bleached beaver, 60% olive rabbit
Rib: Olive thread
Wingcase: Mottled turkey wing quill, lacquered
Thorax: Light olive chenille
Hackle: Ginger hackle, wrapped through thorax, clipped top and bottom, trimmed on sides

MISS TAKE

Originator: Charles Brooks
Hook: TMC 5263, Mustad 9672, size 6, wt.
Thread: Brown 6/0 prewaxed
Tail: Three peacock sword fibers
Rib: Purple wool yarn and gray ostrich herl
Overrib: Fine gold wire
Body: Brown wool yarn
Hackle: Dyed brown grizzly hackle

SWIMMING DAMSEL

Originator: A.K. Best
Tier: Umpqua Feather Merchants
Hook: TMC 400T, sizes 8-12
Thread: Olive 6/0 prewaxed
Tail: Light olive hackle fibers
Rib: Fine copper wire
Body: Olive wool yarn
Wingcase: Olive swiss straw
Thorax: Olive wool yarn
Eyes: Bead chain eyes, painted black
Legs: Dyed olive grizzly hackle fibers

WHIT'S DAMSEL

Originator: Dave Whitlock
Tier: Umpqua Feather Merchants
Hook: TMC 5262, Mustad 9671, sizes 8-14.
  same hook clipped for extended body
Thread: Olive 6/0 prewaxed
Tail: Olive marabou, short
Rib: Fine silver wire
Body: Olive antron dubbing, thin
Wingcase: Olive swiss straw
Legs: Dyed olive hen hackle, tied flat
  under wingcase
Thorax: Olive antron dubbing
Eyes: Mono nymph eyes

OSTRICH DAMSEL

Originator: Fred Arbona
Tier: Umpqua Feather Merchants
Hook: TMC 100, Mustad 94845, sizes 8-12
Thread: Olive 6/0 prewaxed
Tail: Grizzly hackle tips dyed olive
Body: Olive ostrich herl, wrapped over
  monofilament for extended portion
Wingcase: Natural mottled turkey wing quill
Thorax: Olive ostrich herl
Eyes: Mono nymph eyes
Head: Natural mottled turkey wing quill

ATCHISON'S DAMSEL

Originator: Larry Atchison
Tier: Larry Atchison
Hook: TMC 200R, sizes 10-14
Thread: Olive 6/0 prewaxed
Tail: Olive marabou, short
Rib: Fine copper wire
Body: Olive marabou, laid over hook shank
  and wrapped down with wire, tips make
  the tail
Wingcase: Olive marabou
Thorax: Olive rabbit dubbing

MOUNTAIN DAMSEL

Originator: Randall Kaufmann
Tier: Umpqua Feather Merchants
Hook: TMC 300, Mustad 9575, sizes 8-12
Thread: Olive 6/0 prewaxed
Tail: Olive stripped goose, tied short
Shellback: Olive marabou
Rib: Fine gold wire
Body: Dark Green goat dubbing, thin
Wing: Olive marabou, 1/3 body length

DAMSELS,
DRAGONS,
CRUSTACEANS AND
LEECHES

SWIMMING
DAMSEL

OLIVE
DAMSEL

WHIT'S
DAMSEL

PARACHUTE
DAMSEL, olive

OSTRICH
DAMSEL

BRAIDED
BUTT
DAMSEL

ATCHISON'S
DAMSEL

PARACHUTE
DAMSEL, blue

MOUNTAIN
DAMSEL

BLUE DAMSEL

OLIVE DAMSEL

Originator: Scott Dawkins
Tier: Scott Dawkins
Hook: TMC 100, Mustad 94845, sizes 10-12
Thread: Gray 6/0 prewaxed
Body: Natural elk hair
Rib: Tying thread, in bands
Wings: Clear zing (Taiwanese packing tape)
Thorax: Olive tan poly dubbing
Post: White poly yarn
Hackle: Dark dun hackle, parachute style
Eyes: Pearlescent bead eyes

PARACHUTE DAMSEL, olive

Tier: Umpqua Feather Merchants
Hook: TMC 5212, Mustad 94831, sizes 8-12
Thread: Black 6/0 prewaxed
Rib: Black thread
Body: Olive bucktail, tied extended
Hackle: Dark blue dun, wound around base
  of wingcase
Wingcase: Olive bucktail, twisted
Head: Olive bucktail, butts from wingcase

BRAIDED BUTT DAMSEL

Tier: Umpqua Feather Merchants
Hook: TMC 900BL, Mustad 94845,
  sizes 10-12
Thread: Gray 6/0 prewaxed
Body: Braided leader material, colored with
  waterproof markers
Hackle post and Shellback: Pearl blue
  Krystal Flash
Hackle: Grizzly saddle hackle
Body: Light blue dubbing
Eyes: Mono nymph eyes
Head: Light blue poly yarn and butts
  from shellback

PARACHUTE DAMSEL, blue

Tier: Umpqua Feather Merchants
Hook: TMC 5212, Mustad 94831, sizes 8-12
Thread: Black 6/0 prewaxed
Rib: Black thread
Body: Medium blue bucktail, tied extended
Hackle: Light dun, wound around base
  of wingcase
Wingcase: Medium blue bucktail, twisted
Head: Medium blue bucktail, butts
  from wingcase

BLUE DAMSEL

Originator: Scott Dawkins
Tier: Scott Dawkins
Hook: TMC 100, Mustad 94845, sizes 6-10
Thread: Black 6/0 prewaxed
Body: Dyed blue elk hair, extended
Wings: Clear zing, (Taiwanese
  packing twine)
Wing post: White poly pro yarn
Thorax: Blue/gray rabbit dubbing
Hackle: Dark blue dun hackle,
  parachute style
Eyes: Mono nymph eyes

FILOPLUME DRAGON, olive

Originator: Gene Armstrong
Hook: TMC 300, Mustad 36620, size 6, wt.
Thread: Olive 6/0 prewaxed
Tail: Sparse Woodduck flank fibers and dyed olive pheasant rump marabou
Abdomen: Dyed olive pheasant filoplume feathers
Wingcase: Dyed olive pheasant back feather, blue green phase
Thorax: Mixed olive rabbit, goat and antron
Legs: Dyed olive pheasant back, tips from wingcase
Head: Peacock herl

FILOPLUME DRAGON, brown

Originator: Gene Armstrong
Hook: TMC 300, Mustad 36620, size 6, wt.
Thread: Brown 6/0 prewaxed
Tail: Sparse Woodduck flank fibers and brown marabou
Abdomen: Dyed brown pheasant filoplume feathers
Wingcase: Dyed brown pheasant back feather, blue green phase
Thorax: Mixed brown rabbit, goat and antron
Legs: Dyed brown pheasant back, tips from wingcase
Head: Peacock herl

FILOPLUME LEECH, brown

Originator: Gene Armstrong
Hook: TMC 300, Mustad 36620, sizes 4-10, wt.
Thread: Brown 6/0 prewaxed
Tail: Dyed brown pheasant rump marabou
Body: Dyed brown pheasant filoplume feathers
Hackle: Silver badger hackle, palmered through thorax area
Collar: Dyed brown pheasant flank

FILOPLUME LEECH, black

Originator: Gene Armstrong
Hook: TMC 300, Mustad 36620, sizes 4-10, wt.
Thread: Black 6/0 prewaxed
Tail: Dyed black pheasant rump marabou
Body: Dyed black pheasant filoplume feathers
Hackle: Silver badger hackle, palmered through thorax area
Collar: Dyed black pheasant flank

PEACOCK DRAGON

Hook: TMC 300, Mustad 79580, sizes 6-10, wt.
Thread: Black 6/0 prewaxed
Tail: Ringneck pheasant back fibers
Underbody: Dark olive floss, tapered
Body: Peacock herl
Wingcase: Ringneck pheasant tail fibers
Thorax: Muskrat guard hairs, well picked out
Eyes: Mono nymph eyes
Head: Peacock herl

DAMSELS, DRAGONS, CRUSTACEANS AND LEECHES

FILOPLUME DRAGON, olive

WHIT'S DRAGON NYMPH

FILOPLUME DRAGON, brown

LAKE DRAGON

FILOPLUME LEECH, brown

GIERACH DRAGON

FILOPLUME LEECH, black

FLOATING DRAGON, olive

PEACOCK DRAGON

FLOATING DRAGON, brown

WHIT'S DRAGON NYMPH

Originator: Dave Whitlock
Tier: Umpqua Feather Merchants
Hook: TMC 7999, Mustad 36890, sizes 4-8, wt.
Thread: Olive 6/0 prewaxed
Shellback: Olive swiss straw
Rib: Fine gold wire
Body: Dark olive rabbit dubbing and clear antron fibers, mixed
Eyes: Mono nymph eyes
Wingcase: Olive swiss straw

LAKE DRAGON

Originator: Randall Kaufmann
Tier: Umpqua Feather Merchants
Hook: TMC 5263, Mustad 79580, sizes 6-10, wt.
Thread: Olive 6/0 prewaxed
Tail: Olive grizzly marabou, short
Rib: Fine copper wire
Abdomen: 50% olive rabbit, other 50% blue, purple, green, amber, olive, rust, brown goat fur, mixed
Legs: Brown pheasant rump fibers
Wingcase: Dark brown turkey tail, Clipped to "V"
Eyes: Monofilament nymph eyes
Thorax: Same as abdomen, thinner

GIERACH DRAGON

Originator: John Gierach
Hook: TMC 200R, sizes 6-10, wt.
Thread: Black 6/0 prewaxed
Rib: Fine flat gold tinsel
Body: Hare's ear dubbing
Underwing: Dyed dark brown deer hair, tied inverted
Wing: Dark turkey tail, short
Legs: Ringneck pheasant flank fibers
Eyes: Mono nymph eyes
Head: Hare's ear dubbing

FLOATING DRAGON, olive

Originator: Randall Kaufmann
Tier: Umpqua Feather Merchants
Hook: TMC 5263, Mustad 79580, sizes 4-10
Thread: Olive 6/0 prewaxed
Tail: Dyed olive grizzly marabou, short
Body: Olive deer hair, spun and clipped, flat on top and bottom
Legs: Dyed olive grizzly marabou
Wingcase: Dark turkey tail, lacquered and clipped to a "V"
Eyes: Monofilament nymph eyes
Head: Dark olive rabbit haretron dubbing

FLOATING DRAGON, brown

Originator: Randall Kaufmann
Tier: Umpqua Feather Merchants
Hook: TMC 5263, Mustad 79580, sizes 4-10
Thread: Brown 6/0 prewaxed
Tail: Dyed brown grizzly marabou, short
Body: Brown deer hair, spun and clipped, flat on top and bottom
Legs: Dyed brown grizzly marabou
Wingcase: Dark turkey tail, lacquered and clipped to a "V"
Eyes: Monofilament nymph eyes
Head: Dark brown rabbit haretron

FLESH FLY

Tier: Umpqua Feather Merchants
Hook: TMC 300, Mustad 79580, sizes 2-6, wt.
Thread: White 6/0 prewaxed
Tail: White rabbit fur strip and rainbow Krystal Flash
Body: White rabbit fur strip, wrapped

RED LEECH

Hook: TMC 300, Mustad 9575, sizes 4-10
Thread: Red 6/0 prewaxed
Tail: Red Marabou with red and pearl Krystal Flash
Rib: Gold wire
Body: Red goat dubbing, well picked out

ASSAM DRAGON

Originator: Charles Brooks
Tier: Umpqua Feather Merchants
Hook: TMC 5263, Mustad 9672, size 4, wt.
Thread: Black 6/0 prewaxed
Body: Natural brown seal fur, on the hide, wound on
Hackle: Dyed brown grizzly hackle

DON KING

Originator: Greg Carrier
Tier: Greg Carrier
Hook: TMC 5262, Mustad 9671, sizes 2-8, wt.
Thread: Black 6/0 prewaxed
Rib: Medium copper wire
Body: Brown goat dubbing
Wing: Black marabou, matuka style

RABBIT LEECH, black

Tier: Umpqua Feather Merchants
Hook: TMC 300, Mustad 79580, sizes 2-6, wt.
Thread: Black 6/0 prewaxed
Tail: Black rabbit fur strip, with 4 strands of red and blue Krystal Flash
Body: Black rabbit fur strip, wrapped
Topping: 3 strands of red Krystal Flash

DAMSELS, DRAGONS, CRUSTACEANS AND LEECHES

FLESH FLY

RABBIT LEECH, maroon

RED LEECH

FLASH MARABOU LEECH

ASSAM DRAGON

SRI MARABOU DAMSEL

DON KING

MARABOU LEECH

RABBIT LEECH, black

POLLYWOG

RABBIT LEECH, maroon

Tier: Umpqua Feather Merchants
Hook: TMC 300, Mustad 79580, sizes 2-6, wt.
Thread: Maroon 6/0 prewaxed
Tail: Maroon rabbit fur strip, with red and blue Krystal Flash
Body: maroon rabbit fur strip, wrapped
Topping: 3 strands of red Krystal Flash

FLASH MARABOU LEECH

Originator: Bill Black
Tier: Spirit River Inc
Hook: TMC 5263, Mustad 9672, sizes 4-8
Thread: Olive 6/0 prewaxed
Tail: Olive marabou
Body: Olive marabou, wrapped
Wings: Rainbow fly brite and olive marabou
Eyes: Mono nymph eyes
Head: Olive rabbit dubbing

SRI MARABOU DAMSEL

Originator: Bill Black
Tier: Spirit River Inc
Hook: TMC 5263, Mustad 9672, sizes 8-12
Thread: Olive 6/0 prewaxed
Tail: Olive marabou
Rib: Fine gold wire
Body: Olive marabou, wrapped
Wing: Olive marabou, short
Eyes: Mono nymph eyes
Head: Olive marabou

MARABOU LEECH

Tier: Umpqua Feather Merchants
Hook: TMC 300, Mustad 79580, sizes 4-8
Thread: Black 6/0 prewaxed
Tail: Black marabou
Body: Black thread
Mid-wing: Black marabou
Wing: Black marabou, with 6 strands of black Krystal Flash

POLLYWOG

Hook: TMC 300, Mustad 9575, sizes 2-6
Thread: Black 6/0 prewaxed
Body: Peacock herl
Collar: Black marabou, tied forward and pulled back to form head, bullet style

MINI LEECH, olive

Originator: Randall Kaufmann
Tier: John Kistler
Hook: TMC 200, size 10
Thread: Olive 6/0 prewaxed
Tail: Olive marabou, with 4 strands olive Krystal Flash
Body: 3-5 strands of olive Krystal Flash twisted into rope with olive goat dubbing, well picked out

FUZZY BROWN LEECH

Tier: Bill Beardsley
Hook: TMC 5263, Mustad 9672, sizes 6-10
Thread: Black 6/0 prewaxed
Tail: Black marabou
Body: Brown mohair

MINI LEECH, red

Originator: Randall Kaufmann
Tier: John Kistler
Hook: TMC 200, size 10
Thread: Red 6/0 prewaxed
Tail: Red marabou, with 4 strands of red and pearl Krystal Flash
Body: 3-5 strands of red and pearl Krystal Flash twisted into rope with red goat dubbing, well picked out

MINI LEECH, black

Originator: Randall Kaufmann
Tier: John Kistler
Hook: TMC 200, size 10
Thread: Black 6/0 prewaxed
Tail: Black marabou, with 4 strands of black and red Krystal Flash
Body: 3-5 strands of red and black Krystal Flash twisted into rope with black goat dubbing, well picked out

PEACOCK WOOLLY BUGGER

Originator: Doug Jorgensen
Tier: Doug Jorgensen
Hook: TMC 5263, Mustad 9672, sizes 8-10
Thread: Black 6/0 prewaxed
Tail: Black marabou
Rib: Flat silver tinsel
Body: Peacock herl, sparse
Hackle: Black hen hackle, palmered over the body

DAMSELS, DRAGONS, CRUSTACEANS AND LEECHES

MINI LEECH, olive

SLIGHT LEECH, olive

FUZZY BROWN LEECH

SLIGHT LEECH, maroon

MINI LEECH, red

CRYSTAL BUGGER, maroon

MINI LEECH, black

FLASHY BUGGER

PEACOCK WOOLLY BUGGER

RED HEAD

SLIGHT LEECH, olive

Originator: Doug Jorgensen
Tier: Doug Jorgensen
Hook: TMC 5263, Mustad 79580, sizes 8-10
Thread: Olive 6/0 prewaxed
Tail: Olive marabou
Body: Olive marabou, tie in butt ends and wrap forward

SLIGHT LEECH, maroon

Originator: Doug Jorgensen
Tier: Doug Jorgensen
Hook: TMC 5263, Mustad 79580, sizes 8-10
Thread: Maroon 6/0 prewaxed
Tail: Maroon marabou
Body: Maroon marabou, tie in butt ends and wrap forward

CRYSTAL BUGGER, maroon

Tier: John Kistler
Hook: TMC 200, size 10
Thread: Black 6/0 prewaxed
Tail: Maroon marabou with 4 strands of red Krystal Flash
Rib: Fine red wire
Body: Black Crystal chenille
Hackle: Dyed maroon grizzly hackle

FLASHY BUGGER

Originator: Doug Jorgensen
Tier: Doug Jorgensen
Hook: TMC 5263, Mustad 9672, sizes 6-10
Thread: Black 6/0 prewaxed
Tail: Brown olive marabou, and red Krystal Flash
Body: Black crystal chenille
Hackle: Dyed olive grizzly hen hackle, palmered over the body

RED HEAD

Originator: Doug Jorgensen
Tier: Doug Jorgensen
Hook: TMC 5263, Mustad 79580, sizes 8-10
Thread: Red 3/0 monocord
Tail: Black marabou, with copper Krystal Flash on top
Body: Peacock herl, tied sparse
Hackle: Black hen hackle, palmered over the body

WOOLLY BUGGER, olive

Tier: Umpqua Feather Merchants
Hook: TMC 300, Mustad 79580, sizes
  2-10, wt.
Thread: Black 6/0 prewaxed
Tail: Olive marabou, plus 4 to 6 strand of
  pearl Krystal Flash on each side
Body: Olive chenille
Rib: Fine Copper wire
Hackle: Black hackle, palmered over
  the body

WEEDLESS WOOLLY BUGGER

Originator: John Gierach
Tier: Umpqua Feather Merchants
Hook: TMC 5263, Mustad 9672, sizes 4-8
Thread: Black 6/0 prewaxed
Body: Fine dark olive vernille
Hackle: Black hackle, palmered over body
Wing: Black marabou, tied inverted
Topping: Pearl Flashabou
Eyes: Painted, yellow with black pupil

GIRDLE BUGGER

Originator: Tom Travis
Tier: Umpqua Feather Merchants
Hook: TMC 5263, Mustad 9672, sizes
  2-6, wt.
Thread: Black 6/0 prewaxed
Tail: Black marabou
Rib: Clear monofilament
Body: Black chenille, with single strand of
  orange chenille on the belly
Legs: White rubber hackle
Hackle: Black hackle
Wing: Black marabou

WOOLLY BUGGER, black

Tier: Umpqua Feather Merchants
Hook: TMC 300, Mustad 79580, sizes
  2-10, wt.
Thread: Black 6/0 prewaxed
Tail: Black marabou, plus 4 to 6 strands of
  pearl Krystal flash on each side
Body: Black chenille
Rib: Fine silver wire
Hackle: Black hackle, palmered over
  the body

WOOLLY BUGGER, brown

Tier: Umpqua Feather Merchants
Hook: TMC 300, Mustad 79580, sizes
  2-10, wt.
Thread: Black 6/0 prewaxed
Tail: Black marabou, plus 4 to 6 strands of
  pearl Krystal flash on each side
Body: Dark brown wool yarn
Rib: Fine copper wire
Hackle: Black hackle, palmered over
  the body

DAMSELS, DRAGONS, CRUSTACEANS AND LEECHES

WOOLLY BUGGER, olive

JIG-A-BUGGER, white

WEEDLESS WOOLLY BUGGER

JIG-A-BUGGER, red

GIRDLE BUGGER

BLOOD SUCKER

WOOLLY BUGGER, black

LEAD EYED EGG LEECH

WOOLLY BUGGER, brown

EGG SUCKING LEECH

JIG-A-BUGGER, white

Tier: Umpqua Feather Merchants
Hook: TMC 300, Mustad 79580, sizes 6-10
Thread: White 6/0 prewaxed
Tail: White rabbit fur with 4 strands of
  pearl Krystal Flash
Rib: Fine gold wire
Body: Pearl Krystal chenille
Hackle: White hackle, palmered over front
  half of body
Eyes: Nickel plated lead eyes, white with
  black pupil

JIG-A-BUGGER, red

Tier: Umpqua Feather Merchants
Hook: TMC 300, Mustad 79580, sizes 6-10
Thread: Red 6/0 prewaxed
Tail: Red rabbit fur with 4 strands of
  pearl Flashabou
Rib: Fine red wire
Body: Red crystal chenille
Hackle: Red hackle, palmered over front
  half of the body
Eyes: Nickel plated lead eyes, with
  black pupil

BLOOD SUCKER

Tier: Bill Beardsley
Hook: TMC 300, Mustad 79580, sizes
  2-8, wt.
Thread: Black 6/0 prewaxed
Tail: Scarlet wool, short
Body: Black chenille
Hackle: Brown hackle, palmered through
  body, clipped short

LEAD EYED EGG LEECH

Tier: Umpqua Feather Merchants
Hook: TMC 5263, Mustad 9672, sizes 4-8
Thread: Black 6/0 prewaxed
Tail: Black rabbit fur strip
Body: Black rabbit fur strip, wrapped
Eyes: Nickel plated lead eyes
Thorax: Black rabbit dubbing
Head: Fluorescent hot pink chenille

EGG SUCKING LEECH

Hook: TMC 300, Mustad 79580, sizes
  2-6, wt.
Thread: Black 6/0 prewaxed
Tail: Black marabou, with six strands of
  red Krystal Flash on each side
Rib: Fine copper wire
Body: Black crystal chenille
Hackle: Black hackle, palmered over body
Head: Salmon egg glo bug yarn

Chapter 6

Streamers, Bucktails and Sculpins

❖

BLACK MARABOU

Hook: TMC 300, Mustad 9575, sizes 2-6
Thread: Black 6/0 prewaxed
Tail: Red hackle fibers
Body: Black goat dubbing, thin
Throat: Red hackle fibers
Wing: Black marabou

GREEN SIDES MINNOW

Originator: Greg Carrier
Tier: Greg Carrier
Hook: TMC 300, Partridge D3ST, sizes 2-6
Thread: Black 6/0 prewaxed
Body: Bright green frostbite
Throat: White Arctic fox fur
Wing: Dyed olive over dyed red squirrel tail

GRIZZLY KING

Hook: TMC 300, Mustad 9575, sizes 4-12
Thread: Black 6/0 prewaxed
Tail: Red hackle fibers
Rib: Fine flat silver tinsel
Body: Green floss
Throat: Grizzly hackle fibers
Wing: Four grizzly saddle hackles

TETHEROW MINNOW

Originator: Greg Carrier
Tier: Greg Carrier
Hook: Partridge D3ST, Mustad 9674, sizes 2-6
Thread: Black 6/0 prewaxed
Body: Flat silver tinsel
Throat: Arctic fox or badger hair
Underwing: Pearl Flashabou, 6-10 strands
Wing: Dyed olive over gray over dyed red squirrel tail, each longer than the previous section
Eyes: Painted, yellow with a black pupil

HARRIS SPECIAL

Originator: Oliver G. Harris
Hook: TMC 300, Partridge D3ST, sizes 2-6
Thread: Black 6/0 prewaxed
Tail: Golden pheasant tippet fibers
Body: Flat gold tinsel
Throat: Red hackle fibers
Underwing: White bucktail, sparse
Wing: Lemon woodduck flank

STREAMERS, BUCKTAILS AND SCULPINS

BLACK MARABOU

LITTLE BROOK TROUT

GREEN SIDES MINNOW

LITTLE RAINBOW TROUT

GRIZZLY KING

LITTLE BROWN TROUT

TETHEROW MINNOW

BALLOU SPECIAL

HARRIS SPECIAL

MICKEY FINN

LITTLE BROOK TROUT

Originator: Sam Slaymaker
Hook: TMC 300, Mustad 9575, sizes 2-12
Thread: Black 6/0 prewaxed
Tail: Bright green bucktail, with a short piece of bright red floss over
Rib: Flat silver tinsel
Body: Cream wool yarn
Throat: Orange bucktail
Wing: Bucktail, from bottom to top, white, orange, green, with gray squirrel tail over the top

LITTLE RAINBOW TROUT

Hook: TMC 300, Mustad 9575, sizes 4-12
Thread: Black 6/0 prewaxed
Tail: Green bucktail
Rib: Flat silver tinsel
Body: Very pale pink rabbit dubbing
Wing: Bucktail, from bottom to top, white, pink, green, with badger hair over the top
Cheeks: Jungle cock eyes

LITTLE BROWN TROUT

Hook: TMC 300, Mustad 9575, sizes 4-12
Thread: Black 6/0 prewaxed
Tail: Tan ringneck pheasant body fibers
Rib: Oval gold tinsel
Body: White wool yarn
Wing: Orange over yellow bucktail, with dyed brown squirrel tail over the top
Cheeks: Jungle cock eyes

BALLOU SPECIAL

Hook: TMC 300, Mustad 9575, sizes 2-10
Thread: Black 6/0 prewaxed
Tail: Golden pheasant crest feather, curved downward
Body: Flat silver tinsel
Underwing: Red Bucktail, long
Overwing: White marabou
Topping: Peacock herl, 12 strands
Cheeks: Jungle cock eyes

MICKEY FINN

Hook: TMC 300, Mustad 9575, sizes 2-12
Thread: Black 6/0 prewaxed
Rib: Fine oval silver tinsel
Body: Flat silver tinsel
Wing: Bucktail, from bottom to top, yellow, red, yellow

JANSSEN'S RAINBOW TROUT

Originator: Hal Janssen
Tier: Umpqua Feather Merchants
Hook: TMC 5263, Mustad 9672, sizes 2-8
Thread: White 6/0 prewaxed
Tail: Olive marabou
Underbody: Lead tape
Body: Silver mylar piping
Markings: Painted, clear epoxy over

JANSSEN'S THREADFIN SHAD

Originator: Hal Janssen
Tier: Umpqua Feather Merchants
Hook: TMC 5263, Mustad 9672, sizes 2-8
Thread: White 6/0 prewaxed
Tail: Gray marabou
Underbody: Lead tape
Body: Silver mylar piping
Markings: Painted, clear epoxy over

HEN BACK MATUKA

Tier: Tony Fox
Hook: TMC 5263, Mustad 9672, sizes 4-8
Thread: Brown 6/0 prewaxed
Rib: Black thread
Body: Olive wool yarn, slightly tapered
Wing: Two mottled brown hen saddle
   feathers, matuka style
Hackle: Mottled brown hen hackle

OLIVE MATUKA

Tier: Umpqua Feather Merchants
Hook: TMC 5263, Mustad 9672, sizes
   2-10, wt.
Thread: Olive 6/0 prewaxed
Rib: Fine copper wire
Body: Olive chenille
Gills: Red wool yarn
Wing: Four dyed olive hen grizzly saddle
   hackles, tied down over the body with
   the rib
Hackle: Dyed olive hen grizzly hackle
Eyes: Painted, yellow with a black pupil

BLACK MATUKA

Tier: Umpqua Feather Merchants
Hook: TMC 5263, Mustad 9672, sizes
   2-10, wt.
Thread: Black 6/0 prewaxed
Rib: Fine copper wire
Body: Black chenille
Wing: Four black hen saddle hackles, tied
   down over body with the rib
Hackle: Black hen hackle
Eyes: Painted, yellow with a black pupil

STREAMERS, BUCKTAILS AND SCULPINS

JANSSEN'S RAINBOW TROUT

GOLDEN MICKEY

JANSSEN'S THREADFIN SHAD

BLACK NOSE DACE

HEN BACK MATUKA

THUNDER CREEK RAINBOW TROUT

OLIVE MATUKA

THUNDER CREEK SILVER SHINER

BLACK MATUKA

LIGHT EDSON TIGER

GOLDEN MICKEY

Tier: Greg Carrier
Hook: TMC 300, Partridge D3ST, sizes 2-6
Thread: Black 6/0 prewaxed
Body: Flat gold tinsel
Wing: Yellow over red bucktail
Eyes: Painted, yellow with a black pupil

BLACK NOSE DACE

Tier: Brad Burden
Hook: TMC 300, Mustad 9575, sizes 4-12
Thread: Black 6/0 prewaxed
Tail: Red yarn, short
Body: Flat silver tinsel
Wing: Brown bucktail over black bear hair
   over white bucktail

THUNDER CREEK RAINBOW TROUT

Tier: Brad Burden
Hook: Mustad 36620, sizes 2-10
Thread: Red 6/0 prewaxed
Body: Embossed silver tinsel
Wing: Lateral stripe, true pink bucktail;
   top, brown portion of a dyed green
   bucktail; bottom, white bucktail, tied
   forward and pulled back to form head.
Head: Clear varnish with cream eye and
   black pupil

THUNDER CREEK SILVER SHINER

Tier: Brad Burden
Hook: Mustad 36620, sizes 2-10
Thread: Red 6/0 prewaxed
Body: Embossed silver tinsel
Wing: Top, brown bucktail; bottom, white
   bucktail, tied   forward and pulled back
   to form head
Head: Clear varnish with cream eye and
   black pupil

LIGHT EDSON TIGER

Originator: Bill Edson
Tier: Tim Martin
Hook: TMC 300, Mustad 79580, sizes 4-10
Thread: Yellow 6/0 prewaxed
Tag: Fine flat gold tinsel
Tail: Lemon woodduck flank fibers
Body: Peacock herl
Wing: Yellow bucktail
Topping: Two red hackles, tied very short
Cheeks: Jungle cock eyes

GREEN BEAUTY

Originator: Carrie G. Stevens
Tier: Brad Burden
Hook: TMC 300, Partridge Carrie Stevens,
sizes 2-6
Thread: Black 6/0 prewaxed
Tag: Flat silver tinsel
Rib: Flat silver tinsel
Body: Golden orange floss
Wing: Four strands of peacock herl under four
dark green saddle hackles
Throat: White bucktail and two golden
pheasant crests
Sides: Lemon woodduck flank
Cheeks: Jungle cock eyes

FIERY BROWN

Originator: Bob Veverka
Tier: Brad Burden
Hook: TMC 300, Partridge Carrie Stevens,
sizes 2-6
Thread: Black 6/0 prewaxed
Tail: Golden pheasant crest
Rib: Fine oval gold tinsel
Body: Flat gold tinsel
Throat: Red calftail
Wing: Dark badger hackle
Topping: Golden pheasant crest
Cheeks: Jungle cock eyes

ALLIES FAVORITE

Originator: Carrie G. Stevens
Tier: Brad Burden
Hook: TMC 300, Partridge Carrie Stevens,
sizes 2-6
Thread: Black 6/0 prewaxed
Tag: Flat silver tinsel
Rib: Flat silver tinsel
Body: Red floss
Wing: Five strands of peacock herl under
two orange saddle hackles flanked by
two black saddle hackles
Throat: White bucktail then a small bunch
of orange hackle fibers followed by black
hackle fibers
Cheeks: Jungle cock eyes

KENNEBAGO

Tier: Brad Burden
Hook: TMC 300, Partridge Carrie Stevens,
sizes 2-8
Thread: Black 6/0 prewaxed
Body: Flat silver tinsel
Throat: Red, white, and blue bucktail, mixed
Wing: Four black saddle hackles
Topping: Four strands of peacock herl
Cheeks: Jungle cock eyes

DACE

Originator: Herb Burton
Tier: Brad Burden
Hook: TMC 300, Partridge Carrie Stevens,
sizes 2-6
Thread: Black 6/0 prewaxed
Tag: Fine oval gold tinsel
Rib: Fine embossed gold tinsel
Body: Fine black chenille
Throat: Golden yellow hackle fibers
Underwing: Fox squirrel tail
Overwing: Black saddle hackles
Topping: Peacock herl strands
Cheeks: Jungle cock eyes

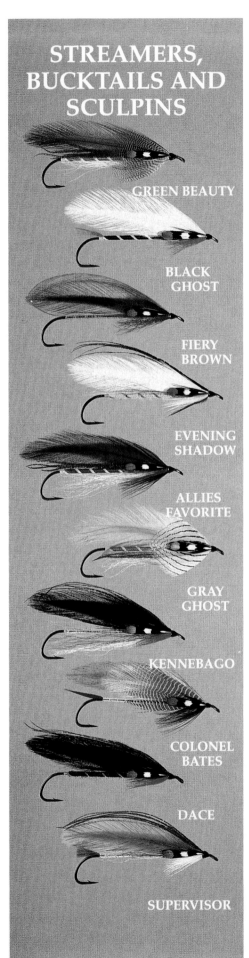

STREAMERS, BUCKTAILS AND SCULPINS

GREEN BEAUTY

BLACK GHOST

FIERY BROWN

EVENING SHADOW

ALLIES FAVORITE

GRAY GHOST

KENNEBAGO

COLONEL BATES

DACE

SUPERVISOR

BLACK GHOST

Originator: Herb Welch
Tier: Brad Burden
Hook: TMC 300, Partridge Carrie Stevens,
sizes 2-10
Thread: Black 6/0 prewaxed
Tail: Yellow hackle fibers, sparse
Rib: Medium flat silver tinsel
Body: Black floss
Throat: Yellow hackle fibers, sparse
Wing: Four white saddle hackle
Cheeks: Jungle cock eyes

EVENING SHADOW

Originator: Herb Burton
Tier: Brad Burden
Hook: TMC 300, Partridge Carrie Stevens,
sizes 2-6
Thread: Black 6/0 prewaxed
Tag: Fine oval gold tinsel
Rib: Fine embossed gold tinsel
Body: Cream mohlon
Throat: Cream hackle fibers and red
marabou
Underwing: Gray squirrel tail
Overwing: Cream saddle hackles
Topping: Peacock herl strands
Cheeks: Jungle cock eyes

GRAY GHOST

Originator: Carrie Stevens
Tier: Brad Burden
Hook: TMC 300, Partridge Carrie Stevens,
sizes 2-10
Thread: Black 6/0 prewaxed
Tag: Fine flat silver tinsel
Rib: Fine flat silver tinsel
Body: Orange floss, thin
Throat: Four strands of peacock herl, white
bucktail, golden pheasant crest
Underwing: Golden pheasant crest
Wing: Four Gray dun saddle hackles
Sides: Two silver pheasant body feathers
Cheeks: Jungle cock eyes
Head: Black with a red band

COLONEL BATES

Originator: Carrie Stevens
Tier: Brad Burden
Hook: TMC 300, Partridge Carrie Stevens,
sizes 2-10
Thread: Black 6/0 prewaxed
Tail: Dyed red goose quill, narrow
Body: Flat silver tinsel
Throat: Dark brown hackle fibers
Wing: Two yellow hackles, flanked by two
white hackles ¾ the length of the yellow,
followed by gray teal flank feathers,
½ the length of the white
Cheeks: Jungle cock eyes

SUPERVISOR

Originator: Joseph F. Stickney
Tier: Brad Burden
Hook: TMC 300, Partridge Carrie Stevens,
sizes 2-6
Thread: Black 6/0 prewaxed
Tail: Red wool yarn, short
Body: Flat silver tinsel
Throat: White hackle fibers
Wing: White bucktail, with four light bright
blue saddle hackles
Sides: Two light bright green saddle hackles
Topping: Peacock herl strands
Cheeks: Jungle cock eyes

YELLOW MARABOU SPRUCE

Originator: A.K. Best
Tier: Umpqua Feather Merchants
Hook: TMC 5262, Mustad 9672, sizes 2-6
Thread: Black 6/0 prewaxed
Tail: Peacock sword fibers
Rib: Copper wire
Body: Rear ½ yellow floss, remainder pea-cock herl
Wing: Yellow marabou and four yellow badger hackle tips
Hackle: Yellow badger hackle

PLATTE RIVER SPECIAL

Tier: Umpqua Feather Merchants
Hook: TMC 300, Mustad 79580, sizes 2-8
Thread: Black 6/0 prewaxed
Rib: Fine gold wire
Body: Brown chenille
Wing: Two yellow saddle hackles, enveloped by two white saddle hackles
Hackle: Brown and yellow hackle, mixed

BLACK ZONKER

Hook: TMC 300, Mustad 79580, sizes 2-8
Thread: Black 6/0 prewaxed
Tail: Unraveled pearl piping, from body
Body: Pearl mylar piping, tied down in back with red thread
Hackle: Black hen hackle
Wing: Dyed black rabbit fur strip, tied down in the back

PURPLE JOE

Hook: TMC 3761, Mustad 3906B, sizes 4-8
Thread: Black 6/0 prewaxed
Tail: Red hackle fibers
Butt: Fine hot orange wool yarn
Body: Purple chenille
Wings: Two badger hackles, flared
Hackle: Badger hackle

BUCKTAIL COACHMAN

Hook: TMC 300, Mustad 9575, sizes 2-10
Thread: Black 6/0 prewaxed
Tail: Red hackle fibers
Butt: Peacock herl
Rib: Fine copper wire
Body: Red wool yarn
Shoulder: Peacock herl
Hackle: Brown hackle
Wing: White bucktail
Eyes: Painted, yellow with a black pupil

STREAMERS, BUCKTAILS AND SCULPINS

YELLOW MARABOU SPRUCE

MIGHTY MINNOW, shad

PLATTE RIVER SPECIAL

MIGHTY MINNOW, golden shiner

BLACK ZONKER

BYFORD'S OLIVE ZONKER

PURPLE JOE

ZONKER

BUCKTAIL COACHMAN

BYFORD'S NATURAL ZONKER

MIGHTY MINNOW, shad

Originator: Bill Black
Tier: Spirit River Inc
Hook: TMC 7999, Mustad 36890, sizes 2-6
Thread: White 6/0 prewaxed
Body: Gray antron dubbing, use black waterproof marker for spots
Throat: White lite brite
Wing: Black over blue over pearl lite brite
Eyes: Mono nymph eyes
Head: Gray antron dubbing

MIGHTY MINNOW, golden shiner

Originator: Bill Black
Tier: Spirit River Inc
Hook: TMC 7999, Mustad 36890, sizes 2-6
Thread: Yellow 6/0 prewaxed
Body: Antique gold antron dubbing, use black waterproof marker for spots
Throat: White lite brite
Wing: Blue over gold over pearl lite brite
Eyes: Mono nymph eyes
Head: Antique gold antron dubbing

BYFORD'S OLIVE ZONKER

Originator: Dan Byford
Tier: Umpqua Feather Merchants
Hook: TMC 300, Mustad 79580, sizes 2-6
Thread: White 6/0 prewaxed
Underbody: Lead tape
Body: Dyed olive pearl mylar piping
Wing: Dyed olive yellow rabbit strip, pliobond to body
Topping: Pearl Krystal Flash
Throat: Dyed olive yellow rabbit fur
Eyes: Painted, yellow with black pupil

ZONKER

Originator: Dan Byford
Hook: TMC 300, Mustad 9674, sizes 2-10
Thread: Black 6/0 prewaxed
Tail: Unraveled silver mylar piping, from body
Body: Silver mylar piping, tied down in back with red thread
Hackle: Grizzly hen hackle
Wing: Natural gray tan stripped rabbit fur, tied down with the red thread at the end of the body

BYFORD'S NATURAL ZONKER

Originator: Dan Byford
Tier: Umpqua Feather Merchants
Hook: TMC 300, Mustad 79580, sizes 2-6
Thread: White 6/0 prewaxed
Underbody: lead tape
Body: Pearl mylar piping
Wing: Natural gray tan rabbit strip, pliobond to body
Topping: Pearl Krystal Flash
Throat: Natural rabbit fur
Eyes: Painted, yellow with black pupil

CLAUSER MINNOW, chartreuse

Originator: Bob Clauser
Tier: Umpqua Feather Merchants
Hook: TMC 800S, Mustad 34007, sizes 1/0-6
Thread: White 3/0 monocord
Eyes: Lead eyes, painted red with black pupil
Throat: White ocean hair
Wing: Chartreuse ocean hair, with pearl Krystal Flash

BUCKTAIL MUDDLER

Originator: John Gierach
Tier: Umpqua Feather Merchants
Hook: TMC 5263, Mustad 9672, sizes 2-8
Thread: Black 6/0 prewaxed
Body: Pearl Flashabou, wrapped
Wing: Black bucktail and pearl Flashabou
Overwing: Peacock herl
Collar: Black deer hair, short and on top only
Eyes: Amber doll eyes
Head: Black deer hair, spun and clipped

BOSS MUDDLER

Hook: TMC 7999, Mustad 36890, size 4-8
Thread: Black 6/0 prewaxed
Rib: Oval silver tinsel
Body: Black rabbit dubbing
Wing: Black marabou
Collar: Orange deer hair
Head: Orange deer hair, spun and clipped

LIGHT SPRUCE

Tier: Umpqua Feather Merchants
Hook: TMC 300, Mustad 9575, sizes 2-10
Thread: Black 6/0 prewaxed
Tail: Peacock sword fibers
Rib: Fine copper wire
Body: Rear 1/2 red wool yarn, front 1/2 peacock herl
Wing: Two badger hackles, tied flared
Hackle: Badger hackle

RED THROAT MATUKA

Hook: TMC 5263, Mustad 9672, sizes 2-8
Thread: Brown 6/0 prewaxed
Rib: Oval gold tinsel
Body: Olive rabbit dubbing, tapered
Throat: Bright red rabbit dubbing
Wing: Four dark dun hackle tips, matuka style
Hackle: Dark dun hackle

STREAMERS, BUCKTAILS AND SCULPINS

CLAUSER MINNOW, chartreuse

CLAUSER MINNOW, sculpin

BUCKTAIL MUDDLER

KRYSTAL FLASH MUDDLER, olive

BOSS MUDDLER

MUDDLER MINNOW

LIGHT SPRUCE

KRYSTAL-FLASH MUDDLER, black

RED THROAT MATUKA

DARK ANGEL

CLAUSER MINNOW, sculpin

Originator: Bob Clauser
Tier: Umpqua Feather Merchants
Hook: TMC 800S, Mustad 34007, sizes 1/0-6
Thread: Brown 3/0 monocord
Eyes: Lead eyes, painted red with black pupils
Throat: Orange bucktail
Wing: Brick red bucktail, with copper Krystal Flash

KRYSTAL FLASH MUDDLER, olive

Originator: John Hazel
Hook: TMC 700, Mustad 9672, sizes 2-10
Thread: Black 6/0 prewaxed
Body: Green glitter body
Underwing: Olive squirrel tail and olive Krystal Flash
Wing: Mottled turkey wing quill
Thorax: Red rabbit dubbing
Collar: Olive deer hair
Head: Olive deer hair, spun and clipped

MUDDLER MINNOW

Originator: Don Gapen
Tier: Umpqua Feather Merchants
Hook: TMC 300, Mustad 79580, sizes 2-14
Thread: Black 6/0 prewaxed
Tail: Mottled turkey quill
Body: Gold diamond braid
Underwing: Gray squirrel tail
Wing: Mottled turkey quill
Collar: Deer hair, spun
Head: Deer hair, spun and clipped

KRYSTAL FLASH MUDDLER, black

Originator: John Hazel
Hook: TMC 700, Mustad 9672, sizes 2-10
Thread: Black 6/0 prewaxed
Body: Black glitter body
Underwing: Black squirrel tail and black Krystal Flash
Wing: Mottled turkey wing quill
Thorax: Red rabbit dubbing
Collar: Black deer hair
Head: Black deer hair, spun and clipped

DARK ANGEL

Hook: TMC 7999, Mustad 36890, sizes 1/0-6
Thread: Black 6/0 prewaxed
Hackle: Black marabou, wrapped
Wings: Red and pearl Krystal Flash, several strands on each side
Collar: Black saddle hackle

SPUDDLER

Hook: TMC 300, Mustad 79580, sizes
   2-10, wt.
Thread: Brown 3/0 monocord
Tail: Brown calftail
Body: Cream wool yarn
Collar: Gray antelope hair, spun and clipped
Underwing: Red fox squirrel tail
Wing: Four dyed dark brown grizzly hackles
Gills: A short band of red wool yarn
Head: Brown antelope hair, spun
   and clipped

TROTH BULLHEAD

Originator: Al Troth
Tier: Umpqua Feather Merchants
Hook: TMC 300, Mustad 79580, sizes
   3/0-6, wt.
Thread: Black 3/0 monocord
Tail: White marabou, with black ostrich herl
   tips from the shellback
Shellback: Black ostrich herl
Body: Cream rabbit dubbing
Collar: Red deer hair, spun
Head: Deer hair, spun and clipped

MARABOU MUDDLER, yellow

Tier: Umpqua Feather Merchants
Hook: TMC 300, Mustad 79580, sizes
   2-10, wt.
Thread: Black 6/0 prewaxed
Tail: Red hackle fibers
Body: Silver diamond braid
Wing: Yellow marabou, with six strands of
   peacock herl over the top
Collar: Spun deer hair
Head: Deer hair, spun and clipped

MARABOU MUDDLER, white

Tier: Umpqua Feather Merchants
Hook: TMC 300, Mustad 79580, sizes
   2-10, wt.
Thread: Black 6/0 prewaxed
Tail: Red hackle fibers
Body: Silver diamond braid
Wing: White marabou, with six strands of
   peacock herl over the top
Collar: Spun deer hair
Head: Deer hair, spun and clipped

WOOLHEAD SCULPIN, black

Tier: Umpqua Feather Merchants
Hook: TMC 300, Mustad 79580, sizes 4-6, wt.
Thread: Black 3/0 monocord
Tail: Black rabbit fur strip and black Krystal
   Flash
Body: Black rabbit fur strip, wrapped
Pectoral Fins: Black hen hackle
Head: Black lambs wool, spun and clipped

STREAMERS, BUCKTAILS AND SCULPINS

SPUDDLER

MARABOU MUDDLER, black

TROTH BULLHEAD

MULTI MARABOU MUDDLER

MARABOU MUDDLER, yellow

WHIT'S SCULPIN, olive

MARABOU MUDDLER, white

WOOLHEAD SCULPIN, olive

WOOLHEAD SCULPIN, black

SRI SCULPIN

MARABOU MUDDLER, black

Tier: Umpqua Feather Merchants
Hook: TMC 300, Mustad 79580, sizes
   2-10, wt.
Thread: Black 6/0 prewaxed
Tail: Red hackle fibers
Body: Silver diamond braid
Wing: Black marabou, with six strands of
   peacock herl over he top
Collar: Spun deer hair
Head: Deer hair, spun and clipped

MULTI MARABOU MUDDLER

Originator: Dave Whitlock
Tier: Umpqua Feather Merchants
Hook: TMC 300, Mustad 79580, sizes 2-8, wt.
Thread: Fluorescent red 6/0 prewaxed
Butt: Red thread
Body: Gold mylar piping
Wing: Brown over yellow marabou
Sides: Orange marabou, short
Topping: Four peacock herl strands
Collar: Dyed deer hair, tips from the head
Head: Brown over orange over yellow deer
   hair, spun and clipped

WHIT'S SCULPIN, olive

Originator: Dave Whitlock
Tier: Umpqua Feather Merchants
Hook: TMC 300, Mustad 9672, sizes
   1/0-8, wt.
Thread: Olive 3/0 monocord
Rib: Medium oval gold tinsel
Body: Light olive wool yarn
Gills: Red wool dubbing
Wing: Two dyed olive grizzly hackles, tied to
   the body with the ribbing
Pectoral Fins: Dyed olive hen mallard breast
   feathers
Collar: Dyed olive deer hair, spun and
   clipped
Head: Dyed olive deer hair with a band of
   dyed black deer hair, spun and clipped

WOOLHEAD SCULPIN, olive

Tier: Umpqua Feather Merchants
Hook: TMC 300, Mustad 79580, sizes 4-6, wt.
Thread: Olive 3/0 monocord
Tail: Olive rabbit fur strip and olive
   Krystal Flash
Body: Olive rabbit fur strip, wrapped
Pectoral Fins: Olive hen hackle
Head: Olive lambs wool, spun and clipped

SRI SCULPIN

Originator: Bill Black
Tier: Spirit River Inc
Hook: TMC 300, Mustad 79580, sizes 2-6
Thread: Olive 6/0 prewaxed
Tail: Olive rabbit strip, stiff monofilament
   tied in under the body and threaded
   through the tail
Body: Olive rabbit strip, wrapped
Eyes: Nickel plated lead eyes
Head: Olive wool, spun and clipped
   to shape

Chapter 7

Steelhead Flies

❖

Atlantic Salmon Flies

❖

Pacific Salmon Flies

❖

AUTUMN GOLD

Originator: Randle Scott Stetzer
Hook: TMC 7999, sizes 2-8
Thread: Black 6/0 prewaxed
Tail: Hot orange hackle fibers
Rib: Fine oval gold tinsel
Body: Antique gold seal or goat fur
Hackle: Hot orange hackle, soft
Wing: White polar bear hair or calf tail
Cheeks: Jungle cock eyes (optional)

POLAR GIBSON

Originator: Dick Williamson
Tier: Dick Williamson
Hook: TMC 7999, Partridge N, sizes 1/0-4
Thread: Black 6/0 prewaxed
Tag: Fine oval gold tinsel
Tail: Golden pheasant tippets
Rib: Fine oval gold tinsel
Body: Rusty orange wool yarn, thin
Hackle: Furnace hackle
Wing: White polar bear or calftail, sparse
Cheeks: Jungle cock eyes

SUPER SKUNK

Originator: Dick Williamson, adaptation
of the Skunk
Tier: Dick Williamson
Hook: TMC 7999, Mustad 36890, sizes 1/0-4
Thread: Black 6/0 prewaxed
Tip: Fine oval silver tinsel
Tag: Fluorescent fire orange wool yarn
Tail: Hot orange hackle fibers
Rib: Fine oval silver tinsel
Body: Black wool yarn, thin
Hackle: Black hackle, soft and sparse
Wing: White polar bear hair or
calftail, sparse
Cheeks: Jungle cock eyes (optional)

STEWART

Originator: Marty Sherman
Tier: Marty Sherman
Hook: TMC 7999, Mustad 36890, sizes 2-6
Thread: Black 6/0 prewaxed
Tail: Golden pheasant tippet fibers
Rib: Fine oval gold tinsel
Body: Black wool yarn
Hackle: Black hackle, soft
Wing: Dyed black squirrel tail, with sparse
orange calftail over the top

REIFF SKUNK

Originator: Bob Aid
Tier: Bob Aid
Hook: Partridge Wilson 01, sizes 6-8
Thread: Black 6/0 prewaxed
Tail: Red hackle fibers
Rib: Oval silver tinsel
Body: Black seals fur or goat dubbing
Hackle: Black hen hackle
Wing: Gray squirrel tail

STEELHEAD FLIES

AUTUMN GOLD
PATRIOT
POLAR GIBSON
PATRICIA
SUPER SKUNK
OTTER BAR PURPLE
STEWART
RICKS REVENGE
REIFF SKUNK
MAXWELL'S PURPLE MATUKA

PATRIOT

Originator: Frank Amato
Hook: TMC 7999, Mustad 36890, sizes 2-6
Thread: Black 6/0 prewaxed
Tail: Red hackle fibers
Rib: Fine oval silver tinsel
Body: Yellow floss, thin
Hackle: Vivid blue hackle, soft
Wing: White polar bear hair, or calftail

PATRICIA

Originator: Randle Scott Stetzer
Hook: TMC 7999, Partridge N sizes 2-8
Thread: Claret 6/0 prewaxed
Tag: Fine flat gold tinsel
Tail: Claret hackle fibers, slight
angle upwards
Rib: Fine oval gold tinsel
Body: Claret seal or goat fur
Hackle: Claret hackle, soft
Wing: White polar bear hair or calftail
Cheeks: Jungle cock eyes (optional)

OTTER BAR PURPLE

Originator: Marty Sherman
Tier: Marty Sherman
Hook: Partridge N, TMC 7999, Mustad
36890, sizes 1/0-8
Thread: Claret 6/0 prewaxed
Tag: Fine flat silver tinsel
Tail: Claret hackle fibers
Rib: Fine flat silver tinsel
Body: Vivid purple wool yarn
Hackle: Claret hackle, long and soft
Wing: Ringneck pheasant tail fibers

RICKS REVENGE

Originator: John Shewey
Tier: John Shewey
Hook: Alec Jackson Spey, sizes 1 ½-7
Thread: Fluorescent orange 6/0 prewaxed
Tail: Fluorescent red floss
Body: Rear ½ fluorescent red floss, remainder
purple goat dubbing, with oval silver rib
Mid-wing: Fluorescent red floss
Hackle: Purple hackle
Wing: Blue over purple over white polar
bear or calftail
Cheeks: Jungle cock eyes

MAXWELL'S PURPLE MATUKA

Originator: Forest Maxwell
Tier: John Shewey
Hook: Alec Jackson Spey, sizes 1 ½-7
Thread: Black 6/0 prewaxed
Rib: Fine oval gold tinsel
Body: Black goat dubbing
Wing: Two purple saddle hackles,
matuka style
Hackle: Purple hackle

UMPQUA RED BRAT

Originator: Polly Rosborough
Tier: Umpqua Feather Merchants
Hook: Eagle Claw 1197 Bronze, sizes 2-8
Thread: Black 6/0 prewaxed
Tail: Mallard flank fibers
Rib: Flat silver tinsel
Body: Red Chenille
Hackle: Mallard flank
Wing: Red calftail

ORANGE SHRIMP

Originator: Polly Rosborough
Tier: Umpqua Feather Merchants
Hook: Eagle Claw 1197 Gold, sizes 2-8
Thread: Black 6/0 prewaxed
Tail: Hot orange hackle fibers
Rib: Flat gold tinsel
Body: Hot orange wool yarn
Hackle: Hot orange hackle
Wing: White calftail

FLASHIN PAT

Originator: Jim Dionne, variation on
the Patricia
Hook: TMC 7999, Partridge N, sizes 2/0-6
Thread: Claret 6/0 prewaxed
Tail: Claret hackle fibers
Rib: Fine flat gold tinsel
Body: Claret chenille
Hackle: Claret hackle, soft
Wing: White polar bear hair with
pearl Flashabou

FALL BRIGHT

Originator: Tim Martin
Hook: Eagle Claw 1197N, sizes 1/0-8
Thread: Black 6/0 prewaxed
Tail: Purple hackle fibers
Rib: Medium flat silver tinsel
Body: Fluorescent red chenille
Hackle: Purple hackle, soft
Wing: Purple Flashabou

STREET WALKER

Originator: Gordon Nash
Hook: Eagle Claw 1197N, sizes 2-8
Thread: Gray 6/0 prewaxed
Tail: Purple hackle fibers
Rib: Oval silver tinsel
Body: Purple chenille
Hackle: Purple hackle, soft
Wing: Pearl Flashabou

STEELHEAD FLIES

UMPQUA RED BRAT

BELLA COOLA BOMBER

ORANGE SHRIMP

SILVER ADMIRAL

FLASHIN PAT

PINK SUNDOWNER

FALL BRIGHT

COAL CAR

STREET WALKER

FREIGHT TRAIN

BELLA COOLA BOMBER

Hook: TMC 7999, Mustad 36890, sizes 1/0-6
Thread: Fluorescent fire orange 6/0
prewaxed
Tail: Fluorescent orange nylon tow yarn,
short
Rib: Fine flat silver tinsel
Body: Fluorescent yellow chenille
Wing: Fluorescent orange nylon tow yarn,
with pearl Flashabou on the sides

SILVER ADMIRAL

Originator: Polly Rosborough
Tier: Umpqua Feather Merchants
Hook: Eagle Claw 1197 Nickel, sizes 2-8
Thread: Black 6/0 prewaxed
Tail: Fluorescent hot pink hackle fibers
Rib: Flat silver tinsel
Body: Fluorescent hot pink wool yarn
Hackle: Fluorescent hot pink hackle
Wing: White calftail

PINK SUNDOWNER

Originator: Bob Wagoner
Tier: Bob Wagoner
Hook: TMC 7999, Mustad 36890, sizes 2-6
Thread: Black 6/0 prewaxed
Tail: Fluorescent pink hackle fibers
Butt: Flat silver tinsel
Body: Fluorescent red depth ray wool
Hackle: Fluorescent pink hackle, palmered
over the body
Wing: Pearl Krystal Flash
Collar: Fluorescent pink hackle

COAL CAR

Originator: Randall Kaufmann
Tier: Doug Canfield
Hook: TMC 7999, Mustad 36890, sizes 2/0-8
Thread: Black 6/0 prewaxed
Tail: Black hackle fibers
Rib: Fine oval silver tinsel
Body: ¼ fluorescent fire orange wool,
¼ fluorescent red wool, front ½
black chenille
Hackle: Black hackle, soft
Wing: Dyed black squirrel tail

FREIGHT TRAIN

Originator: Randall Kaufmann
Tier: Doug Canfield
Hook: TMC 7999, Mustad 36890, sizes 1/0-8
Thread: Black 6/0 prewaxed
Tail: Purple hackle fibers
Rib: Fine oval silver tinsel
Body: 1/4 fluorescent fire orange wool, ¼
fluorescent red wool, front ½ black
chenille
Hackle: Purple hackle, soft
Wing: White calftail, and pearl Krystal Flash

HARRY KARI BUCKTAIL

Originator: Harry Lemire
Tier: Harry Lemire
Hook: TMC 7999, Mustad 36890, sizes 2-6
Thread: Black 6/0 prewaxed
Tail: Red hackle base, short
Body: Alternating, yellow and black chenille
Hackle: Ringneck pheasant shoulder feather
Wing: Black bear hair

BLACK AND GOLDEN

Originator: John Hazel
Tier: John Hazel
Hook: Alec Jackson Spey, sizes 1 ½-7
Thread: Black 6/0 prewaxed
Tail: Golden pheasant crest feather
Rib: Oval silver tinsel
Body: Black goat dubbing
Hackle: Natural guinea hackle
Wing: Golden pheasant rump feather

GOLDEN EDGE, orange

Originator: Harry Lemire
Tier: Harry Lemire
Hook: Partridge N, sizes 1-8
Thread: Orange 6/0 prewaxed
Tag: Fine flat silver tinsel
Tail: Golden pheasant crest feather
Rib: Fine flat silver tinsel
Body: True orange goat dubbing
Throat: Speckled guinea hen hackle fibers
Underwing: Gray squirrel tail, sparse
Wing: Bronze mallard flank
Topping: Golden pheasant crest feather
Cheeks: Jungle cock eyes

SKUPADE

Originator: Joe Butoric
Tier: Bob Aid
Hook: Partridge Wilson 01, sizes 4-6
Thread: Black 6/0 prewaxed
Tail: Natural deer hair
Body: Black chenille
Wing: Natural deer hair
Hackle: Grizzly hackle, collar style

STEELHEAD COACHMAN

Originator: John Hazel
Tier: John Hazel
Hook: Alec Jackson Spey, sizes 1 ½-7
Thread: Black 6/0 prewaxed
Tag: Fine oval silver tinsel
Tail: Golden pheasant crest
Rib: Fine oval silver tinsel
Body: Peacock herl
Hackle: Mottled brown hen saddle
Wing: White polar bear hair or calftail
Cheeks: Jungle cock eyes

STEELHEAD FLIES

HARRY KARI BUCKTAIL

SHOOTING STAR

BLACK AND GOLDEN

THOMPSON RIVER CADDIS

GOLDEN EDGE, orange

LEMIRE'S FALL CADDIS

SKUPADE

ORANGE ROUGHY

STEELHEAD COACHMAN

DAMSELFLY

SHOOTING STAR

Originator: Harry Lemire
Tier: Harry Lemire
Hook: Partridge CS10, sizes 1/0-4
Thread: Black 6/0 prewaxed
Tag: Fine copper wire
Rib: Fine copper wire
Body: Silver glitter body
Throat: White polar bear hair, spun around hook shank
Hackle: Silver doctor blue hackle
Underwing: Dark blue polar bear hair
Wing: Dyed purple guinea hackle strips, short

THOMPSON RIVER CADDIS

Originator: Harry Lemire
Tier: Harry Lemire
Hook: Partridge 01, sizes 4-8
Thread: Black 6/0 prewaxed
Rib: Black nymo thread
Body: Medium olive dubbing
Wing: Two ringneck pheasant back feathers
Collar: Moose body hair
Head: Moose body hair, spun and clipped

LEMIRE'S FALL CADDIS

Originator: Harry Lemire
Tier: Harry Lemire
Hook: Partridge 01, sizes 4-8
Thread: Black "A" nymo
Tag: Fine flat copper tinsel
Rib: Fine flat copper tinsel
Body: Rusty orange seal fur
Underwing: Gray squirrel tail
Wings: Two light mottled brown hen saddle feathers, tied tent style
Collar: Moose body hair, sparse
Head: Moose body hair, spun and clipped

ORANGE ROUGHY

Originator: John Hazel
Tier: John Hazel
Hook: Alec Jackson Spey, sizes 1 ½-7
Thread: Red 6/0 prewaxed
Tail: Golden pheasant breast feather
Body: Yellow orange goat dubbing, picked out in a taper
Wing: Dyed black polar bear hair or calftail
Cheeks: Jungle cock eyes

DAMSELFLY

Originator: Ed Fleming
Hook: Partridge N, sizes 4-8
Thread: Black 6/0 prewaxed
Tail: Very dark deer hair
Rib: Fine oval gold tinsel
Body: Peacock herl
Throat: Very dark deer hair
Wing: Very dark deer hair, tied forward

KALAMA SPECIAL

Originator: Mooch Abrams
Tier: Brad Burden
Hook: TMC 7999, Mustad 36890, sizes 2-8
Thread: Black 6/0 prewaxed
Tag: Flat silver tinsel
Tail: Red hackle fibers
Body: Yellow wool yarn or goat dubbing
Hackle: Badger hackle, palmered over
the body
Wing: White bucktail or polar bear

MAX CANYON

Originator: Doug Stewart
Tier: Brad Burden
Hook: TMC 7999, Mustad 36890, sizes 2-8
Thread: Black 6/0 prewaxed
Tag: Flat silver tinsel
Tail: Orange and white hackle fibers, mixed
Rib: Medium oval gold tinsel
Body: Rear ⅓ orange wool, front ⅔ black wool
Hackle: Black hackle, soft
Wing: White over orange calftail or
polar bear
Cheeks: Jungle cock eyes (optional)

GREEN-BUTTED SKUNK

Tier: Brad Burden
Hook: TMC 7999, Mustad 36890, sizes 1/0-8
Thread: Black 6/0 prewaxed
Tag: Flat silver tinsel
Tail: Red hackle fibers
Butt: Fluorescent green floss
Rib: Fine oval silver tinsel
Body: Black goat dubbing
Hackle: Black hackle, soft
Wing: White calftail or polar bear
Cheeks: Jungle cock eyes (optional)

SKUNK

Tier: Brad Burden
Hook: TMC 7999, Mustad 36890, sizes 2/0-8
Thread: Black 6/0 prewaxed
Tag: Flat silver tinsel
Tail: Red hackle fibers
Rib: Flat silver tinsel
Body: Black chenille or goat dubbing
Hackle: Black hackle, soft
Wing: White calftail or polar bear
Cheeks: Jungle cock eyes (optional)

PURPLE PERIL

Originator: Ken McLeod
Tier: Brad Burden
Hook: TMC 7999, Mustad 36890, sizes 2/0-8
Thread: Black 6/0 prewaxed
Tag: Flat silver tinsel
Tail: Purple hackle fibers
Rib: Fine oval silver tinsel
Body: Purple floss or goat dubbing
Hackle: Purple hackle, soft
Wing: Natural brown deer hair
Cheeks: Jungle cock eyes (optional)

STEELHEAD FLIES

KALAMA SPECIAL

MAX CANYON

GREEN-BUTTED SKUNK

SKUNK

PURPLE PERIL

UMPQUA SPECIAL

SKYKOMISH SUNRISE

BRAD'S BRAT

POLAR SHRIMP

FALL FAVORITE

UMPQUA SPECIAL

Tier: Brad Burden
Hook: TMC 7999, Mustad 36890, sizes 2-8
Thread: Red 6/0 prewaxed
Tag: Flat silver tinsel
Tail: White hackle fibers
Rib: Fine oval silver tinsel
Body: Rear ⅓ yellow wool yarn, front ⅔ red
wool yarn
Hackle: Brown hackle, soft
Wing: White calftail or polar bear
Cheeks: Jungle cock eyes (optional)

SKYKOMISH SUNRISE

Originator: Ken and George McLeod
Tier: Brad Burden
Hook: TMC 7999, Mustad 36890, sizes 2/0-8
Thread: Red 6/0 prewaxed
Tag: Flat silver tinsel
Tail: Red and yellow hackle fibers, mixed
Rib: Fine oval silver tinsel
Body: Red chenille or goat dubbing
Hackle: Red and yellow hackle,
wound together
Wing: White calftail or polar bear
Cheeks: Jungle cock eyes (optional)

BRAD'S BRAT

Originator: Enos Bradner
Tier: Brad Burden
Hook: TMC 7999, Mustad 36890, sizes 1/0-8
Thread: Red 6/0 prewaxed
Tag: Flat gold tinsel
Tail: Orange hackle fibers, with white hackle
fibers over the top
Rib: Medium oval gold tinsel
Body: Rear 1/2; orange goat dubbing, front
1/2; red goat dubbing
Hackle: Dark brown hackle, soft and webby
Wing: Bucktail or polar bear, orange
over white
Cheeks: Jungle cock eyes (optional)

POLAR SHRIMP

Tier: Brad Burden
Hook: TMC 7999, Mustad 36890, sizes 2/0-6
Thread: White 6/0 prewaxed
Tag: Flat silver tinsel
Tail: Fluorescent orange hackle fibers
Body: Fluorescent orange chenille or
goat dubbing
Hackle: Fluorescent orange hackle, soft
Wing: White polar bear hair or calftail
Cheeks: Jungle cock eyes (optional)

FALL FAVORITE

Tier: Brad Burden
Hook: TMC 7999, Mustad 36890, sizes 2-8
Thread: Red 6/0 prewaxed
Body: Flat silver tinsel
Hackle: Red hackle, soft
Wing: Orange polar bear hair, or bucktail

VAN LUVEN

Originator: Harry Van Luven
Tier: Brad Burden
Hook: TMC 7999, Mustad 36890, sizes 2-8
Thread: Black 6/0 prewaxed
Tag: Flat silver tinsel
Tail: Red hackle fibers
Rib: Fine oval silver tinsel
Body: Red wool yarn or goat dubbing
Hackle: Brown hackle, soft
Wing: White calftail or polar bear

RED ANT

Tier: Brad Burden
Hook: TMC 7999, Mustad 36890, sizes 2-8
Thread: Black 6/0 prewaxed
Tag: Flat silver tinsel
Tail: Red hackle fibers
Butt: Peacock herl
Body: Red wool yarn, thin
Hackle: Brown hackle, soft
Wing: Natural brown bucktail
Cheeks: Jungle cock eyes (optional)

DEL COOPER

Originator: Mike Kennedy
Tier: Brad Burden
Hook: TMC 7999, Mustad 36890, sizes 2-6
Thread: Black 6/0 prewaxed
Tag: Flat silver tinsel
Tail: Red hackle fibers
Rib: Fine oval silver tinsel
Body: Purple wool yarn or goat dubbing
Hackle: Red hackle, soft
Wing: White bucktail or polar bear

BURLAP

Tier: Brad Burden
Hook: TMC 7999, Mustad 36890, sizes 1/0-8
Thread: Black 6/0 prewaxed
Tail: Dark deer hair, thick
Body: Burlap sack strand, tapered
Hackle: Grizzly hackle, soft and webby

SILVER HILTON

Tier: Brad Burden
Hook: TMC 7999, Mustad 36890, sizes 2-8
Thread: Black 6/0 prewaxed
Tag: Flat silver tinsel
Tail: Teal flank fibers
Rib: Oval silver tinsel
Body: Black chenille or goat dubbing
Wings: Grizzly hackle tips, flared
Hackle: Teal flank

STEELHEAD FLIES

VAN LUVEN

CUMMING'S SPECIAL

RED ANT

GOLDEN DEMON

DEL COOPER

AUTUMN SPEY

BURLAP

WINTER SPEY

SILVER HILTON

SUMMER SPEY

CUMMING'S SPECIAL

Originators: Ward Cummings and Clarence Gordon
Tier: Brad Burden
Hook: TMC 7999, Mustad 36890, sizes 2-8
Thread: Black 6/0 prewaxed
Tag: Flat silver tinsel
Tail: Golden pheasant crest, optional
Rib: Fine oval silver tinsel
Body: Rear ⅓ yellow floss, front ⅔ claret goat dubbing
Hackle: Claret hackle, soft
Wing: Natural dark brown bucktail
Cheeks: Jungle cock eyes (optional)

GOLDEN DEMON

Originator: C. Jim Pray
Tier: Brad Burden
Hook: TMC 7999, Mustad 36890, sizes 2-6
Thread: Black 6/0 prewaxed
Tag: Flat gold tinsel
Tail: Golden pheasant crest feather
Rib: Fine oval gold tinsel
Body: Medium oval gold tinsel
Hackle: Orange hackle, soft
Wing: Bronze mallard flank
Cheeks: Jungle cock eyes (optional)

AUTUMN SPEY

Originator: John Hazel
Tier: John Hazel
Hook: Alec Jackson Spey, sizes 1½-5
Thread: Black 6/0 prewaxed
Tag: Oval gold tinsel
Rib: Flat gold and oval gold tinsel
Body: Burnt orange goat dubbing
Hackle: Grey Heron hackle or substitute
Throat: Dyed orange guinea hackle
Wings: Bronze mallard flank

WINTER SPEY

Originator: John Hazel
Tier: John Hazel
Hook: Alec Jackson Spey, sizes 1½-5
Thread: Black 6/0 prewaxed
Tag: Oval silver tinsel
Rib: Flat silver and oval silver tinsel
Body: Kingfisher blue goat dubbing
Body-hackle: Kingfisher blue hackle
Hackle: Grey Heron hackle or substitute
Throat: Dyed kingfisher blue guinea hackle
Wings: Bronze mallard flank

SUMMER SPEY

Originator: John Hazel
Tier: John Hazel
Hook: Alec Jackson Spey, sizes 1½-5
Thread: Black 6/0 prewaxed
Tag: Oval gold tinsel
Rib: Flat silver and oval gold tinsel
Body: Claret goat dubbing
Hackle: Grey Heron hackle or substitute
Throat: Claret hackle and red guinea
Wings: Bronze mallard flank

STEELHEAD BEE

Originator: Roderick Haig-Brown
Hook: Partridge 01, sizes 6-12
Thread: Black 6/0 prewaxed
Tail: Fox squirrel tail
Body: Divided into thirds; brown, yellow, brown rabbit dubbing
Wings: Fox squirrel tail, slanted forward and divided
Hackle: Brown hackle, sparse

LEMIRE'S BLACK IRRESISTIBLE

Originator: Harry Lemire
Tier: Harry Lemire
Hook: Partridge 01, sizes 4-8
Thread: Black 6/0 prewaxed
Tail: Dark moose body hair
Body: Black deer hair, spun and clipped
Wing: Dark moose body hair
Hackle: Black hackle, clipped on the bottom

OCTOBER CADDIS

Originator: Bill Bakke
Hook: Partridge 01, sizes 6-10
Thread: Black 6/0 prewaxed
Tail: Golden pheasant crest feather
Body: Orange goat dubbing
Wings: Fox squirrel tail, forward and divided
Hackle: Dark brown hackle, sparse and soft

WAGONER'S STEELHEAD SKATER

Originator: Bob Wagoner
Tier: Bob Wagoner
Hook: Partridge 01, sizes 6-10
Thread: Black 6/0 prewaxed
Tail: Natural light elk hair
Body: Peacock herl
Body-hackle: Grizzly saddle hackle
Wings: Natural light elk hair, tied on underside
Hackle: Grizzly hackle

DISCO MOUSE

Hook: Partridge 01, TMC 7989, sizes 2-10
Thread: Black 6/0 prewaxed
Tail: Black deer hair, tips from body
Body: Black deer hair
Rib: Black thread
Underwing: Pearl Krystal Flash
Wing: Black deer hair
Head: Black deer hair, butts from wing

STEELHEAD FLIES

STEELHEAD BEE

FLUTTERING TERMITE

LEMIRE'S BLACK IRRESISTIBLE

WALLER WAKER

OCTOBER CADDIS

DRAGON FLY

WAGONER'S STEELHEAD SKATER

GREASED LINER

DISCO MOUSE

GREW'S MUDDLER

FLUTTERING TERMITE

Originator: Randle Scott Stetzer
Hook: Partridge 01, sizes 6-12
Thread: Black 6/0 prewaxed
Tail: Fox squirrel tail
Body: Orange poly pro yarn, twisted with sparse burnt orange goat dubbing
Rib: Fine gold wire and medium blue dun hackle, undersized, palmered over body
Wings: Black bear hair, or dark moose body hair
Hackle: Dark blue dun hackle, thick

WALLER WAKER

Originator: Lani Waller
Tier: Umpqua Feather Merchants
Hook: Partridge CS10, TMC 7989, sizes 1-6
Thread: Black 3/0 monocord
Tail: Dark moose body hair
Body: Rusty brown and black deer hair, spun and clipped
Throat: Dark moose body hair
Wings: Natural dark elk hair

DRAGON FLY

Originator: Bill Bakke
Tier: Christine Cutz Baxter
Hook: Partridge 01, TMC 7989, sizes 2-8
Thread: Black 6/0 prewaxed
Tail: Dark deer hair or moose body hair
Body: Depth ray wool yarn, any color
Wings: Dark deer hair or moose body hair
Head: Deer hair, spun and clipped

GREASED LINER

Originator: Harry Lemire
Tier: Harry Lemire
Hook: Partridge 01, sizes 4-8
Thread: Black "A" nymo
Tail: Dark deer hair
Body: Brown seal fur
Hackle: Grizzly hackle, soft and sparse
Wing: Dark deer hair
Head: Dark deer hair, butts from wing

GREW'S MUDDLER

Originator: Bob Grew
Hook: TMC 5263, Mustad 9672, sizes 2-4
Thread: Black 6/0 prewaxed
Wing: Four cree saddle hackles
Collar: Deer hair, spun
Head: Deer hair, spun and clipped

ALBINO MUDDLER

Originator: John Hazel
Tier: John Hazel
Hook: Partridge CS2, sizes 2-6
Thread: White 6/0 prewaxed
Body: Flat copper tinsel
Underwing: Fox squirrel tail
Wing: Light mottled turkey wing quill
Throat: Red goat dubbing
Collar: Bleached deer hair
Head: Bleached deer hair, spun and
  clipped, flat top and bottom

BADGER SKATER

Originator: John Hazel
Tier: John Hazel
Hook: Partridge 01, sizes 4-10
Thread: Black 6/0 prewaxed
Tail: Fox squirrel tail
Body: Badger saddle hackle, tightly wound
Wings: Fox squirrel tail
Hackle: Badger hackle

OCTOBER WULFF

Originator: John Hazel
Tier: John Hazel
Hook: Partridge 01, sizes 6-10
Thread: Black 6/0 prewaxed
Tail: Dyed black squirrel tail
Body: Mixed orange and yellow
  goat dubbing
Wings: Dyed orange polar bear hair
Hackle: Black saddle hackle, stiff

POLAR SKATER

Originator: John Hazel
Tier: John Hazel
Hook: Partridge 01, sizes 6-8
Thread: Black 6/0 prewaxed
Tail: White polar bear hair
Body: Badger saddle hackle, tightly
  wound, undersized
Wings: White polar bear hair
Hackle: Badger saddle hackle, stiff

DICOS SKATER

Originator: John Hazel
Tier: John Hazel
Hook: Partridge 01, sizes 4-6
Thread: Black 6/0 prewaxed
Tail: Dyed orange squirrel tail
Rib: Fine copper wire
Body: Orange poly yarn
Hackle: Dyed orange grizzly hackle,
  palmered over the body
Wings: Dyed orange squirrel tail
Collar: Moose body hair
Head: Moose body hair, spun and clipped

STEELHEAD FLIES

ALBINO MUDDLER

STEELHEAD MacINTOSH

BADGER SKATER

RUSTY BOMBER

OCTOBER WULFF

MOOSE HAIR CADDIS

POLAR SKATER

PURPLE MUDDLER

DICOS SKATER

WATER OUZEL

STEELHEAD MacINTOSH

Originator: John Hazel, variation on
  the MacIntosh
Tier: John Hazel
Hook: Partridge 01, sizes 4-10
Thread: Black 6/0 prewaxed
Tail: Dyed black squirrel tail
Body: Black saddle hackle, tightly wound
Hackle: Dyed orange grizzly saddle hackle

RUSTY BOMBER

Originator: John Hazel, variation on
  the Bomber
Tier: John Hazel
Hook: Partridge 01, sizes 6-8
Thread: Black 6/0 prewaxed
Tail: Fox squirrel tail
Body: Dyed rusty orange deer hair, spun
  and clipped
Wing: Fox squirrel tail
Hackle: Brown saddle hackle, palmered
  over the body

MOOSE HAIR CADDIS

Originator: John Hazel, variation on
  Harry Lemire's Greased Liner
Tier: John Hazel
Hook: Partridge 01, sizes 4-8
Thread: Black 6/0 prewaxed
Tail: Dark moose body hair
Rib: Fine copper wire
Body: Orange poly yarn
Hackle: Dyed orange grizzly hackle,
  palmered over the body
Throat: Dyed orange guinea hackle
Wing: Dark moose body hair, butts form
  the head

PURPLE MUDDLER

Originator: John Hazel
Tier: John Hazel
Hook: Partridge CS2, sizes 2-10
Thread: Black 6/0 prewaxed
Body: Purple glitter body
Underwing: Dyed purple squirrel tail
Wing: Dark mottled turkey quill
Throat: Red goat dubbing
Collar: Dyed purple deer hair
Head: Dyed purple deer hair, spun and
  clipped, flat top and bottom

WATER OUZEL

Originator: John Hazel
Tier: John Hazel
Hook: Partridge 01, sizes 4-8
Thread: Black 6/0 prewaxed
Tail: Natural gray squirrel tail
Body: Dyed brown deer hair, spun and
  clipped
Wings: Natural gray squirrel tail
Hackle: Grey Heron hackle or substitute,
  wrapped over the body, clipped close
  on the top

MOOSE TURD

Originator: Bill McMillan
Hook: Mustad 9672, size 6
Thread: Black 6/0 prewaxed
Tail: White calftail, long
Body: Dyed black deer hair, spun and clipped
Wing: White calftail, the stiff and kinky tip, clipped blunt

STEELHEAD CADDIS

Originator: Bill McMillan
Tier: Bill McMillan
Hook: Partridge 01, sizes 6-12
Thread: Brown 6/0 prewaxed
Body: Hare's mask fur, orangish shade from base of ear, plump
Wing: Mottled turkey quill, tent style over the back
Collar: Deer hair, spun and sparse
Head: Deer hair, spun and clipped, sparse

STEELHEAD SILVER DOCTOR

Originator: Bill McMillan
Tier: Bill McMillan
Hook: Partridge M, sizes 2/0-2, or N, sizes 2-6
Thread: Red 6/0 prewaxed
Body: Flat silver tinsel
Throat: Silver doctor blue hackle
Wing: Red over yellow calftail
Topping: Pintail flank, cupped over the wing

BLACK PALMER

Originator: Bill McMillan, a variation on a Roderick Haig-Brown pattern, the Carpenter Ant
Hook: Partridge N, sizes 1/0-6
Thread: Black 6/0 prewaxed
Tag: Copper wire
Rib: Copper wire
Body: Black seal or goat fur
Hackle: Iron blue dun hackle, palmered over the body

STONE NYMPH

Originator: Bill McMillan
Tier: Bill McMillan
Hook: Mustad 37160, sizes 2-6
Thread: Black 6/0 prewaxed
Tail: Grouse hackle fibers, or brown widgeon flank fibers
Rib: Medium copper wire
Body: Black wool yarn
Thorax: Black rabbit dubbing
Hackle: Grouse hackle, or brown widgeon flank, long and soft

STEELHEAD FLIES

MOOSE TURD

WINTER'S HOPE

STEELHEAD CADDIS

PAINT BRUSH

STEELHEAD SILVER DOCTOR

SILVER AND ORANGE

BLACK PALMER

SILVER AND BLACK

STONE NYMPH

WASHOUGAL OLIVE

WINTER'S HOPE

Originator: Bill McMillan
Tier: Bill McMillan
Hook: Partridge M, sizes 6/0-2/0
Thread: Maroon 6/0 prewaxed
Body: Flat silver tinsel
Hackle: Silver doctor blue hackle, long and soft
Fore-Hackle: Purple hackle, long and soft
Wing: Two yellow hackle tips enclosed by two orange hackle tips
Topping: Golden-olive calftail, sparse

PAINT BRUSH

Originator: Bill McMillan
Tier: Bill McMillan
Hook: Mustad 7970, sizes 1-2
Thread: Red 6/0 prewaxed
Body: Flat gold tinsel
Aft-Hackle: Orange hackle, palmered over the body
Mid-Hackle: Purple hackle, slightly longer than the orange
Fore-Hackle: Silver doctor blue, slightly longer than the purple

SILVER AND ORANGE

Originator: Bill McMillan
Tier: Bill McMillan
Hook: Mustad 7970, sizes 1-2, or Partridge N, sizes 2-6
Thread: Red 6/0 prewaxed
Tail: Orange calftail
Body: Flat silver tinsel
Throat: Orange calftail
Wing: White calftail

SILVER AND BLACK

Originator: Bill McMillan
Tier: Bill McMillan
Hook: Mustad 7970, sizes 1-2, or Partridge N, sizes 2-6
Thread: Black 6/0 prewaxed
Tail: Black calftail
Body: Flat silver tinsel
Throat: Black calftail
Wing: White calftail

WASHOUGAL OLIVE

Originator: Bill McMillan
Tier: Bill McMillan
Hook: Mustad 7970, sizes 1-2, Partridge N, sizes 2-6
Thread: Black 6/0 prewaxed
Tail: Golden-olive calftail
Body: Flat gold tinsel
Throat: Golden-olive calftail
Wing: White calftail

SOL DUC

Originator: Syd Glasso
Tier: Brad Burden
Hook: Partridge N, sizes 1/0-2
Thread: Red 6/0 prewaxed
Tag: Flat silver tinsel
Tail: Golden pheasant crest
Rib: Oval silver tinsel
Body: Rear ⅔ fluorescent orange floss, remainder fluorescent orange goat dubbing
Hackle: Yellow hen hackle
Throat: Teal flank
Wing: Four hot orange hackle tips
Topping: Golden pheasant crest

COURTESAN

Originator: Syd Glasso
Tier: Brad Burden
Hook: Partridge N, sizes 1/0-2
Thread: Red 6/0 prewaxed
Tag: Flat silver tinsel
Rib: Oval silver tinsel
Body: Rear ⅔ fluorescent orange floss, remainder fluorescent orange goat dubbing
Hackle: Brown hen, long and webby
Wing: Four hot orange hackle tips

SOL DUC SPEY

Originator: Syd Glasso
Tier: Brad Burden
Hook: Partridge N, sizes 3/0-2
Thread: Red 6/0 prewaxed
Tag: Flat silver tinsel
Rib: Oval silver tinsel
Body: Rear ⅔ hot orange floss, remainder hot orange goat dubbing
Hackle: Yellow saddle hackle, long and webby
Throat: Black heron hackle or substitute
Wing: Four hot orange hackle tips

ORANGE HERON

Originator: Syd Glasso
Tier: Brad Burden
Hook: Partridge N, sizes 3/0-2
Thread: Red 6/0 prewaxed
Tag: Flat silver tinsel
Rib: Oval silver tinsel
Body: Rear ⅔ hot orange floss, remainder hot orange goat dubbing
Hackle: Grey heron hackle or substitute, palmered over the body
Throat: Teal flank
Wing: Two hot orange hackle tips.

QUILLAYUTE

Originator: Syd Glasso
Tier: Brad Burden
Hook: Partridge N, sizes 1/0-2
Thread: Red 6/0 prewaxed
Tag: Flat silver tinsel
Tail: Dyed Red golden pheasant crest
Rib: Oval silver tinsel
Body: Rear ⅔ fluorescent orange floss, remainder fluorescent orange goat dubbing
Hackle: Teal flank
Throat: Black heron hackle or substitute
Wing: Four golden pheasant body feathers

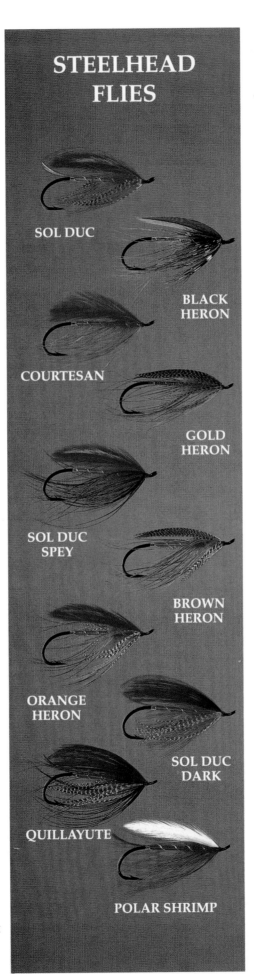

STEELHEAD FLIES

SOL DUC

BLACK HERON

COURTESAN

GOLD HERON

SOL DUC SPEY

BROWN HERON

ORANGE HERON

SOL DUC DARK

QUILLAYUTE

POLAR SHRIMP

BLACK HERON

Originator: Syd Glasso
Tier: Brad Burden
Hook: Partridge N, sizes 1/0-2
Thread: Black 6/0 prewaxed
Tag: Flat silver tinsel
Rib: Oval silver tinsel
Body: Rear ½ flat silver tinsel, front ½ black seal fur
Hackle: Grey Heron hackle or substitute, from second turn of ribbing
Throat: Speckled guinea hackle
Wing: Grey Heron wing quill or substitute

GOLD HERON

Originator: Syd Glasso
Tier: Brad Burden
Hook: Partridge N, sizes 1/0-2
Thread: Orange 6/0 prewaxed
Tag: Flat gold tinsel
Rib: Oval gold tinsel
Body: Rear ⅔ flat gold tinsel, remainder hot orange goat dubbing
Hackle: Grey heron hackle or substitute
Throat: Widgeon flank
Wing: Widgeon flank

BROWN HERON

Originator: Syd Glasso
Tier: Brad Burden
Hook: Partridge N, sizes 1/0-2
Thread: Red 6/0 prewaxed
Tag: Flat silver tinsel
Rib: Oval silver tinsel
Body: Rear ⅔ fluorescent orange floss, remainder fluorescent orange goat dubbing
Hackle: Grey heron hackle or substitute
Throat: Teal flank
Wing: Bronze mallard

SOL DUC DARK

Originator: Syd Glasso
Tier: Brad Burden
Hook: Partridge N, sizes 1/0-2
Thread: Red 6/0 prewaxed
Tag: Flat silver tinsel
Tail: Golden pheasant crest
Rib: Oval silver tinsel
Body: Rear ⅔ fluorescent orange floss, remainder fluorescent orange goat dubbing
Hackle: Yellow hen, long and webby
Throat: Teal flank
Wing: Four golden pheasant body feathers
Topping: Golden pheasant crest

POLAR SHRIMP

Originator: Syd Glasso
Tier: Brad Burden
Hook: Partridge N, sizes 3/0-2
Thread: Red 6/0 prewaxed
Tag: Flat silver tinsel
Tail: Reddish-Hot orange hackle fibers
Rib: Fine oval silver tinsel
Body: Rear ⅔ hot orange floss, remainder dark reddish-orange goat dubbing
Hackle: Hot orange saddle hackle
Throat: Golden pheasant flank feather
Wing: Two white hackle tips

GENERAL PRACTITIONER, Waddington

Originator: Esmond Drury
Tier: John Hazel
Hook: Partridge Waddington Shank
Thread: Red 6/0 and Black 6/0 prewaxed
Tail: Two golden pheasant breast feathers, on the treble
Rib: Oval gold tinsel
Body: Hot orange goat dubbing
Mid-wing: Two golden pheasant breast feathers, and tippet feather cut in a "V"
Wing: Golden pheasant breast feather

MARABOU RED, tube

Originator: John Hazel, variation on Bob Aid's Marabou Spider
Tier: John Hazel
Hook: Copper or Aluminum tube
Thread: Black 6/0 prewaxed
Rib: Oval silver tinsel
Body: Flat silver tinsel
Back-hackle: Fluorescent pink marabou, wrapped
Mid-hackle: Red marabou, wrapped
Front-hackle: Grey Heron hackle or substitute

MARABOU SPIDER, red/orange

Originator: Bob Aid
Tier: Bob Aid
Hook: Alec Jackson Spey Hook, size 1½
Thread: Red 6/0 prewaxed
Body: Flat silver tinsel
Thorax: Orange goat dubbing
Hackle: Orange marabou, followed by red marabou
Collar: Dyed black pheasant rump or saddle hackle

MARABOU SPEY

Originator: John Farrar
Tier: John Farrar
Hook: Partridge CS10, sizes 1/0-4
Thread: Orange 6/0 prewaxed
Body: Rear ⅔, wide flat gold tinsel, front ⅓, orange marabou followed by fluorescent red marabou, wrapped
Hackle: Golden pheasant flank
Wing: Bronze mallard flank

RUSTY SPIDER

Originator: Marty Sherman, adapted from Al Knudson's Spider
Tier: Marty Sherman
Hook: Partridge N, sizes 3/0-2
Thread: Orange 6/0 prewaxed
Tag: Flat gold tinsel
Butt: Bright yellow floss
Rib: Oval gold tinsel
Body: Rusty reddish-brown seal fur, or substitute
Hackle: Natural reddish-brown hackle, palmered over the body
Collar: Mallard flank dyed lemon woodduck

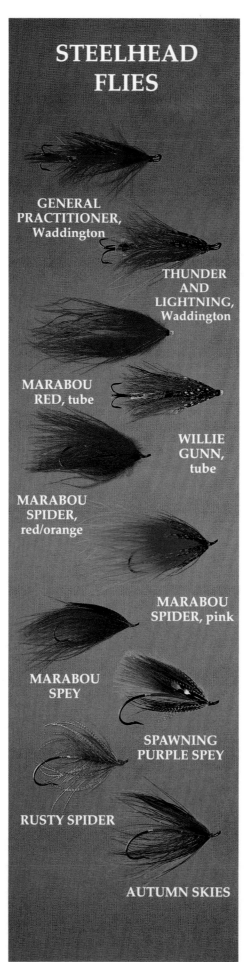

STEELHEAD FLIES

GENERAL PRACTITIONER, Waddington

THUNDER AND LIGHTNING, Waddington

MARABOU RED, tube

WILLIE GUNN, tube

MARABOU SPIDER, red/orange

MARABOU SPIDER, pink

MARABOU SPEY

SPAWNING PURPLE SPEY

RUSTY SPIDER

AUTUMN SKIES

THUNDER AND LIGHTNING, Waddington

Tier: John Hazel
Hook: Partridge Waddington Shank
Thread: Black 6/0 prewaxed
Tag: Oval gold tinsel, on the treble
Tip: Golden yellow floss, on the treble
Butt: Black ostrich herl, on the treble
Rib: Flat gold and oval gold tinsel
Body: Black floss, thin
Body-hackle: Hot orange hackle
Hackle: Grey Heron hackle or substitute
Collar: Dyed kingfisher blue guinea hackle

WILLIE GUNN, tube

Tier: John Hazel
Hook: Copper or Aluminum Tube
Thread: Black 6/0 prewaxed
Tag: Oval silver tinsel
Rib: Oval silver tinsel
Body: Black floss, thin
Wing: Yellow, black and orange polar bear or calftail hair, mixed
Hackle: Natural guinea hackle

MARABOU SPIDER, pink

Originator: Bob Aid
Tier: Bob Aid
Hook: Alec Jackson Spey Hook, size 1½
Thread: Red 6/0 prewaxed
Body: Flat silver tinsel
Thorax: Hot fluorescent pink goat dubbing
Hackle: Cerise marabou
Collar: Red hackle with dyed purple guinea over

SPAWNING PURPLE SPEY

Originator: John Shewey
Tier: John Shewey
Hook: Alec Jackson Spey, Partridge CS10, sizes 3/0-5
Thread: Wine 6/0 prewaxed
Tag: Flat silver tinsel
Body: Flame red single strand nylon floss
Wing: Five "spikes" of purple marabou, laced with dyed purple Krystal Flash
Hackle: Purple neck hackle
Collar: Dyed purple guinea rump
Throat: Teal flank
Cheeks: Jungle cock eyes

AUTUMN SKIES

Originator: John Shewey
Tier: John Shewey
Hook: Alec Jackson Spey, Partridge CS10, sizes 3/0-5
Thread: Wine 6/0 prewaxed
Tag: Flat silver tinsel
Rib: fine flat gold over butt, fine oval gold over body
Butt: ½ orange floss, ½ flame red floss
Body: ½ flame red seal, ½ purple seal
Hackle: Bright red spey hackle over red seal, purple spey hackle over purple seal
Throat: Black spey hackle
Wings: Purple goose shoulder, with thin strips of red goose in the middle of each wing

HALFSTONE

Tier: Kevin Erickson
Hook: TMC 7999, Partridge N, sizes 2-10
Thread: Black 6/0 prewaxed
Tag: Fine flat silver tinsel
Tail: Golden pheasant crest
Rib: Oval gold tinsel
Body: Rear ⅓ yellow seal fur, front ⅔ black seal fur
Hackle: Black hackle
Wing: Gray squirrel tail, from base, short

BLACK BEAR GREEN BUTT

Originator: Harry Smith
Tier: Kevin Erickson
Hook: TMC 7999, Partridge N, sizes 4-10
Thread: Black 6/0 prewaxed
Tag: Fine flat silver tinsel
Tail: Black hackle fibers
Butt: Fluorescent green wool
Rib: Oval silver tinsel
Body: Black wool
Hackle: Black hen hackle, beard style
Wing: Black bear hair

BLACK FAIRY

Tier: Kevin Erickson
Hook: TMC 7999, Partridge N, sizes 2-10
Thread: Black 6/0 prewaxed
Tag: Fine oval gold tinsel
Tip: Golden yellow floss
Tail: Golden pheasant crest
Rib: Oval gold tinsel
Body: Black seal fur
Hackle: Black hen hackle, beard style
Wing: Bronze mallard flank

NIGHT HAWK

Tier: Kevin Erickson
Hook: TMC 7999, Partridge M, sizes 2-10
Thread: Red 6/0 prewaxed
Tag: Fine oval silver tinsel
Tip: Yellow floss
Tail: Golden pheasant crest, with a few short blue hackle fibers
Butt: Fluorescent red floss
Rib: Fine oval silver tinsel
Body: Flat silver tinsel
Throat: Black hackle
Wing: Black bear hair

GREEN PEACOCK

Tier: Kevin Erickson
Hook: TMC 7999, Partridge N, sizes 2-10
Thread: Black 6/0 prewaxed
Tag: Fine flat silver tinsel
Tail: Golden pheasant crest
Rib: Oval silver tinsel
Body: Light blue floss
Throat: Light blue hackle
Wing: Peacock sword fibers

ATLANTIC SALMON FLIES

HALFSTONE

ORANGE BLOSSOM

BLACK BEAR GREEN BUTT

ROGER'S FANCY

BLACK FAIRY

COSSEBOOM

NIGHT HAWK

FIERY BROWN

GREEN PEACOCK

LAXA BLUE

ORANGE BLOSSOM

Tier: Kevin Erickson
Hook: TMC 7999, Partridge M, sizes 2/0-8
Thread: Black 6/0 prewaxed
Tag: Fine oval silver tinsel
Tip: Yellow floss
Tail: Golden pheasant crest
Butt: Black ostrich herl
Rib: Oval silver tinsel
Body: Rear ½ embossed silver tinsel, front ½ yellow seal fur
Hackle: Yellow hackle, palmered over the seal fur
Wing: Light brown bucktail
Hackle: Hot orange hackle, as collar

ROGER'S FANCY

Tier: Kevin Erickson
Hook: Partridge M, sizes 2-10
Thread: Black 6/0 prewaxed
Tag: Fine oval silver tinsel
Tip: Fluorescent green floss
Tail: Peacock sword fibers, short
Rib: Oval silver tinsel
Body: Bright green seal fur
Throat: Bright green hackle over yellow hackle
Wing: Gray fox guard hairs

COSSEBOOM

Originator: John Cosseboom
Tier: Kevin Erickson
Hook: TMC 7999, Partridge M, sizes 2-10
Thread: Red 6/0 prewaxed
Tag: Flat silver tinsel
Tail: Medium olive floss, short
Rib: Flat silver tinsel
Body: Medium olive floss
Wing: Gray squirrel tail
Hackle: Lemon yellow hackle, wound as collar

FIERY BROWN

Tier: Kevin Erickson
Hook: TMC 7999, Partridge N, sizes 3/0-6
Thread: Black 6/0 prewaxed
Tag: Fine oval gold tinsel
Tip: Claret floss
Tail: Golden pheasant crest
Rib: Fine oval gold tinsel
Body: Fiery brown seal fur
Hackle: Light fiery brown hackle, palmered from second turn of tinsel
Wing: Underwing of golden pheasant tippets, veiled by bronze mallard flank

LAXA BLUE

Tier: Kevin Erickson
Hook: TMC 7999, Partridge N, sizes 2-10
Thread: Black 6/0 prewaxed
Tag: Fine flat silver tinsel
Tip: Fluorescent orange floss
Tail: Golden pheasant crest
Butt: Black ostrich herl
Rib: Flat silver tinsel
Body: Bright blue floss
Throat: Pale blue hackle
Wing: Bright blue calftail

RUSTY RAT

Originator: Roy A. Thompson
Tier: Brad Burden
Hook: Alec Jackson, Partridge N, sizes 2-10
Thread: Red 6/0 prewaxed
Tag: Fine oval gold tinsel
Tail: Peacock sword fibers, short
Rib: Oval gold tinsel
Body: Rear ½ yellow floss, front ½ peacock herl
Veiling: Yellow floss, at body joint
Wing: Gray fox guard hair
Cheeks: Jungle cock eyes (optional)
Hackle: Grizzly hackle, collar style

JEANNIE

Tier: Brad Burden
Hook: Alec Jackson, Partridge N, sizes 3/0-2
Thread: Black 6/0 prewaxed
Tag: Flat silver tinsel
Tail: Golden pheasant crest
Rib: Oval silver tinsel
Body: Rear third yellow floss, remainder black floss
Throat: Black hackle
Wing: Bronze mallard flank
Cheeks: Jungle cock eyes (optional)

THUNDER AND LIGHTNING

Tier: Brad Burden
Hook: Alec Jackson, Partridge N, sizes 3/0-6
Thread: Black 6/0 prewaxed
Tag: Fine oval gold tinsel
Tip: Golden yellow floss
Tail: Golden pheasant crest
Butt: Black ostrich herl
Rib: Oval gold tinsel
Body: Black floss
Hackle: Deep orange hackle, from second turn of tinsel
Throat: Dyed blue guinea hackle
Wing: Bronze mallard flank
Topping: Golden pheasant crest
Cheeks: Jungle cock eyes

BLUE CHARM

Tier: Brad Burden
Hook: Alec Jackson, Partridge N, sizes 4-12
Thread: Black 6/0 prewaxed
Tag: Fine flat silver tinsel
Tail: Golden pheasant crest
Rib: Oval silver tinsel
Body: Black floss
Throat: Silver doctor blue hackle
Wing: Bronze mallard flank
Overwing: Teal flank
Topping: Golden pheasant crest
Cheeks: Jungle cock eyes (optional)

MARCH BROWN

Tier: Brad Burden
Hook: Alec Jackson, Partridge N, sizes 2-12
Thread: Black 6/0 prewaxed
Tag: Fine oval gold tinsel
Tail: Brown partridge fibers
Rib: Oval gold tinsel
Body: Rear third yellow wool, remainder hare's ear fur
Throat: Brown partridge hackle
Wing: Hen pheasant tail

ATLANTIC SALMON FLIES

RUSTY RAT

SILVER BLUE

JEANNIE

SILVER DOWNEASTER

THUNDER AND LIGHTNING

LOGIE

BLUE CHARM

HAGGIS

MARCH BROWN

UNDERTAKER

SILVER BLUE

Tier: Brad Burden
Hook: Alec Jackson, Partridge N, sizes 4-10
Thread: Black 6/0 prewaxed
Tag: Flat silver tinsel
Tail: Golden pheasant crest
Rib: Oval silver tinsel
Body: Flat silver tinsel
Throat: Pale blue hackle fibers
Wing: Barred teal flank

SILVER DOWNEASTER

Tier: Kevin Erickson
Hook: TMC 7999, Partridge N, sizes 2-10
Thread: Black 6/0 prewaxed
Tag: Fine oval silver tinsel
Tail: Golden pheasant crest
Butt: Black ostrich herl
Rib: Fine oval silver tinsel
Body: Flat silver tinsel
Hackle: Hot orange hen hackle
Wing: Black bear hair

LOGIE

Tier: Kevin Erickson
Hook: Partridge N, sizes 2-10
Thread: Black 6/0 prewaxed
Tag: Fine oval silver tinsel
Tail: Golden pheasant crest
Rib: Oval silver tinsel
Body: Rear ½ yellow floss, front ½ claret floss
Throat: Light blue hackle
Wing: Fox squirrel tail over dyed yellow squirrel tail

HAGGIS

Originator: Lee Wulff
Tier: Kevin Erickson
Hook: TMC 7999, Partridge M, sizes 2-10
Thread: Black 6/0 prewaxed
Tag: Fine oval silver tinsel
Rib: Oval silver tinsel
Body: Black floss
Throat: Yellow hackle fluff
Wing: Black bear hair, long

UNDERTAKER

Tier: Kevin Erickson
Hook: TMC 7999, Partridge N, sizes 2-10
Thread: Black 6/0 prewaxed
Tag: Fine flat gold tinsel
Butt: Rear ½ fluorescent green floss, front ½ fluorescent orange floss
Rib: Oval gold tinsel
Body: Peacock herl
Throat: Black hackle
Wing: Black bear hair
Cheeks: Jungle cock eyes (optional)

WHITE WULFF

Originator: Lee Wulff
Tier: Kevin Erickson
Hook: Partridge 01, sizes 4-10
Thread: Black 6/0 prewaxed
Tail: White calftail
Body: White goat dubbing
Wing: White calftail, divided
Hackle: White hackle

WULFF SKATER

Originator: Lee Wulff
Tier: Kevin Erickson
Hook: Partridge 01, sizes 12-16
Thread: Black 6/0 prewaxed
Tail: Two grizzly hackle tips
Hackle: Grizzly hackle, palmered
Wing: White calftail, spun and flared

BUCK BUG

Tier: Kevin Erickson
Hook: Partridge CS2, sizes 4-10
Thread: Black 3/0 monocord
Tail: Fox squirrel tail
Body: Deer hair, spun and clipped
Hackle: Brown hackle, palmered
through body

BOMBER

Tier: Kevin Erickson
Hook: Partridge 01, sizes 2-8
Thread: Black 3/0 monocord
Tail: White calftail
Body: Deer hair, spun and clipped
Hackle: Grizzly hackle, palmered
through body
Wing: White calftail

KATE

Tier: Kevin Erickson
Hook: Partridge M, sizes 2-10
Thread: Black 6/0 prewaxed
Tag: Fine oval silver tinsel
Tail: Golden pheasant crest
Rib: Oval silver tinsel
Body: Crimson floss
Hackle: Crimson hackle, palmered
Throat: Lemon yellow hackle
Wing: Golden pheasant tippets, veiled by
bronze mallard flank

ATLANTIC SALMON FLIES

WHITE WULFF

SALMON IRRESISTIBLE

WULFF SKATER

BUTTERFLY

BUCK BUG

PASS LAKE

BOMBER

ABE MUNN KILLER

KATE

MacINTOSH

SALMON IRRESISTIBLE

Originator: Harry Darbee
Tier: Kevin Erickson
Hook: Partridge 01, sizes 4-10
Thread: Black 6/0 prewaxed
Tail: Natural brown bucktail
Body: Deer hair, spun and clipped
Wing: White calftail, divided
Hackle: Brown and grizzly hackle, mixed

BUTTERFLY

Originator: Maurice Ingalls
Tier: Kevin Erickson
Hook: Partridge N, sizes 6-10
Thread: Black 6/0 prewaxed
Tail: Red hackle fibers
Butt: Fluorescent green wool
Body: Peacock herl
Wings: White calftail, divided
Hackle: Brown hackle, wound as collar

PASS LAKE

Tier: Kevin Erickson
Hook: TMC 7999, Partridge M or P, sizes 8-12
Thread: Black 6/0 prewaxed
Tail: Brown hackle fibers
Body: Black chenille
Hackle: Brown hackle
Wing: White calftail

ABE MUNN KILLER

Originator: Abe Munn
Tier: Kevin Erickson
Hook: TMC 7999, Partridge N, sizes 2-8
Thread: Black 6/0 prewaxed
Tag: Fine oval gold tinsel
Tail: Oak turkey wing feather, narrow
Rib: Fine oval gold tinsel
Body: Buttercup yellow wool, smooth
Hackle: Brown hackle, pulled down
for throat
Wing: Oak turkey wing sections

MacINTOSH

Tier: Kevin Erickson
Hook: Partridge 01, sizes 2-10
Thread: Black 6/0 prewaxed
Wing: Fox squirrel tail, from center of shank
Hackle: Brown hackle, thick, from center
of shank

LADY CAROLINE
Tier: Brad Burden
Hook: Alec Jackson, Partridge N, sizes 3/0-2
Thread: Black 6/0 prewaxed
Tail: Golden pheasant breast, sparse
Ribbing: Flat gold, oval silver, oval gold tinsel
Body: Two strand brown, one strand olive wool, twisted and wound together
Hackle: Grey heron hackle substitute, over the body.
Throat: Golden pheasant breast
Wing: Bronze mallard flank

JOCK SCOTT   (see right)
Tier: Bill Chinn
Hook: Partridge M, CS10, sizes 5/0-6
Thread: Black 6/0 prewaxed
Tag: Silver twist and yellow silk floss
Tail: Golden pheasant crest and indian crow
Butt: Black ostrich herl
Body: Yellow silk floss, ribbed with narrow silver tinsel, and butted with toucan above and below, black ostrich herl between, black silk floss ribbed with broad silver tinsel
Hackle: Black hackle over the black floss
Throat: Gallina hackle
Wings: Two strips of black turkey with white tips, golden pheasant tail, bustard, grey mallard, peacock sword fibers, blue swan, yellow and red macaw, bronze mallard over the top
Topping: Golden pheasant crest
Sides: Jungle cock
Cheeks: Blue chatterer
Horns: Blue macaw

AKROYD
Tier: Brad Burden
Hook: Alec Jackson, Partridge N, sizes 3/0-4
Thread: Black 6/0 prewaxed
Tag: Flat silver tinsel
Tail: Golden pheasant crest and tippet
Body: First half, light orange seal fur; second half, black floss
Ribs: Oval silver tinsel over seal fur, flat silver tinsel and twist over floss
Hackle: Lemon yellow hackle over seal fur, black heron hackle substitute over black floss
Throat: Teal flank
Wing: Cinnamon turkey tail strips, set flat
Cheeks: Jungle cock eyes, drooping

PURPLE KING
Tier: Brad Burden
Hook: Alec Jackson, Partridge N, sizes 3/0-2
Thread: Black 6/0 prewaxed
Body: Purple wool, thin
Rib: Flat gold and oval gold tinsel
Hackle: Black heron hackle substitute, over the body
Throat: Teal flank
Wing: Bronze mallard flank.

GREY HERON
Tier: Brad Burdan
Hook: Alec Jackson, Partridge N, Sizes 3/0-2
Thread: Black 6/0 prewaxed
Body: First ⅓; yellow, front ⅔; black Floss
Rib: Flat silver tinsel, oval gold tinsel
Hackle: Gray heron hackle, over the body
Throat: Guinea hackle
Wing: Bronze mallard flank

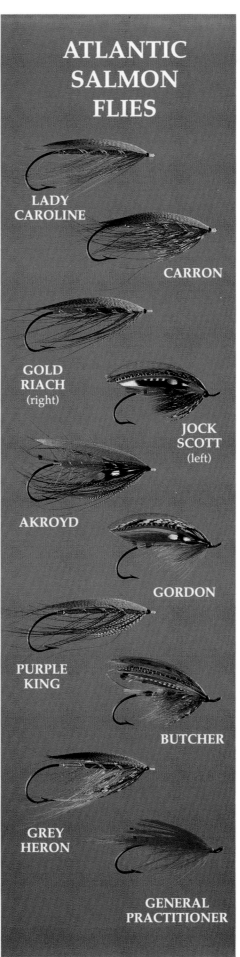

ATLANTIC SALMON FLIES

LADY CAROLINE

CARRON

GOLD RIACH (right)

JOCK SCOTT (left)

AKROYD

GORDON

PURPLE KING

BUTCHER

GREY HERON

GENERAL PRACTITIONER

CARRON
Tier: Brad Burden
Hook: Alec Jackson, Partridge N, sizes 3/0-2
Thread: Black 6/0 prewaxed
Body: Orange wool yarn, thin
Rib: Flat oval tinsel and oval silver tinsel
Hackle: Black heron hackle substitute, over the body
Throat: Teal flank
Wing: Bronze mallard flank

GOLD RIACH   (see left)
Tier: Brad Burden
Hook: Alec Jackson, Partridge N, sizes 3/0-2
Thread: Black 6/0 prewaxed
Body: First ½ orange wool, remainder black wool
Rib: Flat gold, oval gold, and oval silver tinsel
Hackle: Grey heron hackle substitute, over the body
Throat: Widgeon flank
Wing: Bronze mallard flank.

GORDON
Tier: Bill Chinn
Hook: Partridge M, CS10, sizes 5/0-6
Thread: Black 6/0 prewaxed
Tag: Silver twist and yellow silk floss
Tail: Golden pheasant crest and tippet strands
Butt: Black ostrich herl
Body: Rear 1/3; yellow silk floss, front 2/3; claret silk floss
Ribs: Oval silver tinsel and flat silver tinsel
Hackle: Claret hackle, from yellow floss
Throat: Blue hackle
Wings: Pair of golden pheasant sword feathers, yellow blue, and red swan, bustard, amherst pheasant tail
Topping: Golden pheasant crest
Sides: Jungle cock

BUTCHER
Tier: Bill Chinn
Hook: Partridge M, CS10, sizes 5/0-6
Thread: Black 6/0 prewaxed
Tag: Silver twist and yellow silk floss
Tail: Golden pheasant crest and blue chatterer
Butt: Black ostrich herl
Body: Claret floss, light blue, dark claret, dark blue seal fur, equal sections
Rib: Oval silver tinsel
Hackle: Claret hackle, from second turn of tinsel
Throat: Yellow hackle and guinea hackle
Wings: A tippet and breast feather of the golden pheasant, veiled with teal, golden pheasant tail, bustard, yellow, red, and blue swan, mallard
Topping: Golden pheasant crest
Horns: Blue macaw
Cheeks: Blue chatterer

GENERAL PRACTITIONER
Originator: Esmond Drury
Tier: Brad Burden
Hook: Alec Jackson, Partridge N, sizes 3/0-2
Thread: Fire orange 6/0 prewaxed
Tail: Hot orange bucktail, golden pheasant breast,
Rib: Oval gold tinsel
Body: Hot orange seal fur
First Wing: Golden pheasant breast, and tippets cut in V to form eyes
Second Wing: Two golden pheasant breast feathers
Hackle: Hot orange hackle, wound from tail

FLASH FLY

Hook: TMC 800S, Mustad 3407, sizes 2/0-6
Thread: Red 3/0 monocord
Tail: Silver Flashabou
Body: Silver diamond braid
Wing: Silver over purple Flashabou
Hackle: Red hackle

SALMON CREEK SPECIAL

Originator: Irwin Thompson
Hook: Eagle claw 1197N, sizes 2/0-6
Thread: Fluorescent red 6/0 prewaxed
Tail: Black squirrel tail
Rib: Flat silver tinsel
Body: Fluorescent hot orange floss
Wing: Fluorescent orange yarn
Topping: Fluorescent white hackle fibers
Hackle: Fluorescent yellow hackle,
collar style

ORANGE BOSS

Hook: TMC 700, Mustad 36890, sizes 2-6
Thread: Orange 3/0 monocord
Tag: Flat silver tinsel
Tail: Black calftail, long
Rib: Oval silver tinsel
Body: Orange chenille
Hackle: Black hackle
Eyes: Silver bead chain

BRIGHT ROE

Hook: TMC 7999, Mustad 36890, sizes 1/0-6
Thread: Orange 3/0 monocord
Rib: Oval silver tinsel
Body: Fluorescent fire orange chenille
Wing: Fluorescent fire orange tow yarn,
and orange Krystal Flash

BLACK MARABOU

Hook: TMC 7999, Mustad 36890, sizes 2-6
Thread: Black 3/0 monocord
Rib: Oval silver tinsel
Body: Black chenille
Wing: Black marabou

PACIFIC SALMON FLIES

FLASH FLY

BRISTOL BAY MATUKA

SALMON CREEK SPECIAL

COMET

ORANGE BOSS

BLACK BOSS

BRIGHT ROE

GREENHEAD

BLACK MARABOU

WIGGLETAIL

BRISTOL BAY MATUKA

Originator: Don Hathaway
Hook: TMC 7999, Mustad 36890, sizes 1/0-6
Thread: Fire orange 6/0 prewaxed
Rib: Fine oval gold tinsel
Body: Gold diamond braid
Wing: Two fluorescent yellow hackles
enveloped by four red hackles, two on
each side, tied down matuka style
Throat: Fluorescent red marabou
Hackle: Fluorescent orange and yellow
hackle, mixed

COMET

Hook: TMC 700, Mustad 36890, sizes 2-6
Thread: White 3/0 monocord
Tail: Orange calftail and orange Krystal
Flash, long
Body: Silver diamond braid
Hackle: Orange and yellow hackle, mixed
Eyes: Silver bead chain

BLACK BOSS

Hook: TMC 7999, Mustad 36890, sizes 2-6
Thread: Black 3/0 monocord
Tail: Black calftail and black Krystal Flash,
long
Rib: Flat silver tinsel
Body: Black chenille
Hackle: Black hackle
Eyes: Silver bead chain

GREENHEAD

Originator: Rex Collingsworth
Hook: TMC 7999, Mustad 36890, sizes 4-8
Thread: Fluorescent green single strand
floss
Tag: Fluorescent green floss
Tail: Black calftail, long
Rib: Oval gold tinsel
Body: Fluorescent fire orange floss
Hackle: Hot orange hackle
Head: Fluorescent green chenille
Eyes: Gold bead chain

WIGGLETAIL

Hook: TMC 7999, Mustad 36890, sizes 2/0-2
Thread: White 3/0 monocord
Tail: White marabou
Rib: Oval silver tinsel
Body: Hot pink chenille
Skirt: Silver mylar piping, unraveled

SPADE

Hook: TMC 7999, Mustad 36890, sizes 1/0-6
Thread: Black 3/0 monocord
Tail: Natural dark deer hair
Body: Black chenille
Hackle: Grizzly hackle

DENALI

Originator: Tom Elliott
Hook: TMC 7999, Mustad 36890, size 4
Thread: Black 6/0 prewaxed
Tail: Red hackle fibers
Body: Large copper wire
Throat: Yellow hackle
Wing: Bucktail, silver doctor blue on top and bottom, orange in the middle

COHOE GOLDEN

Originator: Roderick Haig-Brown
Hook: Mustad 92608, sizes 3/0-6
Thread: Black 3/0 monocord
Tail: Orange polar bear
Body: Flat silver tinsel
Wing: Olive over white polar bear, with jungle fowl body feathers on each side
Topping: Golden pheasant crest

LAMBUTH CANDLEFISH

Originator: Letcher Lambuth
Hook: Mustad 92608, sizes 3/0-6
Thread: Black 6/0 prewaxed
Body: Flat silver tinsel
Wing: Green over red over blue Fishair

CANDLEFISH FLY

Hook: Mustad 92608, sizes 2-6
Thread: Black 6/0 prewaxed
Body: Silver diamond braid
Wing: Green over white bucktail, and pearl Flashabou

PACIFIC SALMON FLIES

SPADE

GREEN WIENIE

DENALI

SCHAADT EGG SAC

COHOE GOLDEN

PINK PASSION

LAMBUTH CANDLEFISH

FLASHY LADY

CANDLEFISH FLY

COHOE BLUE

GREEN WIENIE

Hook: TMC 7999, Mustad 36890, sizes 2-8
Thread: Fluorescent green single strand floss
Tail: Black calftail
Body: Silver diamond braid
Shoulder: Fluorescent green chenille
Hackle: Fluorescent green hackle
Eyes: Silver bead chain

SCHAADT EGG SAC

Originator: Bill Schaadt
Hook: TMC 700, Mustad 36890, sizes 2/0-8
Thread: Black 6/0 prewaxed
Tail: Black bucktail
Body: Black floss, thin
Shoulder: Fluorescent red chenille
Hackle: Black hackle

PINK PASSION

Originator: Ken Fujii
Tier: Ken Fujii
Hook: TMC 800s, Mustad 34007, sizes 1/0-4
Thread: Fluorescent red 6/0 prewaxed
Body: Pearl diamond braid
Shoulder: Fluorescent red chenille
Underhackle: Pearl Krystal Flash
Hackle: Fluorescent hot pink hackle

FLASHY LADY

Originator: Joe Butoric
Tier: Joe Butoric
Hook: Mustad 92608, sizes 3/0-2
Thread: White 6/0 prewaxed
Head
Wing
Throat: Pearl Flashabou and lavender bucktail tied in over the eye and pulled back and tied down to form head
Eyes: Black Lacquer

COHOE BLUE

Originator: Roderick Haig-Brown
Hook: Mustad 92608, sizes 1/0-6
Thread: Black 6/0 prewaxed
Tail: Two light blue hackle tips
Body: Flat silver tinsel
Wing: Blue over white polar bear, enveloped by two light blue hackles over two badger hackles

FLASHABOU EUPHAUSID

Originator: Gray Strodtz
Hook: TMC 800S, Mustad 3407, sizes 4-10
Thread: White 6/0 prewaxed
Tail: Pearl Flashabou
Body: Pearl diamond braid
Throat: Pearl Flashabou

GREEN AMPHIPOD

Originator: Lloyd Morrell
Hook: TMC 207BL, Mustad 37140, sizes 4-8
Thread: Black 3/0 monocord
Tail: Natural deer hair
Rib: Black thread
Hackle: Two blue dun hackles, palmered
Body: Fluorescent green chenille
Shellback: Natural deer hair

TEENY NYMPH, ginger

Originator: Jim Teeny
Tier: Teeny Nymph Company
Hook: TMC 700, sizes 2/0-8
Thread: Black 3/0 monocord
Body: Bleached ginger pheasant tail, wrapped
Mid-throat: Bleached ginger pheasant tail fibers
Throat: Same
Wing: Same

MIDNIGHT

Hook: Eagle claw 1197 G, sizes 1-4
Thread: Black 6/0 prewaxed
Tail: Black bucktail
Rib: Oval gold tinsel
Body: Flat silver tinsel
Wing: Black over white bucktail

ACKERLAND HUMPY FLY

Originator: Bill Ackerlund
Hook: TMC 800S, Mustad 3407, size 4
Thread: Black 3/0 monocord
Body: Flat silver tinsel
Wing: Pink over white bucktail, long
Eyes: Silver bead chain

PACIFIC SALMON FLIES

FLASHABOU EUPHAUSID

KING'S SHRIMP

GREEN AMPHIPOD

ORANGE SHRIMP

TEENY NYMPH, ginger

BLUE COMET

MIDNIGHT

GLO BUG, orange

ACKERLAND HUMPY FLY

GLO BUG, pink

KING'S SHRIMP

Originator: Grant King
Hook: TMC 800S, Mustad 3407, sizes 2-6
Thread: Fire orange 6/0 prewaxed
Tail: Orange bucktail, long
Hackle: Orange hackle, palmered
Body: Flat silver tinsel
Shellback: Orange bucktail

ORANGE SHRIMP

Originator: Mike Foster
Hook: TMC 207BL, Mustad 37160, sizes 4-12
Thread: Orange 3/0 monocord
Tail: Orange bucktail
Rib: Orange thread
Hackle: Orange hackle, palmered
Body: Hot orange chenille
Shellback: Orange bucktail

BLUE COMET

Hook: TMC 800S, Mustad 3407, sizes 2-6
Thread: Black 3/0 monocord
Tail: Blue calftail, long
Body: Silver diamond braid
Hackle: Blue hackle

GLO BUG, orange

Hook: TMC 2457, Mustad 9174, sizes 4-8
Thread: Fluorescent orange single strand floss
Body: Flame glo bug yarn

GLO BUG, pink

Hook: TMC 2457, Mustad 9174, sizes 4-8
Thread: Fluorescent pink single strand floss
Body: Peachy king glo bug yarn
Eye: Orange glo bug yarn

RUSSIAN RIVER COHO FLY

Hook: Mustad 36717, sizes 2-6
Thread: Black 3/0 monocord
Throat: White bucktail, long
Wing: Red bucktail, long

POPSICLE

Originator: George Cook
Hook: TMC 7999, Mustad 36890, sizes 3/0-2
Thread: Fire orange 6/0 prewaxed
Tail: Fluorescent orange marabou
Mid-Hackle: Cerise marabou, wound on
Hackle: Purple hackle, with fluff
Flash: Gold, electric blue, purple Flashabou, added at tail and mid-hackle

SHOWGIRL

Originator: George Cook
Hook: TMC 7999, Mustad 36890, size 1/0
Thread: Fluorescent orange single strand floss
Wing: Cerise marabou, purple Flashabou, with red and pearl Krystal Flash
Hackle: Purple hackle, with fluff

GREEN ALASKABOU

Originator: George Cook
Hook: TMC 7999, Mustad 36890, size 1/0
Thread: Fluorescent fire orange single strand floss
Wing: Fluorescent green marabou, with green Flashabou and lime Krystal Flash
Hackle: White saddle hackle with fluff

BLACK JACK

Hook: TMC 7999, Mustad 36890, sizes 2/0-4
Thread: Black 6/0 prewaxed
Body: Black diamond braid
Hackle: Black marabou, wound on

PACIFIC SALMON FLIES

RUSSIAN RIVER COHO FLY

PIXIES REVENGE

POPSICLE

DREDGER

SHOWGIRL

ALASKAN POLAR SHRIMP

GREEN ALASKABOU

FIRE CRACKER

BLACK JACK

CHRISTMAS TREE

PIXIES REVENGE

Originator: George Cook
Hook: TMC 7999, Mustad 36890, size 1/0
Thread: Fluorescent fire orange single strand floss
Wing: White marabou, with silver Flashabou and red Krystal Flash
Hackle: Cerise hackle, with fluff

DREDGER

Tier: Umpqua Feather Merchants
Hook: TMC 700, sizes 1/0-4
Thread: Fluorescent green single strand floss
Tail: Fluorescent green marabou, black Krystal Flash, and black marabou
Rib: Fine gold wire
Body: Fluorescent green floss
Hackle: Black hackle, palmered over the body, fluff for collar
Eyes: Nickel plated lead eyes

ALASKAN POLAR SHRIMP

Originator: George Cook
Tier: George Cook
Hook: TMC 7999, Mustad 36890, sizes 2/0-6
Thread: Fluorescent fire orange 6/0 prewaxed
Tail: Hot orange hackle fibers
Rib: Flat gold tinsel
Body: Fluorescent fire orange chenille
Hackle: Hot orange saddle hackle with fluff
Wing: White calftail and pearl Flashabou

FIRE CRACKER

Originator: Jonathan Olch
Tier: Umpqua feather Merchants
Hook: TMC 7999, Mustad 36890, sizes 2/0-6
Thread: White 3/0 monocord
Body: Silver mylar piping, unraveled in back to form tail
Throat: Unraveled body material
Wing: Fluorescent orange over white Fishair

CHRISTMAS TREE

Originator: Jonathan Olch
Tier: Umpqua Feather Merchants
Hook: TMC 800S, Mustad 3407, sizes 1/0-4
Thread: Black 6/0 prewaxed
Tail: Green Flashabou, butts from body
Rib: Black thread
Body: Green Flashabou
Collar: Green Flashabou with silver Flashabou over

Chapter 8

Saltwater Flies

❖

Bass, Panfish and Shad

❖

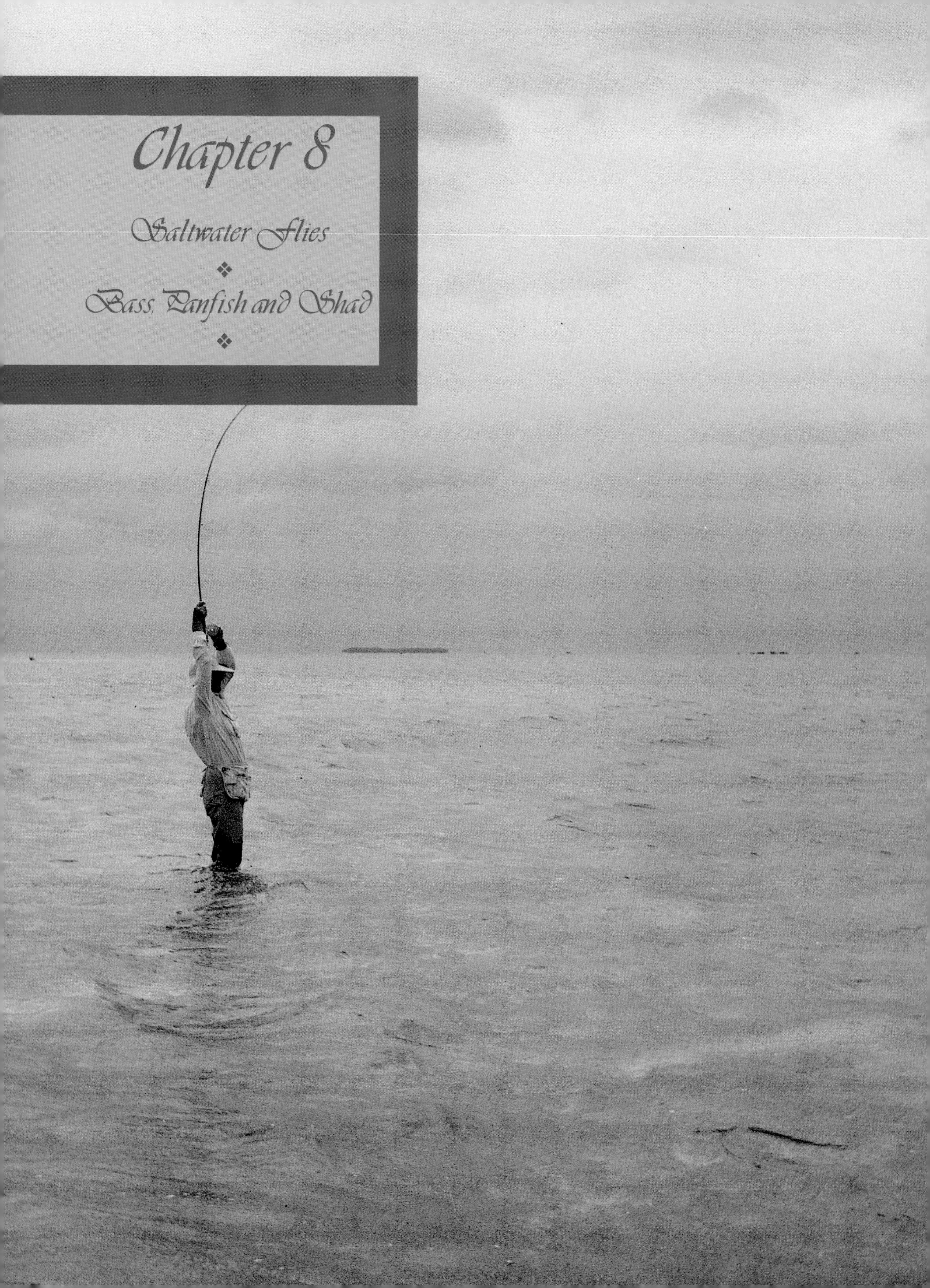

YUCATAN SPECIAL

Tier: Umpqua Feather Merchants
Hook: TMC 800S, Mustad 34007, sizes 2-8
Thread: Fluorscent green single
  strand floss
Butt: Fluorescent orange fuzzy wool
Body: Fluorescent green chenille
Wing: Lime green bucktail, and lime
  Krystal Flash
Sides: Grizzly hackle tips, short

CRAZY CHARLIE, tan

Originator: Bob Nauheim
Hook: TMC 800S, Mustad 3407, sizes 2-8
Thread: White 3/0 monocord
Underbody: Flat pearl tinsel
Body: Clear swannundaze
Wing: Tan calftail, with a few strands of
  pearl Flashabou over the top,
  tied inverted
Eyes: Silver bead chain

GEORGE BUSH

Originator: Jeff Johnston.
Tier: Jeff Johnston.
Hook: TMC 800s, Mustad 34007, sizes 2-8.
Thread: Fluorescent Orange 6/0 prewaxed.
Tail: Dyed yellow pearl Krystal Flash.
Underbody: Fluorescent orange thread.
Body: Dyed yellow pearl Krystal Flash,
  wrapped.
Wing: Dyed yellow pearl Krystal Flash.
Eyes: Gold or silver bead chain, or nickel
  plated lead eyes, depending upon
  currents and depth

GOLD AND BROWN SHRIMP

Originator: Chico Fernandez
Tier: Umpqua Feather Merchants
Hook: TMC 800S, Mustad 3407, sizes 2-8
Thread: Black 6/0 prewaxed
Body: Gold rabbit dubbing
Wing: Natural brown bucktail, copper
  Krystal Flash over the top, tied inverted
Sides: Cree hackle tips
Collar: White thread

MINI SHRIMP, tan

Hook: TMC 800S, Mustad 34007, size 8
Thread: Brown 6/0 prewaxed
Body: Natural tan rabbit dubbing
Wing: Pearl Krystal Flash, ringneck pheas-
  ant tail fibers, and two cree hackle tips

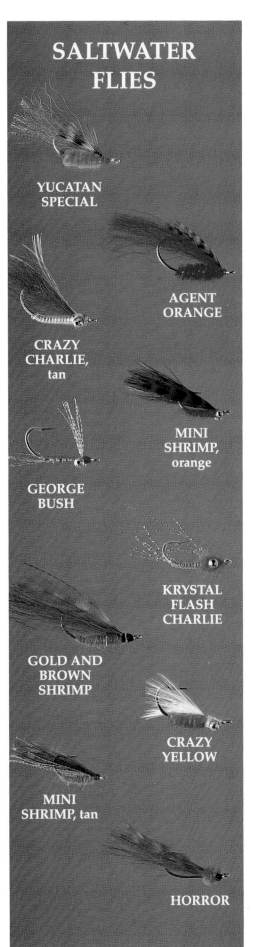

SALTWATER FLIES

YUCATAN SPECIAL

CRAZY CHARLIE, tan

AGENT ORANGE

GEORGE BUSH

MINI SHRIMP, orange

GOLD AND BROWN SHRIMP

KRYSTAL FLASH CHARLIE

CRAZY YELLOW

MINI SHRIMP, tan

HORROR

AGENT ORANGE

Originator: Winston Moore
Hook: TMC 800S, Mustad 3407, sizes 2-8
Thread: Fluorescent fire orange 6/0
  prewaxed
Body: Small orange chenille
Wing: Hot orange calftail, two grizzly
  hackle tips on each side

MINI SHRIMP, orange

Hook: TMC 800S, Mustad 34007, size 8
Thread: Fl. orange 6/0 prewaxed
Body: Hot orange antron dubbing
Wing: Pearl Krystal Flash and four dyed
  orange grizzly hackle tips
Eyes: Silver bead chain

KRYSTAL FLASH CHARLIE

Hook: TMC 800S, Mustad 34007, sizes 4-8
Thread: Yellow 6/0 prewaxed
Tail: Dyed yellow pearl Krystal Flash
Underbody: Dyed yellow pearl Krystal Flash
Overbody: Clear swannundaze
Thorax: Hot yellow rabbit dubbing
Eyes: Gold bead chain
Wing: Dyed yellow pearl Krystal Flash

CRAZY YELLOW

Hook: TMC 800S, Mustad 3407, sizes 2-6
Thread: White 3/0 monocord
Body: Yellow chenille
Wing: Two white hackle tips, with pearl
  Flashabou, tied inverted
Eyes: Silver bead chain

HORROR

Originator: Pete Perinchief
Tier: Umpqua Feather Merchants
Hook: TMC 800S, Mustad 3407, sizes 2-8
Thread: Black 6/0 prewaxed
Wing: Natural brown bucktail and 2 cree
  hackle tips
Head: Yellow chenille

ARBONA'S SHRIMP

Originator: Fred Arbona
Tier: Umpqua Feather Merchants
Hook: TMC 800S, Mustad 3407, sizes 2-6
Thread: Black 6/0 prewaxed
Wing: Pink marabou over orange marabou over fox squirrel tail
Sides: Dyed orange grizzly hackle tips

CRAZY CHARLIE, pink

Originator: Bob Nauheim
Hook: TMC 800S, Mustad 3407, sizes 2-8
Thread: White 3/0 monocord
Underbody: Flat silver tinsel
Body: Clear swannundaze
Wing: Two pink hackle tips, 4 strands of pearl Flashabou on each side, tied inverted.
Eyes: Silver bead chain

TAN MARABOU SHRIMP

Hook: TMC 800S, Mustad 34007, sizes 1/0-4
Thread: Tan 3/0 monocord
Body: Tan frostbite
Wing: Tan marabou and pearl Krystal Flash
Sides: Dyed tan grizzly hackle tips
Eyes: Nickel plated lead eyes

YELLOW MARABOU SHRIMP

Hook: TMC 800S, Mustad 34007, sizes 1/0-6
Thread: Yellow 3/0 monocord
Body: Yellow frostbite
Wing: Yellow over white marabou and pearl Krystal Flash
Sides: Two dyed yellow grizzly hackle tips
Eyes: Nickel plated lead eyes

BONEFISH SPECIAL

Originator: Chico Fernandez
Tier: Umpqua Feather Merchants
Hook: TMC 800S, Mustad 3407, size 4
Thread: Black 3/0 monocord
Tail: Orange marabou, short
Underbody: Flat gold tinsel
Overbody: Clear swannundaze
Wing: White bucktail and pearl Krystal Flash, enclosed by two grizzly hackle tips

SALTWATER FLIES

ARBONA'S SHRIMP

MINI PUFF

CRAZY CHARLIE, pink

WHITE SANDS

TAN MARABOU SHRIMP

PINK SANDS

YELLOW MARABOU SHRIMP

SNAPPING SHRIMP

BONEFISH SPECIAL

HONEY SHRIMP

MINI PUFF

Hook: TMC 800S, Mustad 34007, sizes 2-8
Thread: Fl. pink single strand floss
Wing: Tan calftail pearl Krystal Flash and two grizzly hackle tips
Head: Fluorescent hot pink chenille
Eyes: Silver bead chain

WHITE SANDS

Hook: TMC 800S, Mustad 34007, sizes 2-8
Thread: White 3/0 monocord
Body: Pearl frostbite
Wing: White rabbit fur two white hackle tips and pearl Flashabou

PINK SANDS

Hook: TMC 800S, Mustad 34007, sizes 2-6
Thread: White 3/0 monocord
Body: Pink frostbite
Wing: Pink calftail and pink Krystal Flash and two white hackle tips
Eyes: Nickel plated lead eyes

SNAPPING SHRIMP

Originator: Chico Fernandez
Tier: Umpqua Feather Merchants
Hook: TMC 800S, Mustad 3407, sizes 2-8
Thread: Black 6/0 prewaxed
Butt: Rust synthetic dubbing
Body: Beige synthetic dubbing
Wing: Natural brown bucktail and copper Krystal Flash, tied inverted
Collar: White thread

HONEY SHRIMP

Originator: Chico Fernandez
Tier: Umpqua Feather Merchants
Hook: TMC 800S, Mustad 34007, sizes 4-6
Thread: Black 3/0 monocord
Body: Gold and light olive antron dubbing, mixed
Wing: Gold fishair and gold Flashabou
Topping: Four cree hackle tips

ANDERSON'S McCRAB

Originator: George Anderson
Tier: Umpqua Feather Merchants
Hook: TMC 800S, Mustad 34007, sizes 1/0-4
Thread: Black 6/0 prewaxed
Tail: Tan turkey flats, 2 brown hackle tips,
    and pearl Krystal Flash
Body: Tan deer hair, spun and clipped
Legs: Tan rubber band, knotted
    and clipped
Eyes: Mono nymph eyes
Head: lead eyes, painted brown
Markings: Brown paint

SWIMMING CRAB, tan

Originator: Kaufmann's Streamborn Staff
    and Joe Branham
Tier: Joe Branham
Hook: TMC 800S, Mustad 34007, sizes 2-8
Thread: Tan 6/0 prewaxed
Legs: Orange speckle rubber legs
Claws: Grizzly hackle tips
Antennae: Pearl Krystal Flash
Eyes: Mono nymph eyes
Body: Tan wool, spun and clipped
Head: Lead eyes

SALT CRAB

Originator: Dave Whitlock
Tier: Umpqua Feather Merchants
Hook: TMC 800S, Mustad 3407, sizes 4/0-2
Thread: White 3/0 monocord
Weed Guard: Heavy clear monofilament
Claws: Dark hen saddle feathers, clipped
    and lacquered
Legs: Mottled brown hen saddle feather
Eyes: Large monofilament nymph eyes
Body: Spun and clipped deer hair, white on
    the bottom and natural light and dark in
    bands on the top

SWIMMING CRAB, olive

Originator: Kaufmann's Streamborn Staff
    and Joe Branham
Tier: Joe Branham
Hook: TMC 800S, Mustad 34007, size 2-6
Thread: Olive 6/0 prewaxed
Legs: Olive speckle rubber legs
Claws: Dyed olive grizzly hackle tips
Antennae: Pearl Krystal Flash
Eyes: Mono nymph eyes
Body: Dark olive wool, spun and clipped
Head: lead eyes

ULTRA SHRIMP

Originator: Bob Popovic
Tier: Umpqua Feather Merchants
Hook: TMC 800S, Mustad 34007, sizes 1/0-6
Thread: Tan 3/0 monocord
Tail: Tan ocean hair and copper
    Krystal Flash
Eyes: Burned clear monofilament
Body: Tan thread
Hackle: Ginger hackle, palmered over
    the body
Shellback: Tan ocean hair, epoxy over the
    top, butts out over the eye.

SALTWATER FLIES

ANDERSON'S McCRAB

MOTHER OF EPOXY

SWIMMING CRAB, tan

MOTIVATOR

SALT CRAB

PINK EPOXY CHARLIE

SWIMMING CRAB, olive

PINK SHRIMP

ULTRA SHRIMP

SALT SHRIMP

MOTHER OF EPOXY

Hook: TMC 800S, Mustad 3407, sizes 1/0-4
Thread: Tan 3/0 monocord
Tail: Tan calftail, enclosed by cree
    hackle tips
Underbody: Stiff plastic cut to shape with
    tan floss wrapped over the top
Eyes: Clear doll eyes
Body: Aqua-seal coating the floss

MOTIVATOR

Originator: Jonathan Olch
Tier: Umpqua Feather Merchants
Hook: TMC 800S, Mustad 34007, sizes 4-6
Thread: White 3/0 monocord
Tail: Tan rabbit fur and two cree hackle tips
Body: Pearl diamond braid, coated
    with aquaseal
Eyes: Silver bead chain

PINK EPOXY CHARLIE

Tier: Joe Branham
Hook: TMC 800S, Mustad 34007, sizes 2-8
Thread: Pink 6/0 prewaxed
Body: Pearl frostbite with clear epoxy over
    the top
Eyes: Nickel plated lead eyes
Wing: Pink calftail and pink Krystal Flash
Sides: Dyed pink grizzly hackle tips

PINK SHRIMP

Originator: Joe Brooks
Tier: Umpqua Feather Merchants
Hook: TMC 800S, Mustad 3407, sizes 2-8
Thread: White 3/0 monocord
Tail: Dyed pink hackle fibers
Shellback: Dyed pink bucktail, twisted
Body: Silver diamond braid
Hackle: Pink hackle, palmered over the body
Eyes: Painted, white with a red pupil

SALT SHRIMP

Originator: Dave Whitlock
Tier: Umpqua Feather Merchants
Hook: TMC 800S, Mustad 3407, sizes 3/0-8
Thread: White 3/0 monocord
Weed Guard: Clear heavy monofilament
Antennae: Two dyed olive hackle
    stems, stripped
Tail: Natural dark deer hair and thin
    clear plastic
Rib: Fine gold wire
Shellback: Thin clear plastic
Eyes: Monofilament nymph eyes
Hackle: Dyed olive grizzly hackle
Body: Light olive antron yarn
Throat: Thin clear plastic

BLACK DECEIVER

Hook: TMC 800S, Mustad 34007, sizes 3/0-4
Thread: Black 3/0 monocord
Tail: Four black saddle hackles
Body: Flat silver tinsel
Sides: Wide silver Flashabou
Wing: Black bucktail
Throat: Black bucktail

PALOLO WORM

Hook: TMC 800S, Mustad 3407, sizes
   3/0-2/0
Thread: Tan 6/0 prewaxed
Tail: Bright orange calftail, 1" long
Body: Bright orange chenille
Head: Tan chenille

SURF PERCHER

Originator: John Shewey
Tier: John Shewey
Hook: TMC 800S, Mustad 34007, sizes 1-2
Thread: Fluorescent red single strand
   nylon floss
Tail: Bright yellow marabou
Body: Gold diamond braid
Throat: Bright yellow marabou
Wing: Flame red marabou
Topping: Red Flashabou
Eyes: Silver bead chain

SURF LEECH

Originator: John Shewey
Tier: John Shewey
Hook: TMC 800S, Mustad 34007, sizes 1-2
Thread: Fluorescent orange single strand
   nylon floss
Tail: Three parts; orange Krystal Flash,
   bright red rabbit fur strip, red Flashabou
Body: Bright red rabbit fur strip, wrapped
Collar: Bright yellow saddle hackle
Eyes: Nickel plated lead eyes

BONEFISH BUGGER

Originator: Chico Fernandez
Tier: Umpqua Feather Merchants
Hook: TMC 800s, Mustad 34007, sizes 2-4
Thread: Gray 3/0 monocord
Eyes: Nickel lead eyes
Tail: White marabou and two grizzly
   hackle tips
Body: Pink chenille
Hackle: Grizzly hackle, palmered over
   the body
Topping: 4-6 Strands of pearl Krystal Flash

SALTWATER FLIES

BLACK DECEIVER

SURF CANDY

PALOLO WORM

CANDY EEL

SURF PERCHER

KRYSTAL FLASH

SURF LEECH

SHEWEY'S STREAKER BAIT

BONEFISH BUGGER

SALTY BEADY EYE

SURF CANDY

Originator: Bob Popovic
Tier: Umpqua Feather Merchants
Hook: TMC 800S, Mustad 34007, size 1/0
Thread: White 6/0 prewaxed
Wing: Olive over white ocean hair
Sides: Wide pearl mylar
Eyes: Green and black paste on eyes
Head: Clear epoxy over

CANDY EEL

Originator: Bob Popovic
Tier: Umpqua Feather Merchants
Hook: TMC 800S, Mustad 34007, size 1/0
Thread: White 3/0 monocord
Tail: Badger hackle center, superglue into
   the end
Body: Pearl mylar piping, extended
Wing: Green over white ocean hair
Eyes: Green and black paste on eyes
Head: Clear epoxy over

KRYSTAL FLASH

Originator: Joe Butoric
Tier: Joe Butoric
Hook: TMC 800S, Mustad 34007, sizes 2/0-2
Thread: White 3/0 monocord
Tail: White ocean hair, pearl, yellow, olive
   Krystal Flash, tied forward then
   pulled back
Eyes: Painted, yellow with black pupil

SHEWEY'S STREAKER BAIT

Originator: John Shewey
Tier: John Shewey
Hook: TMC 800S, Mustad 34007, sizes 2/0-2
Thread: White single strand nylon floss
Wing: Bottom to top, as follows; white
   polar bear hair, yellow Krystal Flash,
   chartreuse fishair, silver Krystal Flash,
   blue fishair, and dark blue Krystal Flash
Sides: Dyed green grizzly hackle tips
Body: White single strand nylon floss
Eyes: Yellow audible eyes

SALTY BEADY EYE

Originator: Mathew Vinciguerra
Tier: John Shewey
Hook: TMC 800S, Mustad 34007, sizes 3/0-1
Thread: White 3/0 monocord
Tail: Four white saddle hackle tips
Body: Gold diamond braid
Eyes: Silver bead eye, pupil painted black
Over/underlay: Small silver mylar piping,
   unravel ends around the tail, cover
   entire with epoxy, mix small cut pieces
   of pearl Krystal Flash into epoxy

APTE II

Originator: Stu Apte
Tier: Umpqua Feather Merchants
Hook: TMC 800S, Mustad 3407,
  sizes 4/0-2/0
Thread: White 3/0 monocord
Tail: Four dyed brown furnace hackles, and
  copper Krystal flash
Body: Natural gray squirrel tail, covering
  the whole hook shank

BLACK AND ORANGE

Originator: Winston Moore
Tier: Umpqua Feather Merchants
Hook: TMC 800S, Mustad 3407,
  sizes 4/0-2/0
Thread: Black single strand nylon floss
Tail: Four orange saddle hackle tips,
  enclosed by four black saddle hackle
  tips, flared
Hackle: Black and orange hackle, mixed
Eyes: Large silver bead chain, optional

ORANGE AND GRIZZLY

Originator: Chico Fernandez
Tier: Umpqua Feather Merchants
Hook: TMC 800S, Mustad 3407,
  sizes 4/0-2/0
Thread: Fluorescent orange single strand
  nylon floss
Tail: Four orange saddle hackles enclosed
  by four grizzly saddle hackles, splayed
Hackle: Orange and grizzly hackle, mixed
Eyes: Large silver bead chain, optional

STU APTE

Originator: Stu Apte
Tier: Umpqua Feather Merchants
Hook: TMC 800S, Mustad 3407,
  sizes 5/0-2/0
Thread: Fluorescent fire orange single
  strand nylon floss
Tail: Two bright orange saddle hackles
  enclosed by two yellow saddle
  hackles, splayed, topped by hot
  orange Krystal Flash
Hackle: Bright orange and yellow
  hackle, mixed

WHITLOCK'S BAITFISH

Originator: Dave Whitlock
Tier: Umpqua Feather Merchants
Hook: TMC 800S, Mustad 34007, size 1/0
Thread: White 3/0 monocord
Weed Guard: Heavy clear monofilament
Tail: White and light blue marabou, 2 dyed
  light blue grizzly saddle hackles, with
  silver and light blue flashabou
Hackle: Light blue grizzly hackle
Wing: Silver and light blue Flashabou, short
Throat: Red Flashabou short
Eyes: White audible eyes

SALTWATER FLIES

APTE II

BLUE DEATH

BLACK AND ORANGE

TARPON GLO, orange

ORANGE AND GRIZZLY

TARPON GLO, green

STU APTE

TARPON TAKER, yellow

WHITLOCK'S BAITFISH

TARPON TAKER, white

BLUE DEATH

Tier: Umpqua Feather Merchants
Hook: TMC 800S, Mustad 3407, sizes 4/0-2/0
Thread: Fluorescent blue single strand
  nylon floss
Tail: Four blue saddle hackle tips, enclosed
  by four grizzly hackle tips
Hackle: Blue and grizzly hackle, mixed

TARPON GLO, orange

Originator: Jonathon Olch
Tier: Umpqua Feather Merchants
Hook: TMC 800S, Mustad 3407, size 5/0-3/0
Thread: Fluorescent fire orange single
  strand nylon floss
Tail: Natural brown bucktail
Wings: Four grizzly hackle enveloped by four
  dyed orange hackle, splayed
Hackle: Grizzly and dyed orange hackle
Collar: Fluorescent green single strand
  nylon floss
Eyes: Painted, black with a white pupil

TARPON GLO, green

Originator: Jonathon Olch
Tier: Umpqua Feather Merchants
Hook: TMC 800S, Mustad 3407, size 5/0-3/0
Thread: Fluorescent green single strand
  nylon floss
Tail: Peacock blue fishair
Wing: Four grizzly hackle enveloped by four
  dyed green hackles, splayed
Hackle: Dyed green and grizzly hackles
Collar: Fluorescent fire orange single strand
  nylon floss
Eyes: Painted, white with a black pupil

TARPON TAKER, yellow

Originator: Bill Black
Tier: Spirit River Inc
Hook: TMC 800S, Mustad 34007,
  sizes 4/0-1/0
Thread: Red single strand nylon floss
Tail: Yellow rabbit fur strip
Sides: Grizzly hackle tips, short
Collar: Yellow rabbit fur strip, one wrap
Throat: Pearl and yellow Krystal Flash
Hackle: Red hackle
Body: Red single strand nylon floss
Shellback/Wing: Pearl and yellow
  Krystal Flash
Eyes: Painted, yellow with black pupil

TARPON TAKER, white

Originator: Bill Black
Tier: Spirit River Inc
Hook: TMC 800S, Mustad 34007,
  sizes 4/0-1/0
Thread: Red single strand nylon floss
Tail: White rabbit fur strip
Sides: Grizzly hackle tips, short
Collar: White rabbit fur strip, one wrap
Throat: Pearl and red Krystal Flash
Hackle: Red hackle
Body: Red single strand nylon floss
Shellback/Wing: Pearl and red Krystal Flash
Eyes: Painted, yellow with black pupil

DECEIVER, cockroach

Originator: Lefty Kreh
Tier: Umpqua Feather Merchants
Hook: TMC 800S, Mustad 3407, sizes 4/0-1
Thread: Black 6/0 monocord
Tail: Eight grizzly saddle hackles, with copper Krystal Flash and silver Flashabou
Body: Flat silver tinsel
Throat: Natural brown bucktail
Wing: Natural brown bucktail, also on the sides
Collar: Red thread
Eyes: Painted, yellow with black pupils

DECEIVER, green/white

Originator: Lefty Kreh
Tier: Umpqua Feather Merchants
Hook: TMC 800S, Mustad 3407, sizes 4/0-1
Thread: Black 6/0 prewaxed
Tail: Eight white saddle hackles, with green Krystal flash and silver Flashabou
Body: Flat silver tinsel
Throat: White bucktail
Underwing: White bucktail, also on the sides
Wing: Green bucktail
Topping: 6-8 strands of peacock herl
Collar: Red thread
Eyes: Painted, white with black pupil

DECEIVER, blue/white

Originator: Lefty Kreh
Tier: Umpqua Feather Merchants
Hook: TMC 800S, Mustad 3407, sizes 4/0-1
Thread: Black 6/0 prewaxed
Tail: Eight white saddle hackles, with blue Krystal Flash and pearl Flashabou
Body: Flat silver tinsel
Throat: White bucktail
Underwing: White bucktail, also on the sides
Wing: Blue bucktail
Topping: 6-8 strands of peacock herl
Collar: Red thread
Eyes: Painted, white with black pupil.

DECEIVER, red/yellow

Originator: Lefty Kreh
Tier: Umpqua Feather Merchants
Hook: TMC 800S, Mustad 3407, sizes 4/0-1
Thread: Black 6/0 prewaxed
Tail: Eight yellow saddle hackles, with pearl Krystal flash and pearl Flashabou
Body: Flat silver tinsel
Throat: Yellow bucktail
Underwing: Yellow bucktail, also on the sides
Wing: Red bucktail
Topping: 6-8 strands of peacock herl
Collar: Red thread
Eyes: Painted, white with black pupil

GLASS MINNOW

Originator: Carl Hansen
Tier: Umpqua Feather Merchants
Hook: TMC 800S, Mustad 3407, sizes 2/0-2
Thread: Green 3/0 monocord
Underbody: Flat silver tinsel
Body: Clear swannundaze
Wing: Lime green over white fishair, 4-5 strands of silver Krystal Flash on each side
Topping: Peacock herl
Collar: Red thread
Eyes: Painted, white with a black pupil

SALTWATER FLIES

DECEIVER, cockroach

ABEL ANCHOVY

DECEIVER, green/white

BEND BACK, yellow

DECEIVER, blue/white

BEND BACK, blue

DECEIVER, red/yellow

PINK KEEL BUGGER

GLASS MINNOW

JETTIE JUNKIE

ABEL ANCHOVY

Originator: Steve Abel
Hook: TMC 800S, Mustad 34007, sizes 4/0-2
Thread: Black single strand floss
Body: Pearl diamond braid
Wing: Blue over lime over white bucktail
Topping: Pearl Krystal Flash and peacock herl
Throat: Red Flashabou, short
Eyes: White audible eyes

BEND BACK, yellow

Originator: Chico Fernandez
Tier: Umpqua Feather Merchants
Hook: TMC 800S, Mustad 34007, sizes 2/0-2, bent
Thread: Fluorescent orange single strand floss
Body: Yellow chenille
Wing: Yellow bucktail and pearl Flashabou
Sides: Grizzly saddle hackle tips
Topping: Peacock herl strands
Eyes: Painted, white with black pupil

BEND BACK, blue

Originator: Chico Fernandez
Tier: Umpqua Feather Merchants
Hook: TMC 800S, Mustad 3407, sizes 2/0-2, bent
Thread: Black 3/0 monocord
Body: Fluorescent white chenille
Wing: Peacock blue fishair over white bucktail, tied inverted
Sides: Grizzly hackles with silver and pearl Flashabou
Topping: Peacock herl
Collar: Red thread
Eyes: Painted, white with a black pupil

PINK KEEL BUGGER

Originator: John Shewey
Tier: John Shewey
Hook: Mustad or Eagle Claw keel, sizes 3/0-2
Thread: Fluorescent pink 6/0 prewaxed
Tail: Pink marabou and pink Flashabou
Rib: Fine gold wire
Body: Fluorescent pink chenille
Hackle: Fluorescent pink hackle, palmered over the body.

JETTIE JUNKIE

Originator: John Shewey
Tier: John Shewey
Hook: Keel Hook, sizes 2/0-2
Thread: Fluorescent red single strand floss
Tail: White marabou
Rib: White crystal chenille, and copper wire
Body: Gold diamond braid
Wing: Pearl Krystal Flash, white marabou, pearl Flashabou

WHISTLER, orange/black

Originator: Dan Blanton
Tier: Umpqua Feather Merchants
Hook: TMC 800S, Mustad 3407, sizes 6/0-1/0
Thread: Orange single strand nylon floss
Tail: Black bucktail, thick, enclosed by two black hackle tips
Throat: Black bucktail
Wing: 6 black hackle tips, splayed
Topping: 8 peacock herl strands
Collar: Orange marabou, wound on and pinched off to length
Eyes: Large silver bead chain

REDFISH FLY

Originator: Jonathan Olch
Tier: Umpqua Feather Merchants
Hook: TMC 800S, Mustad 3407, sizes 2/0-2
Thread: Fluorescent red single strand nylon floss
Tail: Four white hackle tips, splayed with silver Flashabou on each side
Collar: Red marabou, wrapped, pinched off to length

SEA DUCER

Hook: TMC 800S, Mustad 3407, sizes 2/0-2
Thread: Red 3/0 monocord
Tail: Six white saddle hackles, splayed, with silver Flashabou on each side
Body: White hackle, palmered over entire hook shank
Hackle: Red hackle

REDFISH ORANGE

Hook: TMC 800S, Mustad 34007, sizes 2/0-4
Thread: Red single strand floss
Tail: Dyed red polar bear hair, thick
Body: Flat silver tinsel
Wing: Dyed orange polar bear hair, thick

WHISTLER, red/white

Originator: Dan Blanton
Tier: Umpqua Feather Merchants
Hook: TMC 800S, Mustad 3407, sizes 6/0-1/0
Thread: Red single strand nylon floss
Tail: White bucktail, thick, enclosed by two white hackle tips
Throat: White bucktail
Wing: Four white and 2 grizzly hackles, splayed, with silver Flashabou on each side
Topping: Peacock herl strands
Collar: Red marabou, wound on and pinched off to length
Eyes: Large silver bead chain

SALTWATER FLIES

WHISTLER, orange/black

STREAKER

REDFISH FLY

TROPICAL PUNCH

SEA DUCER

LIME PUNCH

REDFISH ORANGE

BUNNY BLENNIE

WHISTLER, red/white

BIG FISH FLY

STREAKER

Tier: Gordon Nash
Hook: TMC 800S, Mustad 3407, sizes 4/0-2/0
Thread: Fluorescent green single strand nylon floss
Tail: Green bucktail, with lime and blue Krystal Flash over the top
Rib: Copper wire
Body: Gold diamond braid
Throat: Green bucktail
Underwing: 15-20 strands of peacock herl
Wing: Two matched peacock sword quills, back to back
Cheeks: Blue Krystal Flash

TROPICAL PUNCH

Originator: Dan Blanton
Tier: Umpqua Feather Merchants
Hook: TMC 800S, Mustad 34007, sizes 3/0-2/0
Thread: Fluorescent green single strand floss
Tail: Lime bucktail and lime Flashabou
Body: Lime diamond braid
Wing: Dyed lime pearl Krystal Flash peacock herl and 2 dyed olive grizzly saddle hackles
Throat: Lime hackle fibers
Shellback: Peacock herl
Head: Fluorescent green chenille
Eyes: Silver bead chain

LIME PUNCH

Originator: Dan Blanton
Tier: Umpqua Feather Merchants
Hook: TMC 800S, Mustad 34007, sizes 3/0-2/0
Thread: Red 6/0 prewaxed
Tail: Yellow bucktail and gold Flashabou
Body: Gold diamond braid
Wing: Dyed yellow pearl Krystal Flash, peacock herl and 2 dyed orange grizzly saddle hackles
Throat: Yellow hackle fibers, with fluff
Shellback: Peacock herl
Head: Fluorescent fire orange chenille
Eyes: Silver bead chain

BUNNY BLENNIE

Originator: John Shewey
Tier: John Shewey
Hook: TMC 8089, Mustad 37187, size 2
Thread: Fluorescent orange single strand floss
Tail: Yellow rabbit strip, long
Body: Yellow rabbit strip, wrapped
Legs: Yellow round rubber hackle
Eyes: Nickel plated lead eyes

BIG FISH FLY

Originator: Chico Fernandez
Tier: Umpqua Feather Merchants
Hook: TMC 800S, Mustad 3407, sizes 4/0
Thread: White 3/0 monocord
Tail: White fishair, long
Body: White thread
Throat: White fishair, long
Wing: Bright green fishair with peacock blue fishair over the top, pearl flashabou in-between

BLACK ANN RED BASS BUG

Originator: Dave Whitlock
Tier: Umpqua Feather Merchants
Hook: TMC 8089, Mustad 37187, sizes 2,6,10
Thread: Black 3/0 monocord
Weed Guard: heavy clear monofilament
Tail: two furnace saddle hackles, black and red rubber hackle with a black hen hackle on each side
Butt: Black saddle hackle
Body: Black, red, orange, and white deer hair, spun and clipped
Legs: Black rubber hackle
Eyes: Red audible eyes

DILG SLIDER

Originator: Larry Dahlberg
Tier: Umpqua Feather Merchants
Hook: Mustad 3366, sizes 1/0-6
Thread: Black 3/0 monocord
Weed Guard: Heavy clear monofilament
Tail: Red Flashabou
Rib: Black thread
Wing: Black rabbit fur strip, tied down with the rib, extended
Sides: Two grizzly hackles
Collar: Black deer hair
Head: Black deer hair, spun and clipped
Eyes: Yellow audible eyes

WIGGLE LEGS FROG

Originator: Dave Whitlock
Tier: Umpqua Feather Merchants
Hook: TMC 8089, Mustad 37187, sizes 2,6
Thread: White 3/0 monocord
Rear Legs: Tied on with wire and a cut hook shank, dark green bucktail over white bucktail, lacquered
Body: Predominantly olive deer hair, with yellow and black deer hair, white deer hair underbelly
Front Legs: Four strands of white rubber hackle in each leg, knotted
Eyes: Medium yellow audible eyes

GERBUBBLE BUG

Originator: Dave Whitlock
Tier: Umpqua Feather Merchants
Hook: TMC 8089, Mustad 37187, sizes 2,6,10
Thread: White 3/0 prewaxed
Weed Guard: Heavy clear monofilament
Tail: two dyed yellow and two dyed red grizzly saddle hackles
Butt: Dyed yellow and red grizzly hackle
Body: Orange and yellow deer hair
Sides: Dyed yellow and red grizzly hackles, pulled into the body

CANARY BASS BUG

Originator: Dave Whitlock
Tier: Umpqua Feather Merchants
Hook: TMC 8089, Mustad 37187, sizes 2,6,10
Thread: White 3/0 monocord
Weed Guard: Heavy clear monofilament
Tail: Two yellow hackles enveloped by two white hackles
Hackle: Light grizzly hackle
Legs: Yellow rubber hackle
Body: Two shades of yellow deer hair, spun and clipped
Face: White deer hair, spun and clipped
Eyes: Medium audible eyes

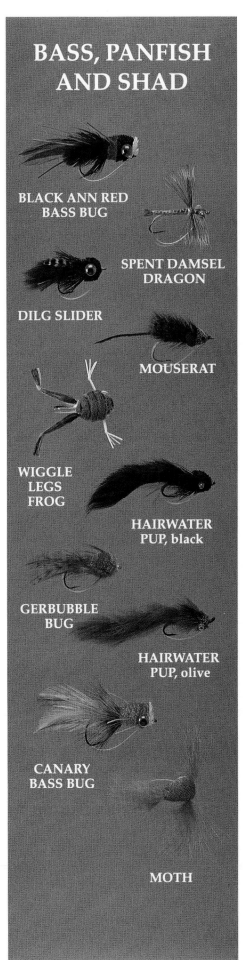

BASS, PANFISH AND SHAD

BLACK ANN RED BASS BUG

SPENT DAMSEL DRAGON

DILG SLIDER

MOUSERAT

WIGGLE LEGS FROG

HAIRWATER PUP, black

GERBUBBLE BUG

HAIRWATER PUP, olive

CANARY BASS BUG

MOTH

SPENT DAMSEL DRAGON

Originator: Dave Whitlock
Tier: Umpqua Feather Merchants
Hook: TMC 8089, Mustad 37187, sizes 2,6,10
Thread: White 3/0 prewaxed
Rib: White thread
Body: Natural light and dark bucktail, tied extended
Wings: Natural light and dark bucktail
Eyes: Yellow audible eyes

MOUSERAT

Originator: Dave Whitlock
Tier: Umpqua Feather Merchants
Hook: TMC 8089, Mustad 37187, sizes 2,6,10
Thread: Black 3/0 monocord
Weed Guard: Heavy clear monofilament
Tail: Dark brown leather strip
Body: Dark deer hair, spun and flared, clipped on the bottom
Ears: Dark brown leather, cut to shape
Collar: Dark deer hair, flared
Head: Dark deer hair, spun and clipped
Whiskers: Dark moose body hair
Eyes: Black waterproof marker

HAIRWATER PUP, black

Originator: Dave Whitlock
Tier: Umpqua Feather Merchants
Hook: TMC 7999, Mustad 36890, sizes 1/0-6
Thread: Red 3/0 monocord
Weed Guard: Heavy clear monofilament
Tail: Black rabbit fur strip, also over the body
Rib: Fine silver wire
Body: Black rabbit dubbing
Throat: Red Flashabou, short
Collar: Black deer hair
Head: Black deer hair, spun and clipped
Eyes: Blue audible eyes

HAIRWATER PUP, olive

Originator: Dave Whitlock
Tier: Umpqua Feather Merchants
Hook: TMC 7999, Mustad 36890, sizes 1/0-6
Thread: Red 3/0 monocord
Weed Guard: Heavy clear monofilament
Tail: Olive rabbit fur strip
Rib: Fine silver wire
Body: Olive rabbit dubbing
Throat: Red Flashabou, short
Collar: Yellow and green deer hair, with black on top
Head: Yellow and green deer hair, spun and clipped
Eyes: Yellow audible eyes

MOTH

Originator: Dave Whitlock
Tier: Umpqua Feather Merchants
Hook: TMC 8089, Mustad 37187, sizes 2,6,10
Thread: Yellow 3/0 monocord
Weed Guard: Heavy clear monofilament
Tail: Yellow marabou
Body: Yellow deer hair
Wings: Yellow marabou

PERCH STREAMER

Originator: Kevin Erickson
Tier: Kevin Erickson
Hook: Keel Hook, sizes 1/0-6
Thread: Yellow single strand nylon floss
Tail: Red Krystal Flash
Body: Pearl diamond braid
Wing: Green marabou over yellow calftail
Sides: Dyed yellow grizzly hackle
Topping: Peacock herl strands
Collar: Olive and orange deer hair
Head: Yellow and olive deer hair, spun and clipped
Eyes: Large audible eyes

DIVING MINNOW

Originator: Larry Dahlberg
Tier: Umpqua Feather Merchants
Hook: TMC 9394, sizes 2-6
Thread: White 3/0 monocord
Weed Guard: Heavy clear monofilament
Body: Silver diamond braid
Wing: White marabou and silver Flashabou
Sides: Two grizzly saddle hackles
Throat: Pearl and red Flashabou, short
Collar: White, with natural and black deer hair
Head: White deer hair, spun and clipped

DIVING BUG

Originator: Larry Dahlberg
Tier: Umpqua Feather Merchants
Hook: TMC 8089, Mustad 37187, sizes 2,6,10
Thread: White 3/0 monocord
Weed Guard: Heavy clear monofilament
Wing: Purple over light blue marabou
Sides: Two dyed blue grizzly hackles enclosed by two dyed purple grizzly hackles, and green Flashabou
Topping: Silver and gold Flashabou and peacock herl
Collar: Purple, blue and black deer hair
Head: Blue and purple deer hair, spun and clipped to shape

UMPQUA SWIMMING FROG

Originator: Dave Whitlock
Tier: Umpqua Feather Merchants
Hook: TMC 8089, Mustad 37187, sizes 2,6,10
Thread: Fluorescent green single strand floss
Weed Guard: Heavy clear monofilament
Tail: 2 lime saddle hackles, four dyed olive grizzly saddle hackles and lime Krystal Flash
Collar: Lime green hackle
Wing: Dark green deer hair
Legs: Yellow and green rubber hackle
Head: Green, black and yellow deer hair, spun and clipped
Eyes: White audible eyes

RABBIT STRIP DIVER

Originator: Larry Dahlberg
Tier: Umpqua Feather Merchants
Hook: TMC 8089, Mustad 37187, sizes 2,6,10
Thread: White 3/0 monocord
Weed Guard: Heavy clear monofilament
Tail: Yellow rabbit fur strip
Topping: Gold Flashabou
Collar: Yellow deer hair, spun and clipped on the bottom
Head: Yellow deer hair, spun and clipped to shape

BASS, PANFISH AND SHAD

PERCH STREAMER

UMPQUA SWIMMING WATERDOG

DIVING MINNOW

HAIRWATER GRUB

DIVING BUG

HARE WORM

UMPQUA SWIMMING FROG

KEVIN'S MOUSE

RABBIT STRIP DIVER

UMPQUA SWIMMING BAITFISH

UMPQUA SWIMMING WATERDOG

Originator: Dave Whitlock
Tier: Umpqua Feather Merchants
Hook: TMC 8089, sizes 2-10
Thread: Fluorescent green single strand nylon floss
Weed Guard: Clear heavy monofilament
Tail: Black rabbit fur strip, with a piece of chartreuse rabbit fur strip glued to the underside of the tip
Sides: Dyed chartreuse grizzly hackle, and chartreuse Krystal Flash
Collar: Black deer hair
Legs: Black and chartreuse rubber hackle
Head: Black deer hair, spun and clipped to shape
Eyes: Chartreuse audible eyes

HAIRWATER GRUB

Originator: Larry Dahlberg
Tier: Umpqua Feather Merchants
Hook: TMC 8089, Mustad 37187, sizes 2,6,10
Thread: Black 3/0 monocord
Weed Guard: Heavy clear monofilament
Tail: Black rabbit fur strip
Body: Black rabbit fur strip, overlapped
Legs: Black rubber hackle, with red and pearl Krystal flash
Eyes: Lead eyes, painted black, white with a red pupil

HARE WORM

Originator: Dave Whitlock
Tier: Umpqua Feather Merchants
Hook: TMC 8089, Mustad 37187, sizes 2-10
Thread: White 3/0 monocord
Weed Guard: Heavy clear monofilament
Tail: Blue rabbit fur strip, long
Body: Blue rabbit fur strips, glued to hook shank, top and bottom
Eyes: White doll eyes

KEVIN'S MOUSE

Originator: Kevin Erickson
Tier: Kevin Erickson
Hook: Keel Hook, sizes 1/0-6
Thread: Orange single strand nylon floss
Tail: Two furnace saddle hackles
Body: Natural deer hair, spun and clipped

UMPQUA SWIMMING BAITFISH

Originator: Dave Whitlock
Tier: Umpqua Feather Merchants
Hook: TMC 800S, sizes 2/0-4
Thread: Red 3/0 monocord
Weed Guard: Clear heavy monofilament
Tail: Four white and two grizzly hackle tips, with pearl and silver Krystal Flash
Sides: Two white hackle, short
Throat: Red Flashabou
Collar: White deer hair on the bottom, with natural deer hair on the top
Head: Orange then red deer hair, spun and clipped to shape
Eyes: Gold doll eyes

LECTRIC LEECH

Originator: Dave Whitlock
Tier: Umpqua Feather Merchants
Hook: TMC 7999, Mustad 36890, sizes 1/0-2
Thread: Black 6/0 prewaxed
Weed Guard: Heavy clear monofilament
Tail: Black marabou
Shellback: Peacock herl, tips over the tail
Rib: Fine gold wire
Body: Black wool yarn
Sides: Electric blue Flashabou, ends as part of tail
Hackle: Black hackle, palmered over the body

CRAYFISH

Originator: Dave Whitlock
Tier: Umpqua Feather Merchants
Hook: TMC 300, Mustad 9575, sizes 1/0-8
Thread: Orange 3/0 monocord
Eyes: Monofilament nymph eyes
Antennae: Two dark moose body fibers
Pinchers: Light speckled hen on top and cream hen on the bottom, flexament together, color top feather with orange waterproof marker
Tail: Dark moose body hair, short
Rib: Copper Wire
Hackle: Dyed orange grizzly hackle
Body: Burnt orange antron yarn, pick out on the sides
Shellback: Orange swiss straw or raffia, extend over the eye to make the tail
Markings: Black waterproof marker

MATCH THE MINNOW

Originator: Dave Whitlock
Tier: Umpqua Feather Merchants
Hook: TMC 300, Mustad 9575, sizes 2-6
Thread: White 6/0 prewaxed
Underbody: Lead tape
Body: Pearl mylar piping, markings are painted on
Wing: Two dyed olive grizzly hackles, glued to body
Sides: Ringneck pheasant back feather, short
Eyes: Yellow doll eyes
Head: White, painted black on top

FUZZABOU SHAD

Originator: Jimmy Nix
Tier: Umpqua Feather Merchants
Hook: TMC 800S, Mustad 34007, sizes 1/0-4
Thread: Gray 6/0 prewaxed
Weed Guard: Heavy clear monofilament
Body: Gray antron dubbing
Wing: Peacock herl and pearl Krystal Flash
Sides: Whole mallard flank feathers
Throat: White and red marabou
Eyes: Lead eyes, painted yellow with black pupil
Head: Gray wool, spun and clipped

BASS BUGGER, yellow

Originator: Kevin Erickson
Tier: Kevin Erickson
Hook: TMC 800S, Mustad 34007, sizes 1/0-6
Thread: Yellow 3/0 monocord
Weed Guard: Heavy monofilament
Tail: Yellow marabou
Legs: White rubber hackle
Body: Yellow chenille
Eyes: Nickel plated lead eyes, painted yellow with a black pupil

BASS, PANFISH AND SHAD

LECTRIC LEECH

EELWORM

CRAYFISH

COTTONMOUTH SNAKEY

MATCH THE MINNOW

FROG BASS BUG

FUZZABOU SHAD

CHAMOIS LEECH

BASS BUGGER, yellow

BASS BUGGER, white

EELWORM

Originator: Dave Whitlock
Tier: Umpqua Feather Merchants
Hook: TMC 7999, Mustad 36890, sizes 1/0-6
Thread: Red 3/0 monocord
Weed Guard: Heavy clear monofilament
Tail: Four black saddle hackles, tied splayed
Body: Black fuzzy wool yarn
Hackle: Black hackle, palmered over the body
Eyes: Large silver bead chain

COTTONMOUTH SNAKEY

Originator: Dave Whitlock
Tier: Umpqua Feather Merchants
Hook: TMC 7999, Mustad 36890, sizes 1/0-2
Thread: White 3/0 monocord
Weed Guard: heavy clear monofilament
Tail: two dyed black and two dyed brown grizzly saddle hackles
Butt: Dyed black and brown grizzly hackle
Body: Light brown and black deer hair, with a white face, spun and clipped
Eyes: White audible eyes

FROG BASS BUG

Originator: Dave Whitlock
Tier: Umpqua Feather Merchants
Hook: TMC 8089, Mustad 37187, sizes 2,6,10
Thread: White 3/0 monocord
Weed Guard: heavy clear monofilament
Tail: 2 white, 2 cree 2 dyed olive grizzly saddle hackles
Collar: Dyed olive grizzly hackles
Body: Olive, black, yellow and white deer hair, spun and clipped
Eyes: Yellow audible eyes

CHAMOIS LEECH

Originator: Dave Whitlock
Tier: Umpqua Feather Merchants
Hook: TMC 7999, Mustad 36890, sizes 1/0-6
Thread: Yellow 6/0 prewaxed
Weed Guard: Heavy clear monofilament
Tail: Fluorescent red floss
Shellback: Brown chamois, over the back of the entire fly and making the long tail
Rib: Fine gold wire
Body: Brown antron dubbing, picked out in a taper
Hackle: Brown speckled hen saddle
Eyes: Silver bead chain eyes

BASS BUGGER, white

Originator: Kevin Erickson
Tier: Kevin Erickson
Hook: TMC 800S, Mustad 34007, sizes 1/0-6
Thread: Maroon 6/0 prewaxed
Weed Guard: Heavy monofilament
Tail: White marabou
Legs: White rubber hackle
Hackle: White saddle hackle, palmered over the body
Body: White chenille
Eyes: Silver bead chain

RUBBER LEGS

Hook: TMC 100, Mustad 94845, size 12
Thread: Yellow 6/0 prewaxed
Body: Yellow sponge bug body
Legs: Yellow rubber hackle

FOAM SPIDER

Originator: Bill Black
Tier: Spirit River Inc
Hook: TMC 100, Mustad 94845, sizes 10-12
Thread: Yellow 6/0 prewaxed
Body: Yellow sponge bug body
Legs: Yellow rubber hackle, 3 strands
　marked with a black waterproof marker
Antennae: Yellow Krystal Flash

LUCKY LEECH, purple

Originator: Bill Black
Tier: Spirit River Inc
Hook: TMC 800B, sizes 2-10
Thread: Black 6/0 prewaxed
Tail: Purple marabou, and pearl
　Krystal Flash
Eyes: Nickel plated lead eyes
Body: Purple rabbit dubbing

JIG-A-BUGGER, purple

Tier: Umpqua Feather Merchants
Hook: TMC 5263, Mustad 9672, size 8
Thread: Black 6/0 prewaxed
Tail: Purple rabbit fur, with purple
　Krystal Flash
Body: Purple crystal chenille
Hackle: Purple hackle, palmered over
　the body
Eye: Nickel plated lead eyes, painted pink
　with black pupil

JIG-A-BUGGER, black

Tier: Umpqua Feather Merchants
Hook: TMC 5263, Mustad 9672, size 8
Thread: Black 6/0 prewaxed
Tail: Black rabbit fur, with black
　Krystal Flash
Body: Black crystal chenille
Hackle: Black hackle, palmered over
　the body
Eye: Nickel plated lead eyes, painted pink
　with black pupil

BASS, PANFISH AND SHAD

RUBBER LEGS

SHAD FLY, orange

FOAM SPIDER

SHAD FLY, green

LUCKY LEECH, purple

FLASH DANCER

JIG-A-BUGGER, purple

LUCKY LEECH, gray

JIG-A-BUGGER, black

BLACK BUSTER

SHAD FLY, orange

Tier: Umpqua Feather Merchants
Hook: TMC 5263, Mustad 9672, sizes 2-6
Thread: Fluorescent fire orange single
　strand floss
Tail: Fluorescent fire orange floss, short
Body: Fluorescent fire orange floss
Eyes: Silver bead chain

SHAD FLY, green

Tier: Umpqua Feather Merchants
Hook: TMC 5263, Mustad 9672, sizes 2-6
Thread: Fluorescent. green single
　strand floss
Tail: Fluorscent green floss, short
Body: Fluorescent green floss
Eyes: Silver bead chain

FLASH DANCER

Originator: Jimmy Nix
Tier: Umpqua Feather Merchants
Hook: TMC 8089, Mustad 37187,
　sizes 2,6,10
Thread: Red 3/0 monocord
Weed Guard: Heavy clear monofilament
Tail: Red marabou
Body: White Chenille
Wing: Pearl Flashabou
Head: Deer hair, spun and clipped

LUCKY LEECH, gray

Originator: Bill Black
Tier: Spirit River Inc
Hook: TMC 800B, sizes 2-10
Thread: Gray 6/0 prewaxed
Tail: Gray marabou, and pearl Krystal Flash
Eyes: Nickel plated lead eyes
Body: Gray rabbit dubbing

BLACK BUSTER

Originator: Bill Black
Tier: Spirit River Inc
Hook: TMC 800B, sizes 1/0-8
Thread: Black 6/0 prewaxed
Tail: Black marabou, with one strand of
　black rubber hackle on each side
Body: Black chenille
Collar: Rubber hackle, black with blue specks
Eyes: Nickel plated lead eyes
Head: Black chenille

Bibliography

Alaska Flyfishers. *Fly Patterns Of Alaska.* Portland, Oregon: Frank Amato Publications, 1983.

Almy, Gerald. *Tying And Fishing Terrestrials.* Harrisburg, Pennsylvania: Stackpole Books, 1978.

Arbona, Fred. *Mayflies, The Angler And The Trout.* Tulsa, Oklahoma: Winchester Press, 1980.

Atherton, John. *The Fly And The Fish.* Rockville Center, New York: Freshet Press, 1971.

Bay, Kenneth E. *Salt Water Flies.* New York, New York: J.B. Lippincott Company, 1972.

Bates, Joseph D., Jr. *Atlantic Salmon Flies And Fishing.* Harrisburg, Pennsylvania: Stackpole Books, 1970.

Bates, Joseph D., Jr. *Streamers And Bucktails.* New York, New York: Alfred A. Knopf, 1979

Bergman, Ray. *Trout.* New York, New York: Alfred A. Knopf, 1976.

Best, A.K. *Production Fly Tying.* Boulder, Colorado: Pruett Publishing, 1989.

Blades, William F. *Fishing Flies And Fly Tying.* Harrisburg, Pennsylvania: Stackpole Books, 1979.

Borger, Gary. *Designing Trout Flies.* Wausau, Wisconsin: Tomorrow River Press, 1990.

Brooks, Charles E. Nymph *Fishing For Larger Trout.* New York, New York: Nick Lyons Books, 1976.

Brooks, Joe. *Trout Fishing.* New York, New York: Harper & Row, 1979.

Combs, Trey. *Steelhead Fly Fishing And Flies.* Portland, Oregon: Frank Amato Publications, 1976.

Dennis, Jack. *Western Trout Fly Tying Manuel.* Jackson Hole, Wyoming: Snake River Books, 1974.

_____. *Western Trout Fly Tying Manuel Volume II.* Jackson Hole, Wyoming: Snake River Books, 1980.

Ferguson, Bruce and Les Johnson and Pat Trotter. *Fly Fishing For Pacific Salmon.* Portland, Oregon: Frank Amato Publications, 1985.

Flick, Art. Flick's *Master Fly Tying Guide.* New York, New York: Crown Publisher, Inc., 1972

Fly Tyer Quarterly. *Fly Tyer Pattern Bible.* North Conway, New Hampshire: Saco River Publishing Corporation, 1985.

Fulsher, Keith and Charles Krom. *Hair-Wing Atlantic Salmon Flies.* North Conway, New Hampshire: Fly Tyer Inc., 1981.

Hafele, Rick and Dave Hughes. *The Complete Book Of Western Hatches.* Portland, Oregon: Frank Amato Publications, 1981.

Haig-Brown, Roderick L. *The Western Angler.* New York, New York: William Morrow & Company, 1947.

Hanley, Ken. California *Fly Tying And Fishing Guide.* Portland, Oregon: Frank Amato Publications, 1991.

Harder, John. *Index of Orvis Fly Patterns.* Manchester, Vermont: The Orvis Company, 1978.

_____. *Index Of Orvis Fly Patterns Volume 2.* Manchester, Vermont: The Orvis Company, 1987.

_____. *The Orvis Fly Pattern Index.* New York, New York: Viking Penquin, 1990.

Hellekson, Terry. *Popular Fly Patterns.* Salt Lake City, Utah: Peregrine Smith Books, 1984.

Hughes, Dave. *Western Streamside Guide.* Portland, Oregon: Frank Amato Publishing, 1987.

_____. *American Fly tying Manuel.* Portland, Oregon: Frank Amato Publications, 1986.

Inland Empire Fly Fishing Club. *Flies Of The Northwest.* Spokane, Washington: Inland Empire Fly Fishing club, 1979.

_____. *Flies Of The Northwest.* Portland, Oregon: Frank Amato Publications, 1986.

Jennings, Preston J. *A Book Of Trout Flies.* New York, New York: Crown Publishers, Inc., 1935.

Jorgensen, Poul. *Modern Trout Flies.* Garden City, New York: Nick Lyons Books, 1979.

_____. *Dressing Flies For Fresh And Salt Water.* Rockville Center, New York: Freshet Press, 1973.

_____. *Salmon Flies.* Harrisburg, Pennsylvania: Stackpole Books, 1978.

_____. *Modern Fly Dressing For The Practical Angler.* New York, New York: Winchester Press, 1977.

Kaufmann, Randall. *American Nymph Fly Tying Manual.* Portland, Oregon: Frank Amato Publications, 1975.

_____. *The Fly Tyers Nymph Manual.* Portland, Oregon: Western Fishermans Press, 1986.

_____. *Tying Dry Flies.* Portland, Oregon: Western Fishermans Press, 1991.

Kaufmann's Streamborn Catalog. Tigard, Oregon, 1991, 1992.

Koch, Ed. *Fishing The Midge.* Rockville Center, New York: Freshet Press, 1972.

Kreh, Lefty. *Saltwater Fly Patterns.* Fullerton, California: Maral, Inc.

LaFontaine, Gary. *Caddisflies.* New York, New York: Nick Lyons Books, 1981.

Leiser, Eric. *The Book Of Fly Patterns.* New York, New York: Alfred A. Knopf, 1987.

Leonard, J. Edson. *Flies.* New York, New York: A.S. Barnes, 1960.

Mathews, Craig and John Juracek. *Fly Patterns Of Yellowstone.* West Yellowstone, Montana: Blue Ribbon Flies, 1987.

McKim, John F. *Fly Tying, Adventures In Fur, Feathers And Fun.* Missoula, Montana: Mountain Press, 1982.

McMillan, Bill. *Dry Line Steelhead.* Portland, Oregon: Frank Amato Publications, 1987.

Meck, Charles R. *Meeting And Fishing The Hatches.* New York, New York: Winchester Press, 1977.

Nemes, Sylvester. *The Soft-Hackled Fly.* Old Greenwich, Connecticut: The Chatham Press, 1975.

Patrick, Roy. *Pacific Northwest Fly Patterns.* Seattle, Washington: Patrick's Fly Shop, 1970.

Pryce-Tannatt, T.E. *How To Dress Salmon Flies.* London, England: A & C Black, 1977.

Rosborough, E.H. "Polly". *Tying And Fishing The Fuzzy Nymphs.* Harrisburg, Pennsylvania: Stackpole Books, 1978.

Schwiebert, Ernest G., Jr. *Matching The Hatch.* New York, New York: MacMillan Publishing Company, 1955.

Scott, Jock. *Greased Line Fishing For Salmon (And Steelhead).* Portland, Oregon: Frank Amato Publications, 1982.

Shaw, Helen. *Fly Tying.* New York, New York: John Wiley & Sons, 1979.

Slaymaker, S.R., II. *Tie A Fly, Catch A Trout.* New York, New York: Harper & Row, Publishers, 1976.

Solomon, Larry and Eric Leiser. *The Caddis And The Angler.* Harrisburg, Pennsylvania: Stackpole Books, 1977.

Spirit River Incorperated Catalog, Roseburg, Oregon, 1992.

Stewart, Dick. *Universal Fly Tying Guide.* Westfield, Massachusetts: Universal Vise Corporation, 1979.

Surette, Dick. *Trout and Salmon Fly Index.* Harrisburg, Pennsylvania: Stackpole Books, 1978.

Swisher, Doug and Carl Richards. *Tying The Swisher/Richards Flies.* Harrisburg, Pennsylvainia: Stackpole Books, 1980

_____. *Selective Trout.* New York, New York: Crown Publishers, Inc., 1971.

_____. *Emergers.* New York, New York: Lyons & Burford, 1991.

Talleur, Dick. *The Versatile Fly Tyer.* New York, New York: Lyons & Burford, 1990.

Umpqua Feather Merchants Catalog. Glide, Oregon, 1990, 1991.

Wulff, Lee. *The Atlantic Salmon.* New York, New York: Nick Lyons Books, 1983.

Fly Pattern Index

Index of Fly Tiers and Originators